FORTUNA DOMUS

FORTUNA DOMUS

A SERIES OF LECTURES

DELIVERED IN

THE UNIVERSITY OF GLASGOW

IN COMMEMORATION OF

THE FIFTH CENTENARY OF ITS

FOUNDATION

1952

PUBLISHED BY THE UNIVERSITY

Printed in Great Britain
By Robert MacLehose and Company Limited
The University Press, Glasgow

This volume presents, substantially as they were given, the lectures delivered in the course of the fifth centenary year, in which Professors of 1951 surveyed the development in the University of certain major disciplines, and noted the contribution of the University to each.

It was possible to arrange only sixteen lectures. There are now seventy-five separately organized departments of study within the University, and there might be more. Hence the grouping of departments for purposes of these historical discourses involved some omissions, and other somewhat arbitrary assignments. Nor in any case would it have been possible, within the limits of an hour's lecture, to report in full the vicissitudes, proliferations and achievements of any one important subject. The lectures therefore must be read for what they are—brief historical reviews of specific areas of study which exclude almost all but inescapable references to the present and even to the quite recent past. But the lectures in delivery excited much interest: and are issued in the belief that graduates and friends of the University who could not hear them will find in reading them equal interest and even entertainment.

The Senate of the University issues this book as part of its contribution to the Fifth Centenary celebrations. It desires to express its obligations to those of its members who prepared and gave the lectures, and to Mr. J. B. Neilson, Secretary of the Fifth Centenary Committee, for his editorial labours.

Hector Hetherington.

Principal

EDITOR'S NOTE

The note on Political Economy and
the section on Anatomy were not part
of the lecture series, but supplemen-
tary contributions for this volume.

J.B.N.

CONTENTS

vii

CONTENTS

DIVINITY

by

J. G. Riddell
Professor of Divinity

These Commemorative lectures are designed to recall the teachers of the past and the record of achievement which their service to the University presents. One of the greatest of those whom it is my privilege thus to commemorate—John Caird—emphasised the distinction between branches of knowledge in which we are independent of the past and those into which an historical element necessarily enters. In the study of human achievements, individual or corporate, we must know the stages through which the thought and culture of the world have passed to become what they are. 'The form of time', wrote Caird, 'has dropped from those intellectual and moral struggles, those events and actions which through successive ages have distilled themselves into great movements of thought; but there is not one of them which, in its vital results, has not been absorbed into the progressive life of the world.' At the end of five centuries we have learned not lightly to disparage the past but rather to gain all we may from those who stand before us in the long sequence of the years.

There is, none the less, a certain embarrassment in the very length of the record. Twenty-three names appear in the list of Professors of Divinity between 1640 and 1947. To these must be added the six Divinity Principals, as Dr. H. M. B. Reid entitled them, who were responsible for all teaching in Theology from 1574 till 1640, and, in the later period, three holders of the Chair of Divinity and Biblical Criticism from 1863 onwards. A total of thirty-one names makes it impossible to deal in detail with each individual, especially since the contemporary political and ecclesiastical situation has often to be taken into account. All that can be attempted is to set forth in broad outline the main trends of the Glasgow School of Theology and note something of the influence of successive teachers of Divinity in its development.

THE PRE-REFORMATION PERIOD, 1451-1560

There is specific provision in the Bull of Pope Nicholas V, by which the University was established, for theological study. There is, however, no clear evidence of the effective existence of a Theological faculty in the pre-Reformation period. Instruction for the priesthood continued, presumably, under the care of the teaching Orders, particularly the Black Friars. Contacts between the Church and the University were incidental rather than regular, taking the form of occasional lectures delivered in the University by members of the Religious Orders.

THE REFORMATION TO THE RESTORATION, 1560-1660

While the University may have had little direct contact with the pre-Reformation Church in theological teaching, it was largely maintained by ecclesiastical revenues. Its finances, even more than its teaching methods, were immediately affected by the Reformation. There was such marked disparity, indeed, between the ideal of academic attainment which the Reformed Church envisaged and the practical limitations which poverty imposed that the new scheme of University reform could be dismissed as 'a devout imagination.' Neither John Davidson, who was Principal at the Reformation, nor his acting successor, Blackburn, was able to begin the needed reconstruction of the whole University system or to undertake serious theological teaching. Both tasks awaited the coming to Glasgow in 1574 of the great Andrew Melville.

The General Assembly set Melville apart as a Doctor, to discharge the office of interpreter of Holy Scripture in the University, and he was directed to visit Glasgow, see the beginning of a College there, and hear what conditions should be offered to him. The University proved co-operative, and Melville thus became not only a Doctor but also *Praefectus Collegii*. His first step in securing financial stability for the College was to obtain revenues from the Parish of Govan, in return for which he and his successors were to preach there each Sunday. With academic versatility which matched his administrative skill, Melville not only reorganised the teaching in Arts but undertook responsibility for 'his awin ordinar profession the Holy Tongues and Theologie. He teachit the Hebrew Grammar, first shortlie and syne mor accurately; thereafter the Chaldaic and Syriac dialects, with the practice thereof in the Psalms and works of Solomon, etc. He past throu the haill commonplaces of Theologie verie exactlie and accuratlie; also throu all the Auld and New Testament.' For this he had been prepared by studies at St. Andrews, Paris and Geneva. That he should have carried it though successfully, with the work of the Principalship and the Ministry of Govan Parish, is a remarkable achievement even for one who is rightly regarded as the Restorer or Second Founder of the University.

Melville's programme, embodied in the *Nova Erectio*, was the pattern for his immediate successors, but with changing circumstances and with lesser men it became necessary to modify it in various ways. Thomas Smeaton and Patrick Sharp indeed attempted it from 1580 till 1614. They were different types—Smeaton the abler theologian, Sharp the superior in administration. In Smeaton's time the tensions of the Reformation period had not begun to disappear. He himself had been slow to break with the Roman Church, but he emerged in the end as a champion of Protestantism with his *Orthodoxa Responsio* to an attack by one Archibald Hamilton on Scottish Calvinism.

Patrick Sharp devoted himself more to the duties of the Principalship than to the theological controversies of the time. His brief account of Christian doctrine can still be consulted in our Library. It is somewhat dull reading and is said to afford no proof of the literary attainments which its author is known to have possessed. More colourful theology reappeared in the Glasgow School under its next two Principals—Robert Boyd and John Cameron. Both of them had studied and taught on the Continent, but the meteoric appearance of Cameron for a single session in Glasgow was much less important than the influence of his predecessor's seven years' teaching.

Robert Boyd, the first Edinburgh graduate to teach theology in Glasgow, had clear ideas as to the duty both of the student and of the professor. He drew up seventeen regulations for students, of which I quote only two. The student ought to be teachable, attentive and modest in time of lecture, not talkative or noisy, not laughing or using slangy or unreasonable speech, nor requiring his professor to repeat what has just been uttered. He should never postpone till to-morrow the task of to-day, but render daily his due. Boyd's method combined dictation with explanation and discussion varied by an occasional formal lecture. His interests lay in exposition and in Practical Divinity and Casuistry rather than in traditional theological doctrine. He protested against the impossible combination of duties laid down in the *Nova erectio,* and as a result of his efforts the Principal was relieved of parochial responsibilities in Govan 'that he might the more diligently employ his whole labour in public doctrine, in private colloquies with his auditors and disciples, and in government of the College.' Before the new arrangement came into force, however, Boyd was forced to resign on his refusal to accept the Five Articles of Perth which, in H. M. B. Reid's phrase, 'touched the very nerve of Presbyterian consciences.'

The full result of Boyd's criticisms of existing practice was

4

seen in the course of John Strang's long tenure of office from 1626 till 1651. The separation of the Principalship from parish duty in Govan became effective. The College authorities included in a list of *desiderata* submitted to the Privy Council in 1637 the appointment of Divinity Professors additional to the Principal. The University approached the General Assembly asking that they should furnish a competent number of Professors, especially of Theology, and David Dickson, minister at Irvine, was appointed and took up duty as Professor of Divinity in March, 1640.

In 1641 a second chair of Divinity was instituted and Robert Baillie was appointed as Dickson's colleague. The two had much in common. Both were natives of Glasgow, educated in the University, deeply influenced by Boyd. With Strang, who had been called from the parish of Errol to the Principalship in 1626 and continued to teach Divinity, they provided a much more adequate theological course than had hitherto been attempted, and the Glasgow School entered on one of its great periods. Strang had already shown himself not only a man of affairs but a competent teacher of theology, though, according to Wodrow, 'a source of weariness in the pulpit.' As Principal, in view of his continued responsibility for theological teaching, he received the title of Professor Primarius of Divinity. The other Professors would properly be *S.S. Theologiae Professores ordinarii*, Senior and Junior. Although the Principal rarely exercised his teaching functions in Divinity after this period, they remained a nominal responsibility at least until the passing of the Universities (Scotland) Act, 1858, which laid it down that 'The Principals in the Universities of Glasgow, Aberdeen and Edinburgh, appointed in time to come, shall not, as such, be or be deemed Professors of Divinity.' The later title, Primarius Professor, relates to ceremonial precedence only and dates from 1727.

Dickson's exegetical lectures were published as expositions of the Epistles, the Gospels and the Psalms. His *Therapeutica*

Sacra, one of the few Scottish contributions to the literature of the cure of souls, was derived partly from his own spiritual experiences in the Covenanting period, but still more from the revivalist movement in his Irvine ministry known as the 'Stewarton sickness.' It deals mainly with the emotional experience of conversion, but there was no unhealthy spirit in Dickson's approach either to his parish ministry or to his pastoral work. At Irvine, we are told, he was seen to run twice, very fast, round the Manse garden and go into the pulpit straight, in order, as he said, to awaken his spirit. He came to the University almost directly from a strenuous period of chaplaincy duty in the Covenanting army. Baillie's linguistic ability was outstanding in a period when few professors or students in Scotland showed interest in the ancient tongues. He also had been a chaplain in the 1639 war and was grieved, as he tells us, that in the Covenanting Army there was not only sound from the tents of singing psalms and reading the Scriptures, but also of swearing and cursing and brawling. He hoped, however, if their camp had been a little settled, to have got some way of remedying these misorders. His knowledge of Chronology and of doctrinal questions qualified him not only for his teaching responsibilities but for membership of the Westminster Assembly to which he was appointed one of the Scottish Commissioners.

The partnership between Strang, Dickson and Baillie was broken in February, 1650, when Dickson was appointed to the Chair of Divinity in Edinburgh. In the following April, Strang resigned the Principalship, and was succeeded by Patrick Gillespie. Baillie had been proposed for the Principalship, but refused nomination and became instead the Senior Professor Ordinarius. The appointment of his junior raised an interesting issue. The College had set its Principal free from the duties of minister in Govan, but no general decision had been taken to prevent either the Principal or the Professors of Divinity from retaining or accepting another ministerial charge. There were special circumstances at that particular period which made it desirable to avoid a plurality, but opportunity was taken to go further still and claim the freedom of the College to choose any qualified person, apart from his ecclesiastical status, to be Principal or Professor of Divinity. Thus it came about that in 1653 John Young, who had been a Regent in Arts since 1645, was appointed to the junior Chair in Divinity although he had not been ordained by the Church as a minister or set apart as a Doctor.

No theological test seems to have been required of the Principal either in the Charter of 1573 or in the *Nova Erectio,* nor of the Professors of Divinity when their Chairs were instituted. Baillie refused to accept his successor on the ground that he was not properly qualified, and, since he was by no means on friendly terms with the Principal, the Divinity staff was seriously divided. Young, however, was appointed to the Senior Chair when Baillie himself became Principal, and retained his office after the Restoration of Charles II.

THE RESTORATION TO THE UNION OF PARLIAMENTS, 1660-1707

John Young was succeeded by the first of the Divinity Professors appointed in the Episcopalian period, Gilbert Burnet, a graduate of Aberdeen and minister of Saltoun. Burnet is better known as Bishop of Salisbury and author of a *History of His Own Times,* but during the five years (1669-1674) he occupied the Chair in Divinity he showed himself a notable teacher. The second Chair had to be discontinued for lack of funds, as a result of ecclesiastical disturbances which again affected University revenues, but Burnet undertook the whole programme of teaching single-handed. He dealt with the body of Divinity in Latin, expounded the Gospels in English, the Psalms in Hebrew, explained the constitution and ritual of the Church and opened the Apostolical Canons, as well as conducting a sermon class and dealing with students' questions. 'Everyone,' he says 'approved of the scheme, only they thought it ought to be the work of two or three men. . . . Thus I applied myself for eight months in the year to answer the ends of a Professor with the diligence of a schoolmaster.'

None of Burnet's successors in the Episcopalian period was equal to him in distinction or ability. Two of them, like himself, were graduates of Aberdeen, David Liddell who taught from 1674 till 1682, and Alexander Ross, who was appointed Principal of St. Mary's College, St. Andrews, in 1687. The third, James Wemyss, was deposed in 1690 under the new requirements of the Revolution Settlement. The number of students had greatly declined, in spite of Burnet's influence, for, as he had found, the West of Scotland was Presbyterian at heart, 'and in league with hillmen and field conventiclers . . . " so much so that when the news of the landing of William and Mary reached Glasgow the students burned the effigy of the Pope along with effigies of the Archbishops of Glasgow and St. Andrews. The re-establishment of Presbyterianism brought with it a new era both for Church and University. The Confession of Faith was approved by the Scottish Parliament on 26th May, 1690. On 4th July it was enacted that no Principal or Professor or Office-bearer should be admitted to the Universities or allowed to continue in his office without subscribing to the oath of allegiance, the Confession of Faith, the Presbyterian Form of Church Government and being of a pure, loyal and peaceable conversation. It was added, as a kind of afterthought, that he must be of sufficient scholarship for his employment.

Under these conditions, which Wemyss refused to accept, James Wodrow was appointed to the single Chair of Divinity in 1692. He had studied under Baillie and did much to revitalise the theological school in a time when large number of men were required to fill the vacancies left by the abolition of Episcopacy. His break with normal tradition in using English as well as Latin in his teaching and his training of students to read for themselves were of great value. His insistence that there should be less formal lecturing and more discussion between professors and students has a modern sound. He went the length, indeed, of suggesting that there should be two Professors of Divinity, 'one to lecture, the other, and far more important one, to talk and train.'

THE UNION OF PARLIAMENTS TO THE DISRUPTION, 1707-1843

Wodrow's plea for a larger teaching staff was answered not in the way he proposed, but perhaps more effectively, after his death by the establishment of Chairs in Oriental Languages, in 1709, and in Ecclesiastical History, in 1716. Three of the lines of teaching developed by Strang, Dickson and Baillie were thus separated, and Divinity, as such, could be more narrowly defined—much too narrowly as it turned out. It was unfortunate that new interests in linguistic and historical study should coincide with a growing scholasticism in theology. The Confession of Faith had come to exercise an influence which Robert Baillie, as one of its authors, would not have desired. It became a text-book of religion, the conclusions of which were not to be questioned. Neither intellectual effort nor Biblical study was expected to throw light on theological issues which were held to have been decided with a finality that the Confession itself refused to claim. The reaffirmation in the Treaty of Union in 1707 of the Tests imposed in 1690, together with conformity to the discipline and worship of the Established Church, underlined on the political side the theological atmosphere of the time. Men held by the strict formula of subscription dare not deviate from the narrow pathway of orthodoxy as thereby defined.

How strict was the supervision of theological teaching in the early eighteenth century the University soon found out, for it became involved immediately in a heresy hunt, the victim being John Simpson, Wodrow's successor as Professor of Divinity. Simpson was twice libelled in the Church Courts for teaching contrary to the Confession of Faith. On the first occasion he was attacked for Socinian and Arminian errors, as well as for believing that the moon might be inhabited. The second case concerned his doubts regarding the necessary existence of the Second Person of the Trinity. The General Assembly of 1729 suspended him from all ecclesiastical functions, and declared that it was 'not fit nor safe that he be further employed in teaching Divinity, and instructing of youth designed for the Holy Ministry of this Church.'

Quite serious issues might have been raised had Simpson been deposed. The actual outcome of his suspension, however, was somewhat ludicrous, for he continued to hold his Chair although forbidden to teach. For twelve years he had the ideal situation of a professor without students—and a professor whom the visiting Committee of 1727 had just declared should take first place in point of ceremony after the Principal. The Principal himself, as Professor Primarius of Divinity, had to undertake the duties of the Chair, for which he later claimed some payment, only to be told that he was and always had been obliged to teach Divinity. The final incident in this strange interlude throws a light on the circumstances of the time. Having no other employment, Simpson desired to keep a cow or cows in the College precincts, and a special Committee was appointed to investigate the possibility of conveniently building a byre for the Professor of Divinity without prejudice to his then next door neighbour, the Professor of Humanity.

The harm which resulted from these unfortunate events was not greatly mitigated by the appointment in 1740, on Simpson's death, of Michael Potter, a man of almost seventy, who died three years later. William Leechman, minister of Beith and a graduate of Edinburgh, followed, and held the Chair from 1744 till he was appointed Principal in 1761. He was succeeded by the newly-appointed Professor of Oriental

Languages, Robert Traill, whose thirteen years' tenure was noteworthy more for the part he took in controversies within the College than for his theological achievement. Traill's successor, James Baillie, died three years after his appointment, and William Wight, transferred from the Chair of Ecclesiastical History, taught Divinity during four sessions only. Robert Finlay, then aged sixty-one, followed, and remained in active service for thirty-two years—until he was over ninety-three, engaging in three notable controversies —the first against various misrepresentations of the Sacred Books and Josephus by the celebrated M. Voltaire; the second against pluralities in University and Church appointments; the third against a denial of the divine inspiration of the Hebrew historians by a Roman priest—Alexander Geddes—who had received facilities to study the valuable Clementine Octateuch Manuscript in the University Library.

Stevenson MacGill, who succeeded Finlay in 1814, continued the protest against pluralities by dissenting from the admission of Duncan Macfarlane as Principal on the ground that he had also been presented to the charge of the Cathedral, and intended to accept both appointments. On the theological side, MacGill was the author of a series of letters to young clergymen, which seem to have been more interesting than his formal lectures. He gave evidence before the Universities Commission, appointed in 1826, urging the institution of a Chair of Biblical Criticism, and also pleading that the Principal should again discharge at least some of his duties in the teaching of Divinity. Fifty years were to pass before his first proposal was adopted. The second seems to have been disregarded, and MacGill was left unaided until his death in 1840.

The teaching of Divinity during the eighteenth and early nineteenth century was, for the most part, traditional and unadventurous. Sometimes, particularly in Leechman's time, there had been suspicions of undue sympathy with deistic teaching and of an optimism regarding man's capacities which true Covenanting Calvinism could not have approved. Leechman, however, safeguarded himself by giving 'no dictatorial opinion, no infallible judgment,' so that 'none of the students knew the particular opinion of this venerable Professor.' David Hume passed his judgment, for what it is worth, on two of the eighteenth century Professors. Dr. Traill, he declared, is dead, and now knows whether there be any truth in all these doctrines which he taught, and of which he did not believe a word while alive. Dr. Wight he commended for the Chair of Divinity as sensible and good humoured, and as sound and orthodox as you could wish.

The brief tenure of the Chair by some of its holders, and the over-long incumbencies of others did not help in a time of theological stagnation which, we must remember, was not peculiar to Glasgow. In Scotland as a whole in this period, according to Sir William Hamilton's deliberate judgment, for two centuries Theology had ceased to exist as a scientific study.

The dead hand of orthodoxy for its own sake was the main reason for this impoverishment. But there were other contributory and connected causes. The life of the Scottish Church provided no very stimulating atmosphere. It lacked the power to encourage theological enquiry, or even to secure a reasonable standard of academic attainment. There may have been shortcomings in the Divinity Halls, but there was little excuse for conditions which led the Commissioners of 1826 to animadvert on 'the laxity of the Church, which till recently allowed students who merely enrolled their names in the books of the professors . . . without hearing a lecture or receiving any instruction in Theology, to be taken on trial by the Presbytery for license to preach.' The sectarianism of the Scottish Church, moreover, had a retarding effect on its theological development. All living and powerful theological thinking is Catholic rather than sectarian or specialised. The party struggles, political and ecclesiastical alike, that make up so much Scottish Church history inevitably narrowed and thwarted theological enquiry in the true sense and led to a dangerous neglect of contemporary thought in it wider and more fruitful developments.

The first half of the nineteenth century marks the beginning of a new movement which was to transform both Scottish theological teaching and the life of the Presbyterian Church. On the theological side revival may be said to have begun with John M'Leod Campbell—'a heretic,' who in the long run converted the Church. In the parishes of the Church of Scotland a comparable revitalising movement culminated in the work of Thomas Chalmers. Sectarian divisions remained, and were indeed aggravated in 1843 but, even so, they ceased to have a merely negative influence and came to stimulate wider theological enquiry and a richer life within the Church.

THE DISRUPTION TO THE REUNION, 1843-1929

In the Glasgow Divinity classes the full effects of these movements did not become manifest until well after the middle of the century. For the vacancy in the Chair of Divinity created by Stevenson MacGill's death in 1840, two nominations were made—Thomas Chalmers and Alexander Hill, son of an outstanding leader of the Moderate party. With the Disruption only three years ahead and ecclesiastical controversy growing more acute it must have been an anxious choice. What would have happened had Thomas Chalmers been appointed is a matter of speculative interest—like the possibilities that might have followed Gilbert Burnet's remaining in Glasgow in the seventeenth century. Hill was appointed, but the keenness of the contest is indicated by the fact that the Rector of the period travelled specially from London to support him. Chalmer's biographer, Dr. Hanna, commented bitterly that the University made as great a mistake in rejecting Chalmers as it had done in refusing the Chair of Logic to Edmund Burke—on which H. M. B. Reid remarks that in both cases it may have been wise to

prefer efficiency to eloquence. The latest writer on the period,
Dr. Hugh Watt, is probably correct in saying that neither
eloquence nor efficiency entered deeply into the choice, but
that the dominant factor was ecclesiastical politics.

Hill taught for over twenty years, covering the period
in which the Free Church College, established in 1856,
brought rivalry in theological teaching closer to the University than before. He had studied under his father, author of
the famous St. Andrews plan of theological teaching, and
brought not only his father's tradition and methods but a
good deal of his lecture material to the work of the Glasgow
chair. 'Few men,' says H. M. B. Reid, 'passed through the
Disruption period with greater steadiness or dignity.' None
the less, teaching on the Scheme of Salvation; the Disease
and the Remedy, following a plan devised sixty years before,
had become outmoded long before Hill's retirement. The
welcome which awaited John Caird in 1862 was a measure
of the growing impatience of the nineteenth century with a
tradition that went back to the seventeenth and had ceased
to have vitality and power.

Caird's inaugural address deliberately broke with tradition and made it evident that there was to be as great a
change in the theological atmosphere of the Divinity Hall
as in its impending geographical removal from High Street
to Gilmorehill. It inauguarted a half-century of achievement
in which Caird and his successors, Dickson and Hastie,
with their colleagues in Oriental Languages, Ecclesiastical
History and Biblical Criticism, recaptured the traditions of
Strang, Dickson and Baillie in the early period of Glasgow's
theological renown.

From the outset it was plain that Caird was not content
to follow the traditional lines of Alexander Hill, his own
teacher, to whom, none the less, he referred with great respect.
He did not regard it as his function to give his students 'an
irresistible and logically infallible system of Divinity,' . . .
but 'to supply the principles upon which alone a true inter-

pretation of the Christian system could be founded.' These principles were based on his conviction that 'an uncritical, unreasoned, and unexplained faith was insufficient.' In his inaugural lecture he asserted that while it may be necessary to check the self-sufficiency of reason it does not follow that 'because human intelligence cannot comprehend God, it can have no real knowledge of Him; because it cannot "find out the Almighty to perfection," it can never know Him at all.' This defence of the place of reason in relation to faith, as contrasted with acceptance of a formula authoritatively imposed, was further developed in Caird's endeavour to find in philosophy grounds on which faith could be shown to be both intelligent and intelligible. Reflective reason, he believed, might well lead to a modification of traditional teaching, but such modification would not touch anything which was really essential to religious life, or to Christianity.

If traditional theology had ignored the claims of reason in the realm of faith, it had no less forgotten the need for constant study of the Bible from which its dogmas claimed authority. Caird's exposure of the first of these errors found a needed counterpart in the work of William Dickson, appointed first holder of the Chair of Divinity and Biblical Criticism, in 1863, and Professor of Divinity from 1873 till 1895. In his New Testament teaching, Dickson insisted that neither traditionalism, on the one hand, nor desire for novelty, on the other, should replace a conscientious regard for truth as the deepest interest of Christian scholarship. Such scholarship, he believed, could not be disregarded in the teaching of Divinity. The supreme standard of doctrine is the Word of God, and the Christian theologican must try to 'revert to the Scriptural basis of the science and to ascertain the origin, development, mutual relations and organic connection of the truths set forth in the New Testament.' His own distinctive contribution lay in the study of Biblical Theology—'a subject,' as he said, 'which has not been much handled, so far as is known to me, in this country.' His programme, says

H. M. B. Reid, was 'that of an accomplished scholar who knew the country to be traversed, and knew also that a Christian theology stands or falls with Holy Scripture.'

The enrichment of theological studies by the results of New Testament scholarship which Dickson thus initiated was continued by his successors in the Chair of Divinity and Biblical Criticism, William Stewart and George Milligan.

Stewart had heard the inaugural lectures of Caird and Dickson of which he spoke with enthusiastic approval. While minister of St. George's in the Fields, he published a booklet interpreting the order of paragraphs in the Third Gospel, partly in the light of incidents recorded at the beginning of certain key passages and partly by an ingenious alphabetical scheme of arrangement. Professor G. H. C. Macgregor, to whom I am indebted for guidance in dealing with his predecessors in the Chair of Divinity and Biblical Criticism, points out that while Stewart's theory is quite fantastic in the light of modern synoptic scholarship, it is worked out with great skill and with no little persuasiveness. In addition to his New Testament teaching, Stewart served assiduously in University administration, and from 1911 until his death in 1919 he held the Office of Dean of Faculties.

George Milligan, one of the most distinguished New Testament scholars of the past half-century, is still remembered with gratitude by his students for the clarity of his exposition, his sympathy with the views of others, his genial humour and dignified kindness. Like his predecessor, he took a full share in University administration and was prominent also in the service of the Church of Scotland, being Moderator of the General Assembly in 1923. The foundations of his scholarship were laid during his parish ministry at Caputh, but it was during his tenure of the Chair that Milligan began to throw a flood of light on many New Testament words and grammatical forms from the hitherto unused papyri unearthed by modern archæological research. He wrote, not only as a scholar for scholars, but with a skill and imagination which held the interest of the ordinary man. His *magnum opus, The Vocabulary of the Greek Testament,* was begun in 1911 in collaboration with Professor James Hope Moulton. Each section was published as it was completed, and after Moulton's tragic death in 1917 Milligan continued alone until the eighth and final part was issued in 1929— 'a noble piece of work, nobly done.'

During the period of Stewart and Milligan, the Divinity Chair was occupied by William Hastie, H. M. B. Reid, and my own predecessor, Dr. William Fulton. While Caird had linked the teaching of Theology with contemporary philosophical systems, and Dickson had insisted on its basis in Biblical study, it remained for Hastie to make plain the importance of modern theological movements in the reformulation of doctrine. His linguistic skill enabled him to appreciate all that was best in the thought of his time. Dr. Fulton, in an appreciation of his own teacher, has recalled Hastie's masterly expositions of modern German thought and his persuasion that the movement of theology must ever advance, without rest and without haste. At the same time 'he loved the Reformed Theology with a deep and even passionate love, born of ancestral piety,' and 'was zealous in vindicating its principles in the face of modern knowledge.' 'The Theology of the Reformed Church,' wrote Professor Flint, in his Preface to Hastie's Croall Lectures, 'had early taken possession of Dr. Hastie's mind and heart and absorbed his interest more and more as the years went on.' Within that theology the Scottish tradition had a special place, as Hastie's inaugural lecture emphasised. 'In the Scottish Church,' he said, 'the distinctively Reformed faith most livingly and purely survives. It is a sacred trust, a holy inheritance which we do well jealously to guard. . . . May it be ours to take some small share in this important work of preparing theologically for the future triumph and closer union of our Reformed Church.'

Such closer union was encouraged in Scotland nowhere

more cordially than in the Glasgow Divinity Hall, where it was clearly recognised that mere sectarianism was hostile to every interest of Theology. Caird encouraged the attendance of students belonging to Churches other than the Church of Scotland, and paid a special tribute to their presence as conducing to that mutual respect and kindly feeling between the future ministers of the various Churches which it ought to be every good man's aim to promote. Dickson, more than once, underlined the success of the Glasgow regulations for the degree of B.D., which had virtually affiliated the extra-mural theological halls to the University. It was in recognition of Hastie's catholicity of spirit that the friends who founded the lectureship that bears his name insisted that the choice of lecturers was not to be restricted to one church alone.

The revitalising of Church life in Scotland sent an increasing number of men to the study of theology. Growing sympathy between the teachers of theology sent, in turn, a body of men into the ministry for whom sectarian differences became less and less significant in comparison with doctrinal unity. Caird, Dickson and Hastie earned the gratitude of generations of students for their teaching. They received the thanks of the University for their loyalty to its service, Dickson in particular for his devoted interest in its Library. They deserved, perhaps, more recognition than they received for their influence in the movement towards unity in Scottish Presbyterianism which was to reach its fulfilment after their time.

In the same period noteworthy contributions to theological study and to the life of the Church were made by successive holders of the Chair of Ecclesiastical History. Professor Norman Sykes, in his inaugural lecture as holder of the corresponding Chair in Cambridge, noted with a measure of envy the early date of the Glasgow foundation in 1715. He noted also that some of the earlier holders of the Chair had not been exempt from the infirmity and frailties even of ecclesiastical human nature. In the later period, however,

William Lee, Robert Herbert Story, James Cooper and Archibald Main each contributed fresh and scholarly insight to the record of Scottish Church History from which theologian and ecclesiastic alike could draw wise guidance for their immediate tasks.

For his inaugural address in October, 1904, Hastie's successor in the Chair of Divinity, Dr. H. M. B. Reid, chose as his subject 'A Scottish School of Theology.' The characteristics of the Scottish School in his judgment were, first, its emphasis on the doctrine of the Church, and, second, its insistence on Scripture as the norm of authority. To these essentials were added a conviction of the reality of spiritual experience; a practical interest in what God requires of man as well as what man requires of God; a demand for logical presentation of doctrine; and approval of rational method in discussion of great religious themes. This was, as Reid described it, the heritage into which Scottish Theology entered, the work of men like those whom we commemorate to-night.

Twenty-one years ago the reunion of the Scottish Churches opened the way for the blending of two theological traditions which, though separated, had never been so far apart as the ecclesiastical jealousy and rancour which Caird deplored had often made them appear. In the carrying out of these negotiations we in Glasgow owe very much to Dr. Reid's successor and my own predecessor, Dr. William Fulton, happily with us tonight.

Such in broad outline is the factual record of five hundred years. Their inner meaning and spiritual significance are less easily assessed. Two things, however, may be said. In the first place, the teachers of Divinity in Glasgow have sought to blend Catholic and ecumenical scholarship with the distinctive qualities of the Scottish tradition. In so doing they have claimed from the University and from the Church due recognition of the place of sacred learning and have sent scholars of note to serve in many spheres throughout the world. Secondly, they have kept their study of the Church's Faith always in close contact with its life and work. It could not be otherwise in a University within sight and sound of the streets, the shipyards and the factories of a great city. Thus they have provided the Church with men not only trained in the study of theological doctrine, but prepared to take the truths of the classroom into the life of the community, there to be tested and proved in their adequacy and power.

I began with a quotation on the significance of history from John Caird's Gifford Lectures. Let me close with characteristic words taken from his introductory lecture in the first session of teaching here in Gilmorehill. 'Need we fold our hands as if the work of the theologian were ended, and that ever-growing process and freshness of results, which is the stimulus and reward of intellectual labour in every other sphere of thought, were here no longer possible—as if the last stone had already been placed on the temple of truth, the last sheaf gathered from the Master's field? No, it is not so. . . . The great living temple that has been slowly rising through the ages is still far from complete; and when, on its stately walls and uprising towers, hands that can work no more have left off to build, we are now called to resume and carry on the noble task. The field where generations of reapers have gathered in such rich results is still waving luxuriantly with a perennial harvest of thought; and still, to the youngest and latest come of His servants, the Master's voice is calling, "Go thou also into the vineyard".'

CLASSICS

by

C. J. Fordyce
Professor of Humanity

Classical scholarship, in the usual meaning of the phrase, begins with the recovery of the Latin classics and the return of Greek to the West. But all Europe did not rediscover antiquity at once: the movement which for convenience, but sometimes misleadingly, we call the Renaissance, was a slow and gradual process which covered more than a century. When this University was founded in 1451, the Renaissance had begun in Italy. The current of enthusiasm for the long-lost past was already flowing strong; the passion for manuscripts, for finding them, reading them, copying them, was in full career, and the Pope who granted our bull of foundation was himself the founder of the Vatican Library. In the succeeding century the movement was gaining strength and spreading over Western Europe. But Scotland was then, even more than it is now, a remote corner of Europe: it was detached from the spiritual and intellectual forces which were changing the face of Italy, France and even England. Like most things, the Renaissance came late to Scotland: it came about a century late and coincided with the Reformation. So far as the Universities were concerned, it was at Glasgow, by a series of happy accidents, that its first impact was made. When Alexander Hume published his *New Grammar* in 1612, he acknowledged his indebtedness to one James Fullarton, with whom he had had a profitable discussion of a problem which had been perplexing him. This James Fullarton was no professional scholar: at this time he was a Gentleman of the Household of the Duke of York, and he continued to serve the same master when he came to the throne as Charles I. But he had been one of the first group of Glasgow graduates who had been trained in the new learning, for whom dead languages had come to life, and who had not only Latin but Greek and Hebrew at their command.

To understand what had happened, one must look back for a moment. Latin, of course, had been the language of University life. It was the common speech of educated men: it had been the vehicle not only of academic instruction but also of academic conversation since Universities began, and in that use it continued long after the Reformation. The first lectures in English were given by Francis Hutcheson in 1730, and students in College were required, in theory at least, to speak in Latin to one another. But of Latin literature there had been very little knowledge and of Greek there had been none. The course of study had been confined within the narrow limits of scholastic doctrine: its basis, on the secular side, was the logical, the ethical and, in part, the scientific works of Aristotle, read—or rather first dictated and then read—in Latin versions.

England had been more fortunate, and there the new learning was already at home. Some of the first humanists, Poggio and Chrysoloras, had visited England themselves; the fifteenth century had already seen a great patron of learning in Humphrey, Duke of Gloucester, and men like Gray and Gunthorpe, Linacre, Colet and More had brought the scholarship of Italy to the North. Early in the sixteenth century it was established in the Universities; in 1516, when he founded Corpus Christi College, Oxford, Bishop Fox provided for the teaching of Latin and Greek; at Cambridge the Readership in Greek was founded at the same time and the Regius Professorship a little later. These were the days of Roger Ascham and Gabriel Harvey, and a host of translators of the classics testifies to the new demand. But the Scottish Universities were still pursuing their ancient ways. With the aid of Paris, Scotland had indeed produced in

George Buchanan a humanist of European reputation, whose birth and schooling we are proud to claim as St. Andrews claims his later years. No less a judge than Scaliger pronounced him the best writer of Latin verse in Europe: his Latin version presented the Psalms in real elegiac and lyric poetry, and the sapphics he wrote on Mayday were a revelation to Wordsworth. Greek he served by translating the *Medea* and the *Alcestis* into Latin and Linacre's Grammar into English. But he did curiously little to promote humanism in his own country. In 1563 he had drawn up a scheme of reform for St. Andrews, but nothing came of it, and even when he returned there as Principal of St. Leonard's in 1566 he did nothing to implement it. Our own regent James Melville complains of his St. Andrews days: 'I wold haiff gladlie bein at the Greik and Hebrew toungs, because I red in our Byble that it was translated out of Hebrew and Greik, bot the langages war nocht to be gottine in the land.' At Glasgow the story was the same.

The revolution was the work of one man, Andrew Melville. When he had gone up to St. Andrews and followed the regular mediæval curriculum there, he already knew more than his teachers: for, thanks to a French refugee settled at Montrose, he knew Greek and, while they were dictating the Latin version of Aristotle, he was reading the Greek. Leaving St. Andrews as he found it, he went abroad to plunge enthusiastically into the new learning and the new philosophy, the world of Turnebus and Ramus, Scaliger and Beza, all of them his friends. Ten years later he returned to plant the new seed in his own country, and to bring Scotland into line with Europe, and in 1574 he was called to be Principal Regent at Glasgow. His indefatigable energy went with singular personal charm. Unyielding in principle but brimful of fun, taking on himself an incredibly heavy load of teaching and preaching but hospitable and fond of company, he is an unexpectedly debonair figure in the gallery of Reformation divines. No one could have been better qualified for his task: he knew what he wanted and he had the knack of getting his way. The first tide of the Reformation had left the College almost deserted: Melville found it in the hands of Peter Blackburn, a St. Andrews man who had been put in to keep things going. He knew only the old ways in which he had been trained and was suspicious of the new regime: if the new Principal had been of a different sort there might have been an awkward situation. But this gay, determined little man disarmed suspicion and turned Blackburn into his devoted second-in-command. Then he set to work with a small picked group of new students, and Greek was taught for the first time in a Scottish University. To make a new start, he had to do all the work himself. But work was nothing to Melville; he brought his pupils through Latin and Greek and on to philosophy and mathematics, and it was only when he had gathered a team of juniors trained in his own methods that he could hand over the Arts teaching to others and concentrate on what he regarded as his real function, the teaching of theology and oriental languages. But he first put Arts teaching on a new foundation. The old system of regenting which made the regent a jack-of-all-trades, who took one year of entrants right through their course, had fitted the old scholastic discipline well enough, but it did not answer the claims of the new humane learning. Melville swept it away and put his regents in charge of subjects, not of years. The teaching of Greek and Latin literature was now one man's function: his pupils were reading Virgil and Horace, Cicero's speeches and philosophical works, Homer and Hesiod, Plato, Isocrates, Theocritus. The omission of Greek drama is notable: the reason was not an objection to drama itself, for Terence was (with Cæsar and Ovid) read at school. The languages were still regarded as ancillary to the study of theology, but not all Melville's pupils became ecclesiastics and the list of them includes men of affairs like Sir Gideon Murray and Sir Edward Drummond as well as academics and divines.

Not the least interesting among them is the black sheep of the flock, Mark Alexander Boyd, who, coming with a bad record from the Grammar School, proceeded at College to make it worse. After a lamentable story of truantry and insubordination—we have it from his kindly regent, who tried hard to think, and make, the best of him—he turned his back on Glasgow and went abroad. There, in the course of a colourful vagabondage which took him over all France and some of Italy as student and soldier of fortune, he found time (or so he says) to turn Cæsar into Greek in the style of Herodotus. This *tour de force* has not survived, and the reason which he gives for having destroyed it, that he preferred deserving fame to achieving it, shows that modesty was not conspicuous among his virtues. But we have a volume of Ovidian verse which he published at Bordeaux in 1590; there fifteen elegiac epistles in the manner of the *Heroides* and twelve hexameter poems on various flowers and plants are prefaced by a dedication to King James. They are not great poetry, but their ease and their learning put them high in an art in which Scotland was outstanding for a century. After all his adventures Boyd came home to Scotland, and he died an Ayrshire laird.

So the opening of the seventeenth century saw the classics well established at Glasgow, and we realise what a difference a few years could make when we find a young man who proposes to visit France studying the vernacular with the aid of the Greek text of Plutarch and a French translation. Melville's successors were not men of his stature: they were preoccupied with theological contention and with the issues of church and state. But they were accomplished scholars, widely read and able to turn an epigram on a friend or (more often, perhaps) an enemy or to greet an occasion in a sapphic ode. Patrick Sharp had been master of the Grammar School when Melville was in Glasgow and had absorbed his ideas then: he declared himself that he had learned more from Melville 'craking and pleying for understanding of the

authors quhilk he teatched in the scholl nor be all his com-
mentares.' Robert Boyd, his successor, was Melville's equal
in scholarship. He had taught as a regent at Montauban,
where his inaugural lecture had been on Persius and where
he had instructed his students that class lectures were not
enough and they they must use books for themselves—advice
which shows how far the mediæval system was now left
behind. In John Cameron, the 'walking library' (as Sir
Thomas Urquhart called him), the town of Glasgow itself
—the Saltmarket—produced a Greek scholar of European
reputation whose scholarship gained him the friendship of
Casaubon: if he had given himself to Greek studies, his life
would have been a happier and a longer one. Apart from one
year in a regentship which he found irksome and one stormy
year in the Principalship which he was forced to resign, he
spent his days in France: there his learning became a legend
and his erastianism cost him his life at the age of forty-six.

Such were the Principals. Of the day-to-day work of the
regents we should like to know more. The College records of
these unsettled years are tantalisingly incomplete, but such
glimpses as we have do them credit. When Robert Blair
became regent in 1616, three years after taking his degree,
the advice he got was what a young teacher would get to-day:
'My elder colleagues,' he says, 'urged me to peruse all classical
authors.' And, when he settled in College, he took them at
their word: he had read the whole of Plautus when the chance
discovery of St. Augustine turned his thoughts into new
channels. A little later, idly turning over a Petronius which
he had bought when he was equipping himself for his work,
he was moved to renounce the classics and devote himself to
the service of the Church. The conversion is easy to parallel:
the significant thing is that he had been encouraged to read
Petronius as Latin. The seventeenth-century College was
more broad-minded in its taste and more catholic in its
learning than one might have supposed.

Early in the century, by 1637 at any rate, the professions of

Humanity and Greek were separated and so, with some breaks due to lack of funds, they have continued to this day. The scheme of studies and examinations in Arts which was drawn up in 1648 provides for Latin studies in the first year and for Greek in the second. In both languages there are exercises in composition, in prose and for 'those who have the faculty' in verse: at the beginning of each year the work of the previous year is tested by a 'theme' prescribed by the Principal, to be rendered by the bejans into Latin, but the semis into Greek. In the higher years, practice in the languages did not cease. In 1672 the Privy Council passed a singularly unenlightened enactment forbidding the teaching of Greek outside the Universities, on the ground that such teaching prejudiced the Universities by 'rendering some of their professions altogether useless.' In the West of Scotland at least the prohibition does not seem to have been enforced, but the attitude which it represented had the effect of retarding the development of classical studies in Scotland for more than a century.

The seventeenth century had been a time of intense intellectual vitality in Scotland, but it was also a time of unsettlement in Church and State, and besides its share in the national troubles the College had had its domestic trials. Of the period which succeeded great things might have been expected. In England, the eighteenth century was the great era of classical scholarship: it was the age of Bentley and Porson and—what was no less significant than the appearance of these giants—it was also the great age of the non-professional scholar, in which as much scholarly work was done outside the Universities as in them and in which two able textual critics of the Greek dramatists were to be found in Devon, the one a practising physician and the other a town clerk. Scotland has nothing comparable to show. It had five Universities to England's two; the grammar schools and the parish schools were doing their work and putting Latin at any rate within the reach of everyone. But the zest and enthusiasm for humane studies had gone: there was no advance, and hardly anything of that critical scholarship which in England laid the foundations for all that has followed. As for that astonishing summer of Latin poetry which moved Dr. Johnson to say that it 'would have done honour to any country' and that 'the English had very little to oppose,' it had faded: the poets of the *Deliciae* had no successors.

A critic in the *Edinburgh Review* of 1821, writing just when a change was about to happen, assigns two reasons for this state of things—'the nature of our Church Establishment' and 'the forms of our academic tuition.' As for the first, while in England the Church is the main support of learning and such of her endowments 'as are every now and then bestowed upon real merit and attainments operate in a wide circle as vouchers to Hope and spurs to Industry,' in Scotland 'for wise reasons . . . the ecclesiastical profession is stripped of all these substantial attractions which incite the ardour of Southern divines. . . . Hence the very general distribution of knowledge to a certain degree of excellence and, at the same time, the extreme rarity of anything approaching to perfection.' As for the second, he laments that young men 'come to College by no means qualified to profit by a system which is restricted to public lecturing and occasional examination.' He finds this weakness of schooling most obvious in Greek, and the fact that he regards Greek as a more difficult language to acquire than Latin—a judgment with which few modern teachers would agree—suggests that he had suffered from it himself. There is no reason, he thinks, why 'as large a proportion of sound and elegant scholars should not be produced in Scotland as at an English University: all that is needed is a little more trouble and a little more activity in the incumbents of the chairs, who would do well to 'blend something of the character of an English tutor with the dignity of a Scotch Professor.' 'It is to such as aim at a really high proficiency in classical learning that we would have the Professor devote a portion of that plentiful leisure which remains to him after the discharge of the ordinary duties of his chair.'

There is something in this diagnosis, but it cannot represent the whole truth. It is true that in Scotland the scholar had no deaneries to spur his endeavour and could not hope to emulate John Randolph, who from holding simultaneously three Oxford professorships proceeded to hold successively three bishoprics. But in fact few of the English scholars were clerics; Porson, Markland, Dawes, Heath, Musgrave, Wakefield, Tyrrwhit—none of these was in orders. No doubt the Scottish professor could have an easy life: but the Oxford and Cambridge colleges were not hives of industry, and the offer made by Ross at Glasgow, of which I shall speak in a moment, shows that there at any rate the will to provide something beyond routine lecturing was not wanting. It is true that there was nothing like an examination for honours: but there was none at Oxford, and at Cambridge it was in mathematics that classical scholars were somewhat perfunctorily examined. No doubt Greek teaching was not on the level of Latin, but from some schools at any rate Glasgow was drawing students who had been taught Greek. The explanation must lie deeper. And one remembers on the one hand that the nadir of Scottish classics coincided with the zenith of Scottish philosophy: on the other, that political economy and law were flourishing in Glasgow while classical studies were in decline. A new interest in metaphysics and morals, the fact that Scotland was realising itself as a commercial country, and the growth of a certain materialism—these were as potent causes as any for the sterility of classical scholarship.

Andrew Ross, who came to the profession of Humanity from Edinburgh in 1706, was a not inconsiderable scholar. His inaugural lecture was devoted to the definition of Humanity and the pragmatic defence of that title for Greek and Latin learning as being the key on the one hand to the New Testament, on the other to the science of law, the two things which have done most to make civilised man what he is. Five years later, in a Latin public lecture—one of the first of a series of weekly public lectures given by members of the Faculty—he gave an outline of his plans for his teaching and for his own work. His interest is in Latin idiom and he takes Terence as his text: he has sensible remarks on the principles of translation and learned disquisitions by the way on the status of freedmen, on ancient flutes, on the authenticity of the prologues. Of the state of classical studies he has two complaints—that teaching in the schools is ineffective and that students are going straight into the Greek class, side-stepping Humanity, or even avoiding Greek and going direct to Philosophy—and he takes advantage of the opportunity of appealing to the clerical members of his audience to use their influence to remedy these evils. Teaching in the schools should be rationalised: presenting the rules of Latin grammar in Latin is conveying *obscurum per obscurius;* Latin should be taught in English and so taught that the beginner is not bewildered by a mass of detail and can master one stage at a time. But teaching cannot be improved until there are good teachers, and those who are in a position to advise parents should urge them to see that their sons continue their classical studies at College and make themselves good scholars instead of impatiently hurrying on to philosophy. He himself, he says, will be glad to do what he can to improve things by giving 'private Colleges'—that is, tutorial instruction—in Latin literature to students of philosophy in the senior years who wish either to make up what they missed in their ill-considered haste or to go further in studies which have interested them. How successful this appeal was and how many took advantage of his offer, we do not know, but there was no obvious result. His Greek colleague, Alexander Dunlop, was more interested in University politics than in scholarship, but he was a good grammarian and a vigorous teacher. The two worked well together, and in 1712 they produced a scheme for making the teaching of their languages more effective by dovetailing their classes into one another, so that the student pursued both for two years. A few years later Ross showed still more enterprise by persuading the Faculty to launch an appeal for books—'copies of the rarer classick authors for the use of the young gentlemen.' So in the Honours Class and the Class Library Andrew Ross has his memorials.

We have a pleasant side-light on Ross's first year of teaching from a son of the Laird of Johnstone, James Houston, who came to College in 1706, 'diverted himself' (as he says) for five years in Arts, proceeded to a doctorate in Medicine at Leiden, and thereafter pursued a lively career as a merchant-adventurer in Africa and the West Indies. Writing of his year in the Humanity class he says: 'Our Regent understood his Profession exceedingly well, but was a little upon the volatile taste, and wanted to infuse lofty notions into his disciples of the grandeur and magnificence of the old Romans. I remember he told us "that there was more money expended and more men employed in cleaning a common sewer in Rome than all the charges and number of men in the whole confederate Army amounted to under the great Duke of Marlborough." But I don't remember to have read any such account in Roman authors. However, it took with me, for I like much to hear stories and read of the exploits of the ancients and this year I passed with profit and pleasure.' One would like to know the context of Ross's remark; at least he could interest a wayward pupil and leave him something to remember after forty years of adventuring. When he went on to Greek next year, Houston was not so happy: 'I never knew so much of the Greek language as to be master of any author.' Greek was lagging far behind Latin. When Ross came, the Faculty had resolved that he should not teach grammar and that students entering his class must have done their grammar at school. Dunlop was spending almost the whole of his time on grammar and such reading of authors as he did was no more than a grammatical exercise. Cosmo

Innes's stricture is well deserved: students so handled could but poorly maintain the character of a school in which Andrew Melville had taught Greek and John Cameron had learned it.

In 1727 the excitements of a Rectorial Election upset Ross's mental equilibrium: 'it is a question if ever he be in case for teaching,' says Wodrow, 'and he was come to a considerable exactness in his business of Latin.' Of his son George, who was his understudy for sixteen years and his successor for three, there is not much to note except the filial piety which induced him to hand over his stipend to his father and the innocence which led him to complain to the College that he had nothing left for himself. The next pair of professors, George Muirhead in Humanity and James Moor in Greek, have derived an adventitious fame from their share in the development of Greek printing. Moor, who owed his bad eyesight to measles and his bad temper (so it was supposed) to an excessive addiction to tea, had been tutor to Lord Kilmarnock and was Librarian of the College when in 1745 he went to London and interceded, without success, for his unfortunate pupil. He was interested in the Greek mathematicians and shared that interest with his fellow-eccentric Robert Simson, Professor of Mathematics, who, like himself, still 'kept chambers' in College. He collated two Paris manuscripts for the edition of Apollonius of Perga which Simson published in 1749 and contributed his scholarship to Simson's Euclid of 1756. Moor himself projected an edition of Archimedes but it never went beyond a first volume containing the Psammites. Apart from it, he published only a work on prepositions, a few literary essays, and a translation of Tyrtæus, dedicated, under the title of 'Spartan Lessons,' to 'the young gentlemen lately bred at the University of Glasgow at present serving their countrymen as officers of the Highland Battalions now in America.' Most of his energies were devoted to the enterprise in which he was associated with his colleague Muirhead, with Alexander

Wilson, who curiously combined the offices of Type-founder to the University and Professor of Astronomy, and with the brothers Andrew and Robert Foulis, both graduates of the University and its Printers by appointment.

The series of Foulis classics had begun with a Demetrius in 1743, and in 1744 the press had produced a Pindar, a Marcus Aurelius, and the so-called 'immaculate' Horace, in which George Ross had been concerned. These were followed by Xenophon, Sophocles, Aristotle, Aeschylus and Theocritus: Cicero in twenty duodecimo volumes appeared in 1749. The climax was to be a great Plato, the text edited by Moor and the type designed by Wilson on the model of Stephanus' founts. The work was advertised in 1751; much material was collected—the Foulises met scholars and obtained notes and collations from them in Holland and in Paris, and as late as 1764 they were getting collations from the Vatican—but no use was ever made of it. Owing to Foulis's other commitments—especially the ill-fated Academy of Art—the project had to be abandoned, and the greatest achievement of the press remained the folio Homer which appeared in four volumes in 1756 and 1758, one of the finest pieces of Greek printing ever produced. Gibbon said of it, 'As the eye is the organ of fancy, I read Homer with more pleasure in the Glasgow edition: through that fine medium the poet's sense appears more beautiful and transparent.' The College was justly proud of the work which had been done within its walls, and the list of those to whom it sent presentation copies contains, in surprising conjunction, the names of William Pitt and the King of Spain. Moor and Muirhead were responsible for the text; it was a reprint of Samuel Clarke's, the last English edition, but the care taken over proof-reading (there were seven independent readings) set a new standard in accuracy. After Homer came a series of the historians in forty-one volumes, with Greek text and Latin translation on facing pages, intended, as the publishers say, 'to render the reading of the historians more convenient for gentlemen in active life.' The work of the Foulises and their editors should not be forgotten: for though no original work was done on the texts, by providing convenient, readable and accurate editions of most of the major authors, and some minor ones, they did a real service to classical studies. But the printing-house never recovered from the disaster which befell the Academy of Art, and Moor himself fell a victim in 1766 when his library, which he had pledged as security to the Foulises, was seized by them to stave off their own creditors.

Moor held the chair for eight years more, but his failing health prevented him from performing its duties, and for some time the teaching was done by his pupil John Gillies, a man who in the course of his long life acquired a reputation beyond his merits. He deserves remark as the author of one of the first works on Ancient History published in Britain. His *History of Greece* and Mitford's appeared at the same time, but that work and the *History of the Ancient World* from Alexander to Augustus which followed it are uncritical, common-place and turgid. He makes no attempt to distinguish history from mythology, and the tenour of his dedication to George III—that Greek history 'evinces the inestimable benefits resulting to Liberty itself from the lawful domination of hereditary kings'—says more for his loyalty than for his acumen. It is to his credit that his survey includes literature and philosophy—and even a chapter on art—but his priggish prejudices are no less obvious there, and it is hard to believe that one who described the Old Comedy as 'this odious and disgusting form' was a sympathetic teacher of Greek. Still, as a historian he was a pioneer, and he has another title to note, if not to great esteem. It was given to him late in life to translate Aristotle's *Ethics* into English for the first time: his Aristotelianism is as uncritical as his history, and he believes that everything that is not Aristotelian is wrong with a simple sincerity which is more like the thirteenth century than the reign of King George IV.

Moor's successor in the Chair of Greek was John Young, an enthusiast not only for his own subject but in the fields of Italian literature and music as well. It was not for nothing that he was a passionate devotee of the stage: he brought to his work not only some good scholarship but something of the gifts of the actor, and he made an impression on his pupils which was more than that of a schoolmaster. He could make his class laugh heartily with him over Aristophanes and move them to tears with his reading of Homer: he could pass all of a sudden (so Lockhart says) 'from a transport of sheer verbal ecstasy about the particle ἄρα into an ecstasy quite as vehement and a thousand times more noble about the deep pathetic beauty of one of Homer's conceptions in the expression of which that particle happens to occur.'

William Richardson, his Humanity colleague, was as sedate as Young was lively: he stood out among his colleagues as a man of the world, and something of a *poseur*. He was a man of letters rather than a scholar or, as a contemporary describes him with contemporary elegance of phrase, 'he would have preferred the character of the Addison to that of the Porson of the age.' He was in no danger of being taken for a Porson: how much of an Addison he was is for others to say. It is for his work in Shakespearian criticism that he has his importance, but the notes which he printed to accompany his Lectures on Latin Literature and Roman Antiquities show that he took pains with his teaching and that, if it was not as adventurous and stimulating as Young's, it was systematic and sound. As were the Professors, so were their best pupils—Thomas Campbell, John Gibson Lockhart, 'Christopher North.' They were not scholars, but they had a good knowledge of classical literature. When Campbell, as Rector, established a prize in the College, it was for original Latin verse that he gave it. And a certain competence in the languages was presumed in other departments of teaching; Quintilian was read in Latin in the class of Logic and Rhetoric under Jardine and

Aristotle in Greek in the class of Moral Philosophy under Mylne.

Richardson was a man of clear distinction of mind: his successor, Josiah Walker, was an undistinguished dilettante who was hoisted into the chair from the post of Collector of Customs at Perth. The voluminous notebooks of his which we possess are filled with superficialities on all manner of subjects; his published work was some pompous verse and the worst life of Burns ever written; his lectures were profuse in quotation of parallels from modern poetry, but for scholarship he did nothing at all.

Reform was now in the air. When the Chair of Greek was vacant by Young's death in 1820, the writer of the article in the *Edinburgh Review* which I have mentioned urged that a Professor of Greek should be relieved of the routine of elementary teaching and pointedly suggested how the Glasgow electors should use their opportunity. During the vacancy the Faculty took the hint and decided to appoint a teacher of elementary Greek: but just before the election that enlightened decision was rescinded and for many years —until the end of the century—the Professor of Greek had to be prepared to teach the alphabet himself or employ someone to do it for him. The new Professor, Daniel Keyte Sandford of Christ Church, was the first teacher to come to Glasgow from an English University, and had made a name for himself by his gift of rhetoric. 'A paragon of academic eloquence,' a pupil calls him after thirty years, but eloquence is no substitute for scholarship. An English reviewer in the *Westminster Review* of 1832 found Sandford's scholarship an easy target, and left him no comfort except that of knowing that his colleagues at St. Andrews and Edinburgh, under the same unkind but not unjust scrutiny, came off no better than he did. When Sandford deserted Greek for Sir Robert Peel and the Reform Bill, he gained a knighthood and Glasgow did not lose very much. In reaching his conclusion that Greek was 'in its infancy in

Scotland,' the same reviewer put his finger on the radical weakness—that for most students the Universities were still doing in Greek what should have been done at school.

When the Chair of Humanity next fell vacant in 1831, the ideal appointment was made—a young Glasgow graduate who had gone on to Cambridge and who had distinguished himself in both Universities: seven years later he was joined by another Cambridge man in the Chair of Greek, and Glasgow had a pair of professors who not only outshone all their predecessors but vastly outshone their contemporaries in the other Universities. James Bryce, writing of his student days under William Ramsay and Lushington, declares that when he went to Oxford he found there, in its much larger body of teachers, none superior, if indeed any equal, to them. They were very different men. Ramsay combined the best in the Scottish and English traditions. He was an exact scholar with a wide range of learning; he was interested in every aspect of ancient life; his lectures were full of his own vitality and he tried to bring home to the student's mind all that lay behind the words he read, to help him to recapture all the associations that they were written to evoke. His books on prosody and on antiquities gave new tools to the student and both sharpened and broadened his understanding: and his edition of the *Mostellaria* laid the foundations of Plautine study in Britain, the study which some fifty years later was to reach its climax in the work of another Glasgow man, that prodigy of light-hearted learning, Wallace Martin Lindsay. Lushington's scholarship was of a severer kind. In his inaugural lecture he made it clear that he regarded language as the subject of his chair. 'The study of a language,' he said, 'opens the mind's eye to a survey of its own operations, training it gradually to perceive and comprehend its own energies,' and he went on to emphasise the relations between the study of language and that of philosophy, and the value of linguistic study as an exercise in the analysis of thought. His was an austere discipline, but it was a much-needed corrective to the pretentious dilettantism which had taken the place of scholarship for most of a century. And the two professors were complementary to each other. From Ramsay the student got a wide view of the whole field of antiquity and learned to fit into its place everything that threw light on ancient life: from Lushington he had the patient exegesis of a text and acquired, slowly, perhaps,—for there were still many for whom Greek began at College—a sensitivity to the value of words, an awareness of idiom as a reflexion of thought. At last Glasgow had a school in which scholars could be made. And they were made. One was Charles Badham, son of the Professor of Medicine, editor of Euripides and Plato: the quarrelsome temper which he inherited from his father lost a fine scholar to this country but deserves the gratitude of Australia where, as the first Professor of Greek, he established the strong classical tradition which still survives. Another was W. Y. Sellar, Fellow of Oriel, whom we gave to St. Andrews and Edinburgh, a sensitive and sober critic of Latin poetry, a third his successor at St. Andrews, Lewis Campbell, Fellow of Queen's, the editor of Sophocles and Plato; a fourth was D. B. Munro, Provost of Oriel; it was Lushington who first turned his thoughts to Homeric studies. A fifth was Sir James Frazer, Fellow of Trinity, who declared that his life work was determined by the influence of William Ramsay. The introduction of Honours examinations in 1861 made less difference in practice than might be thought: for the Blackstone Examination, in which each candidate made his own profession of work, was already producing a width of reading and accuracy of knowledge which probably only the best undergraduates of contemporary Oxford and Cambridge could rival.

When Lushington, after a reign of thirty-seven years, retired in 1875, he was succeeded by another brilliant Cambridge classic of the same College, Richard Claverhouse Jebb, who was already a Cambridge teacher of some standing and Public Orator of the University. He came to Glasgow for a year's trial of the place, and one of the main inducements to stay was 'the six months' annual freedom from all official duties.' That, alas, has gone, and so has the other attraction which he found in Glasgow, the view from the windows of No. 5 'across the valley to the setting sun.' It was in Glasgow that he began his work on Sophocles, the greatest single contribution to Greek scholarship in Britain for many years: the *Introduction to Homer* was written for the needs of his Junior class: from here he worked for the establishment of the Hellenic Society and for the foundation of the *Journal of Hellenic Studies*. Though he took no interest in academic politics, he realised the peculiar qualities of Scottish University life, and he was quick to defend the Scottish Universities against attempts to turn them into English ones or German ones; he justified the drudgery of elementary teaching, which he did not pretend to enjoy, by pointing out that local conditions still made it a regrettable necessity, though it was less of a necessity than it had been, and that its removal would make a gulf between school and University. He was a tireless worker and the claims of his pupils were never sacrificed to those of his own interests, but he lacked the sympathy that makes a great teacher and in his dealings with his students he was too self-conscious to be natural. They respected his learning and the pains he took for them, but his fourteen years at Glasgow left less impression than they might have done.

His successor was an Oxford man who added to consummate scholarship the qualities which he had lacked. Of him I need say little, for the New College don who came here in 1889 and charmed Glasgow at the age of twenty-three is happily with us still, and there is no need for me to enlarge on the debt which Greek studies owe to Gilbert Murray, especially in this place where there are those who remember him with gratitude and affection. The same house in which Jebb's Sophocles was begun saw the beginning of

Murray's Euripides: a house has become a monument for less than that.

Nor shall I speak at length of the remaining names in our *fasti,* of George Ramsay's robust championship of the classics in education, of the shy, ironic fastidiousness of Gilbert Davies. I shall not embarrass the present Dean of Faculties, even at a distance, by speaking of the part he played in maintaining here one of the foremost schools of Greek in Britain. But in this room I must speak a personal word of John Swinnerton Phillimore. I shall not attempt to weigh the peculiar qualities of mind which were evident in everything he did, as editor, critic, translator and poet: I simply acknowledge the debt which I, and many others, owe to a Latinist who could make Latinists, whose scholarship had a sweep that embraced all Latinity and a subtlety that first amazed and then delighted.

I have tried to trace in this rough survey the phases through which the classical disciplines here have passed—the first period of rapturous apprehension of a new world, when men would give everything for Greek, and Latin was again the language of poetry; a second in which the vigour and excitement had faded into a stiff and unadventurous competence; a third in which Glasgow was brilliantly revitalised by Oxford and Cambridge and did something to repay her obligation. I have tried to recall the major figures in the story, some of them the possessors of that quality which, in Bentley's words, 'neither length of years nor assiduity of toil can give, but only nature and a lucky star.' I should like my last word to be of others, of those nameless students of four centuries who have taken from this place, not the elegancies of the scholar or his learning, but a love of the classics and some understanding of what they have to teach. These also are our pride.

40

HISTORY

by

Andrew Browning
Professor of History

It is not unfitting that the lecture on History in this series
should follow immediately after those on Divinity and
Humanity, for it was largely under the shadow and protection of these older disciplines that History made its first
entrance into the academic world. History was not a subject
of study at the mediæval university. Like the kindred subject
of Political Economy it has always been a study peculiarly
appropriate to the man of affairs, and its rise to prominence
has thus coincided with the appearance of the educated lay-
man, which was one of the consequences of the Renaissance
and Reformation, and with the immense development of the
administrative hierarchy, which has been one of the features
of the nineteenth and twentieth centuries.

Even as early as the sixteenth century, instruction in History
was not unknown in the University. Possibly under the
inspiration of George Buchanan, who was then engaged on
his *History of Scotland,* Andrew Melville, on becoming Principal of the University in 1574, included in the very elaborate
curriculum which he drew up 'a view of universal history,
supplemented by chronology and the composition of public
documents, such as charters, treaties and the like'; and apparently in the assignment of subjects at which he aimed associated this historical survey with Divinity. But the effective
connection seems rather to have been with Humanity. By
the visiting commissioners appointed by the General Assembly of 1639 it was expressly provided that 'the Master of the
Humanity Class shall go through a compendium of History';

while towards the close of the same century a determined
effort was made to secure the establishment of a professorship
of Humanity and History combined.

So novel, one must suppose, was the idea of giving such
recognition to History that the Faculty, in minuting their
resolution, deemed it prudent to record their reasons for what
they were doing. 'Taking into their consideration . . . that
a profession of Civil History for this University would much
tend to the better instruction of the youth, and especially of
those of the best quality, who may be called to serve their
country in civil employments, and may in a more pleasant
and taking manner instil the principles of virtue, and increase
that knowledge which may most fit men for an active life,
and that such a profession will be to the advantage and
ornament of the University,' and that the two professions of
Humanity and History may very well be exercised by one
professor, they resolve 'that there be immediately elected a
fit person to be Professor of Humanity and History, who
shall teach the same in such manner as the Faculty shall
enjoin him, and who shall be accounted one of the Masters
of this University as the Professors of Humanity used to be.'

Unfortunately the funds on which reliance had been placed
proved insufficient, and the election provided for could not at
that time be made. Among the competitors for a vacant
regency in 1690, however, there had been several who had
greatly impressed the Faculty, and on one of these it was
proposed to confer a purely exceptional appointment, which
available funds would justify, and which would serve one
of the purposes for which the joint professorship had been
designed. The resolution is minuted under date May 30,
1692. 'The Faculty this day taking into consideration the
condition of Mr. William Jameson, who had been born
blind, yet having been educated at this University hath
attained to great learning, and particularly is well skilled in
History, both civil and ecclesiastical, and having no estate
to subsist by, and the Faculty considering that he may be

useful in these sciences, therefore they have thought fit to allow to the said Mr. William Jameson 200 merks Scots per annum for two years commencing from the first of April last, the said Mr. William Jameson employing himself according to his capacity at the direction of the Faculty.' To William Jameson belongs the double distinction of having been the first Lecturer (as distinct from a Regent or Professor) at this University, and the first individual to hold any position within the University the sole duty connected with which was to give instruction in History.

Taken by itself the appointment appears to have been a success. On December 19, 1692, the Faculty determined 'that Mr. William Jameson have a public prelection of Civil History once a week on the Thursdays at three of the clock in the afternoon,' in the Laigh Common Hall and in Latin. On July 15, 1696, they raised his salary to 400 pounds Scots. But this perpetuation of his lectureship, which does not seem to have been originally intended, inevitably meant the abandonment of the proposed Chair of Humanity and History. When in 1706 it became possible to appoint a professor, his duties were defined as giving instruction in 'Humanity and the Roman Antiquities,' and History was thrown back on its earlier association with Divinity.

This was the more unfortunate inasmuch as the reign of George I was marked by a strong movement in favour of the study of Modern History, which not merely led to the establishment of Chairs at Oxford and Cambridge but affected Scotland too. In the peculiar circumstances prevailing at Glasgow, however, it was almost inevitable that any Chair founded should be a Chair of Ecclesiastical History, and that even to such a Chair no appointment could well be made so long as Jameson remained alive and active. The date of Jameson's death is unknown, but it was probably about 1720. In 1716 the Chair was founded, in 1721 the first appointment was made, and on October 31 of that year the first professor, William Anderson, delivered his inaugural

address 'on *The Credibility of History,* in the presence of the
Rector and other members of the University and in the public
hall of the College to the very great satisfaction of the members of the University.' In this way was established the earliest
permanent provision for instruction in History.

According to his commission the occupant of the new
Chair was both Professor of Ecclesiastical History and Lecturer on Civil History; but it is to be feared that the obligations of the latter position sat lightly upon him. It is true
that the fourth occupant of the Chair, Hugh Macleod, when
in 1797 he felt himself growing past his work, had an assistant
and successor appointed in the person of William McTurk,
the arrangement being that McTurk should undertake the
lectures on Civil History, while Macleod continued as long
as he could the lectures on Ecclesiastical History. It is equally
true that McTurk's successor, James S. Reid, devoted his
short but busy life to a three-volume *History of the Presbyterian
Church in Ireland,* which is by no means confined to ecclesiastical affairs, and has not yet been superseded; and that
Robert H. Story, later to become Principal of the University,
established his reputation with several historical works, the
most permanently valuable of which has proved to be his
life of his own distant connection, William Carstares, the
chief Scottish adviser of William III. But McTurk had to
admit to a royal commission in 1827 that in actual fact
Macleod had never lectured on Civil History at all; that he
himself had not done so for twenty-five years; and that the
sole advantage of the obligation to lecture on Civil History
was that whereas he was required by the terms of his appointment to deliver four lectures a week he could really get off
with two, on the basis that the other two were the lectures
on Civil History which he did not give. Reid's successor,
Thomas T. Jackson, went rather further, openly announcing
that his solitary course of instruction was not on History in
any accepted sense, but on 'historical theology or theology
historically developed.' Story seems to have ignored Civil

History altogether. One cannot but feel that History would have done much better had it retained the association with Humanity which at one time had promised so well.

The third, and last, foster-parent of History was Law. History and Law have always been intimately connected, and at Edinburgh a Chair of Universal Civil History, combined with Greek and Roman Antiquities, had been established as early as 1719, which was in the hands of the lawyers from the very first, and was recognised as belonging to the Faculty of Law in 1858. At Glasgow the historical aspirations of the lawyers manifested themselves somewhat later, and took the form of the establishment in 1878 of a Lectureship on Constitutional Law and History, to provide instruction in a subject just made compulsory for the degree of LL.B. This was a genuine history lectureship, not merely dealing with the main principles and organs of the English constitution, but tracing their development from the Anglo-Saxon migrations to the reign of Queen Victoria; and it was held, like most Law lectureships in Scotland, by a succession of very distinguished men, among them Alexander Ure, later Lord Strathclyde, Solicitor-General for Scotland, Lord Advocate, and President of the Court of Session. But these lecturers were almost without exception lawyers rather than historians, and were too deeply immersed in actual legal practice to have much time to spare for purely academic pursuits. It was therefore a fortunate chance when in 1894 the appointment fell to one of Ure's most distinguished students, William S. McKechnie, whose interests lay primarily in History, and who was prepared to leave the affairs of his own legal firm in the hands of his partner while he devoted himself to his University duties.

It would thus be a serious mistake to conceive of the University as having made no provision for historical studies before the close of the nineteenth century. Not merely had the Professorship of Ecclesiastical History and the Lectureship on Constitutional Law and History been for some time in existence, but the Professor of Humanity had continued to give instruction in Ancient History, and in many less important ways encouragement had been extended to the historical student. As early as 1827 Thomas Campbell, the poet, had emphasised in his rectorial address 'the vast importance of attending to Civil History, and above all to that of our own Empire.' 'This,' he declared to the students, 'will guide you to form sound political opinions, and in good time to become influential members of the class to which you belong, a class on whose opinions and free principles public happiness is more dependent than on those of any other part of the community.' So impressive had this adjuration proved that James Ewing, himself an alumnus of the University, had been inspired by it to found the first University prize in History, the Ewing Gold Medal, awarded for the best essay on a prescribed historical subject. In similar fashion Gladstone's election as Lord Rector had been commemorated in 1880 by the foundation of the Gladstone Historical Prize, awarded after examination in English History. There was also the Luke Historical Prize, founded in 1863, and awarded after examination in Ancient History. The University produced eminent historical scholars long before the close of the nineteenth century. George Finlay, the historian of Greece, received his training at Glasgow, though in the Faculty of Law, not in the Faculty of Arts. So also did his less famous predecessor in the same field, John Gillies, later Historiographer Royal for Scotland, who was a classicist by training, and was for some time in charge of the Greek Department.

The real trouble was not so much a lack of provision for historical studies as the aimless and ineffective way in which existing provision had been made, and the fact that History was not recognised as a subject at all within the curriculum of the Faculty of Arts, its natural home, where students for it would normally be found. Prior to 1892 the curriculum of the Faculty of Arts was of the most rigid and exclusive description. All candidates for the degree of Master had to secure passes in seven prescribed subjects, three of them—Humanity, Greek and Mathematics—after two sessions of study, and the remaining four—Logic, Moral Philosophy, Natural Philosophy and English—after one session of study. The reforms flowing from the Universities (Scotland) Act of 1889 involved a considerable relaxation of the rigidity among the old subjects, and also the introduction of several new subjects which are now taken for granted as essential features of any Arts curriculum. The number of subjects required was retained at seven, but these were now defined as Latin *or* Greek, Logic *or* Moral Philosophy, Mathematics *or* Natural Philosophy, English *or* History *or* a Modern Language, a fifth subject which had to be chosen from among the first three pairs, and two more subjects which were unrestricted. In 1893 steps were taken to give practical effect to this readjustment by the institution of a Professorship of History in the Faculty of Arts, and in 1894 the University invited applications for the new Chair.

Scotland at the time was by no means without historians. In proportion to its size, indeed, it had probably produced a larger volume of sound historical work than England. But most of its historians were amateurs, few had ventured far beyond the field of Scottish History, and fewer still were prepared to make the teaching and writing of History their profession. For candidates for their new posts, Glasgow and the other Scottish Universities had accordingly to turn to England, where interest in probable appointments in Scotland had been developing for some years. The English Universities were still few in number; the salaries they paid were extremely low; and the summer vacation they allowed was much shorter than that in Scotland. The prestige of a Scottish Chair, indeed, stood higher than that of any Chair outside, or even perhaps inside, Oxford or Cambridge, and the response to the Scottish advertisements was in consequence most gratifying. At Glasgow alone the candidates included W. J. Ashley, then Professor of Economic History at Harvard; Oscar Browning, at the height of his reputation at Cambridge; H. A. L. Fisher, who had not yet reached his thirtieth year; Richard Lodge; D. J. Medley, and many others whose names are now in the front rank of historical scholarship. It was on this occasion that the famous remark was made by one of the electors to one of the candidates— that the great majority of the latter were completely ruled out by their personal appearance alone. The recipient of this confidence was D. J. Medley, and the only candidates who reached the high standard of personal appearance required by their critic were Medley himself, H. A. L. Fisher, and presumably Richard Lodge, for it was in favour of Lodge that the decision was eventually given.

The task immediately confronting Lodge on his appointment was that of establishing the Ordinary Class which is the centre of every important department in a Scottish University, and the danger was that no students at all might be forthcoming, for History at that time was even more inadequately taught in the Scottish schools than it is to-day. About numbers, however, it was soon apparent that there was going to be little trouble, if for no other reason than that History was one of the very first classes to be thrown open on an equal footing to both men and women students. Hitherto women students had been excluded from the University buildings, and had been required to attend classes at Queen Margaret College, some ten minutes' walk away, where they were seldom visited by any professor, and had to be content with the ministrations of junior lecturers. Lodge, however, who constituted the entire staff of his Department, strongly objected to the needless duplication of lectures which this system in his case would have involved, and insisted on taking all his students in one class in the University. The innovation was regarded with considerable disfavour by many of the older professors, and also by Mrs. Elder, to whose generosity the founding of Queen Margaret

College was due; but it was very popular with the students, many of whom were attracted by it to a class which they might otherwise not have considered, but about the merits of which they had no doubt once they had heard Lodge lecture. In his first year, when Lodge and his subject were alike unknown, and when his class met in the Law Classroom at the highly unpopular hour of half-past five in the afternoon, only nineteen students attended, of whom one was a woman. In the following year, when Lodge grasped the fact that half-past five in Glasgow was a very different thing from half-past five in Oxford, and changed the hour of meeting to eleven in the morning, the number of students rose to fifty, of whom eight were women. Three years later seventy were attending, of whom eighteen were women. The subject of study in the class, throughout Lodge's period in Glasgow, remained a general course in British History, spreading towards its end into a sketch of European History in the time of Louis XIV.

Less immediately important than the establishment of an Ordinary Class was the establishment of an Honours Class and the formation of an Honours Group in History; and here a serious difficulty had to be surmounted, for an Honours Group necessarily involved the association of two separate subjects under separate instructors. Lodge, however, was fortunate. English Literature, although established in 1862, had hitherto been unable to develop an Honours school for lack of a second subject. It now united with History to form the group English Language, Literature and History, which has continued in various forms to the present day. The undesirable feature of this group, in the eyes of the historians, was that Literature was officially regarded as being of equal importance to Language and History combined, and in reality counted for a good deal more. But here again fortune smiled, for, owing to the appointment of McKechnie almost at the same time as Lodge, History had another possible partner besides English. Constitutional Law and History, in origin a Law subject, was recognised as being also a subject within the Faculty of Arts, and another Honours group of History and Constitutional Law and History was established, which similarly has continued in various forms to the present day. During the years 1896-8 the pioneer candidates in these groups presented themselves. In English there was one First—J. L. Morison, who was to become Professor of History successively at Queen's University, Ontario, and at King's College, Newcastle-upon-Tyne. In History there were three Firsts—Morison again; William M. R. Pringle, who later established an immense, if ephemeral, reputation in the political world, and might have reached high office had it not been for the Liberal collapse in 1918 and his own premature death at the age of forty-four; and Gavin Scott, declared by Lodge to have gained the highest marks in History in the Civil Service examination that had ever been awarded. It was at least an auspicious beginning.

Unfortunately Lodge was a life-long sufferer from asthma, and the atmosphere of a great industrial city soon proved to be more than he could endure. Had he been prepared to live some distance from the University this difficulty might have been avoided; but the idea had not yet been accepted that it was legitimate for a professor to do so; neither motor cars nor even electric trams had appeared to solve the problem of transport; and before he fully realised how serious the problem was Lodge had sunk more of his capital than he cared to remember in building for himself the house at 10 University Gardens which now most fittingly accommodates his old associates among the Departments—Constitutional History, Ancient History, and English Language. Thus when the opportunity offered he felt there was no course open to him but to transfer to Edinburgh, and in July, 1899, his resignation was intimated to the University Court. The loss was a serious one, for though never among those who suffer fools gladly, Lodge was a man whom it was impossible not to admire, and difficult, once one got to know him, not to like. An unhappy fate has coupled his name almost exclusively with a *Student's Modern Europe* little loved by undergraduates. In reality his historical work was of the very highest quality, distinguished throughout by an extraordinary lucidity; and the only pity is that the innumerable administrative duties undertaken by him during his long and busy life prevented him from writing more than he did.

Lodge had laid the solid foundation of the History Department at Glasgow; but his brief stay had scarcely enabled him to raise much of a superstructure, or to do anything towards providing his own successor. His most brilliant students, indeed—J. L. Morison and John Edgar, who for eight years was to occupy the Chair of History at Cape Town—had scarcely had time to complete their course before he left. Thus the problem of making an appointment to the Glasgow Chair was substantially the same in 1899 as it had been five years earlier. Scottish candidates were still lacking, and as the summer advanced somewhat the same band of English historians as previously, in response to advertisements, again took the highroad leading to Scotland, reinforced on this occasion by a man no longer young, whose reputation in spite of that was still largely to make, Thomas Frederick Tout, Professor of Mediæval and Modern History at Manchester. In October, just before the new session commenced, the choice of the electors was made, and fell upon D. J. Medley. Three months earlier, McKechnie had had his period of office extended for a further five years. In this way was formed a second partnership of historians which was to continue until the outbreak of the first World War.

It was a fortunate chance which entrusted the early destinies of the Honours History school at Glasgow to two such masters of lucid exposition as Lodge and McKechnie, and an even more fortunate chance which ensured that though so alike in this all-important respect they should be unlike in almost every other. Lodge was a pure historian, McKechnie largely a lawyer. Lodge was interested primarily in foreign affairs, McKechnie in constitutional development. Lodge's favourite period was the eighteenth century, McKechnie's the twelfth and thirteenth. Only by the peculiarly complementary character of their training and outlook were they enabled, without assistance from any one else, to build up a comprehensive and well-balanced Honours school. Eight papers sufficed—two on British History to 1837, two on European History from 1714 to 1815, two on the general history of the English Constitution, and two on the Constitutional History of the seventeenth century. Medley brought to his work a friendliness which contrasted strangely with Lodge's aloofness, and won him the affection of generations of students. His enthusiasm and sense of humour were as successful as Lodge's lucidity in making his lectures effective. But as a partner with McKechnie he suffered from the fact that his interests lay too much along the same lines. Both men were constitutionalists, for Medley had established his reputation with his *Student's Manual of English Constitutional History,* which made its first appearance in 1894, and was to pass through no fewer than six editions. Both were at heart mediævalists. In 1901 McKechnie abandoned his special study of seventeenth-century constitutional history, and substituted, as the subject for his Honours Class, the early constitution to the death of Edward I. Immediately afterwards Medley abandoned Lodge's prescription for the Ordinary Class, and substituted Mediæval European History from 476 to 1453. The changes in themselves were admirable. The one placed at the service of students all the research work which was going to lead in 1905 to the publication of McKechnie's *Magna Carta.* The other opened up to students a period and aspect of History which they had never before heard of, and which under Medley's guidance they found absolutely enthralling. But in the absence of other members of staff to conduct alternative classes the effect was to unbalance the whole Honours school. Of the eight papers appreciably more than four became constitutional, and approximately five mediæval. No modern History was studied after 1880.

The first serious challenge to this system came with the rise of Scottish History as an independent subject of study with claims of its own. Lodge in his inaugural address had made a strong plea for the study of Scottish History, and paid a high tribute to his predecessors in that field. 'To every man,' he declared, 'the history of his native land must always be of pre-eminent interest and importance.' But, although he devoted a surprising proportion of his time to instruction in Scottish History, it was impossible for him, and for Medley after him, to cover, unaided, the whole field of History, and also give to Scotland what might reasonably be considered its due in a Scottish University. The important event, therefore, was the development of a movement in favour of a separate Scottish History Chair. During the years 1910-1913 six short courses of lectures on Scottish History and Literature were given by eminent Scottish historians and men of letters, the most important being one by Andrew Lang on the Scottish Reformation, remarkable for the large number of clergymen who crowded to hear the first lecture, and the small number who attended thereafter. In 1913 the first Professor of Scottish History and Literature was appointed—Robert S. Rait, who was later to become Historiographer Royal for Scotland and Principal of the University. The choice was a particularly happy one. Among scholars Rait's reputation must rest on his monumental *Parliaments of Scotland,* and on the *Acts and Ordinances of the Interregnum,* which he edited in conjunction with Sir Charles Firth. But much more influential have proved the innumerable smaller books and articles which he wrote with such consummate ease, and which can be read with similar ease. Rait was pre-eminently one of those who maintain that in order to be accurate it is not necessary to be obscure and dull.

The second challenge came with the outbreak of the first World War in 1914. That event, and the problems which it raised, inevitably confronted historians in universities with the vital question of their primary purpose in teaching History. Was it to produce historians, who would themselves presumably produce more historians, who would in due course produce still further historians; or was it to produce enlightened citizens and men of affairs, who as a result of their historical training might be of some real service to mankind? In common with the majority of History teachers, Medley decided in favour of the latter view, and his decision involved an immediate and radical change from mediæval to modern history. In 1915 the Ordinary Class went over, in 1916 the Higher Class, and shortly afterwards the general balance of the whole Honours School. Fortunately this did not involve a complete abandonment of serious mediæval studies, for an expansion in the staff made special mediæval appointments possible, and the University has had since then a remarkable succession of able mediæval lecturers, among them D. C. Douglas, the historian of the Norman Conquest, who has held Chairs of History successively at Exeter, Leeds and Bristol, and G. O. Sayles, the historian of the early English Parliament, now professor at the Queen's University of Belfast.

The third and last challenge came with the appointment of McKechnie to the Chair of Conveyancing in 1916. This made possible what otherwise would have been extremely difficult, a complete reconstruction of the Honours History School. The place given to Constitutional Law and History was reduced in importance, and in due course Constitutional Law and Constitutional History were separated from each other, to the advantage of both. Scottish History and other branches and aspects of History on which increased staff had made it possible to give instruction were introduced. The whole area covered by the Honours School was greatly extended.

Throughout this process of expansion and reconstruction the University has never failed to keep in mind its duty to produce historical scholars. History is an immensely wide subject, and the particular character assumed by historical research in any university is apt to be determined by local circumstances. At London and Edinburgh the decisive factor has been the possession of the national archives; at Oxford, Cambridge and Manchester the existence of large libraries of printed and manuscript material; at Southampton the presence of the Department of the Ordnance Survey; at Newcastle the neighbourhood of the Roman Wall. From such influences Glasgow, for good or ill, has been conspicuously free. Only in connection with Romano-British studies does it owe anything to favourable circumstances, and even there it probably owes more to the energy and perseverance of the scholars who have been associated with it—George Macdonald, who was Lecturer on Greek for twelve years; and Steuart Miller, who was Lecturer on Roman History for twenty. As a result Glasgow has never developed, and probably never will develop, a school of History in the sense of a body of scholars working more or less in the same field. The historians it has produced have indeed made their reputations in the most diverse fields—J. L. Morison in Imperial History; J. B. Black in the Elizabethan period; David Ogg in the seventeenth century; Denis Brogan in foreign and American History; Sir David Keir in modern constitutional history; G. O. Sayles in early parliamentary history; G. P. Insh and Henry Hamilton in Scottish economic history; Annie Dunlop in Scottish history of the fifteenth century.

But it would be a mistake to associate History in any university exclusively with such as these, who have either been trained or have held posts in an actual History Department. History is not a subject requiring some vast apparatus of technical equipment; or perhaps one should say the equipment of the historian is so immense that no one man can possibly possess it all, and any individual who is fortunate enough to possess some part of it may therefore in his own sphere surpass all others. Every educated man is more or less a historian, and in this, as in other universities, there have been many great historians who have had no official title to be called so. John Major, that 'storehouse of all the learning of the Middle Ages,' author of the *History of Great Britain, both England and Scotland,* was Principal of the early College. Robert Wodrow, author of *The History of the Sufferings of the Church of Scotland from the Restoration to the Revolution,* a mine of information even to modern scholars, was University Librarian. Gilbert Burnet, the historian of the English Reformation, was Professor of Divinity, and wrote his first and most characteristic work, the *Memoirs of the Lives and Actions of James and William, Dukes of Hamilton,* while he occupied his Chair. In more recent times W. R. Scott, the historian of British commercial development and the biographer of Adam Smith, was Professor of Political Economy, and W. B. Stevenson, the historian of the Crusades, Professor of Semitic Languages.

It is related of A. F. Pollard that when he ventured to foretell to his colleagues in the University of London a day when there would be many professors of History in that institution, his words were received with prolonged and incredulous laughter. Time has more than justified his vision, and the end of the development of historical studies, in other universities no less than in London, has not yet been reached. History is not a static subject. New history is being made every day; communities rise and fall; and the historian (as distinct from the antiquarian) must devote his attention to those developments which he thinks will best repay study. When Lodge was appointed to the Chair of History at this University more than fifty years ago anything more recent than the French Revolution was regarded as scarcely History at all; the United States, it was freely declared, had had no History; Asia and Africa were merely fields for commercial enterprise. Now Modern History begins with the Russian

Revolution. The United States, China and Russia bulk larger and larger. Not a little of the History that once seemed so important appears to have lost its point. It is the function of the historian to try to understand these and similar changes, and to adjust his studies to suit, neither confining himself to purely modern events on the one hand, nor, on the other, grubbing without aim or purpose exclusively in the distant past. Only by so doing can historians justify the increasingly important position accorded to them in universities.

MATHEMATICS
(AND ASTRONOMY)

by

T. M. MacRobert
Professor of Mathematics

Before the seventeenth century the curricula of schools in Scotland and England were almost entirely confined to Latin Grammar and Literature—hence the name Grammar Schools. Indeed, at the beginning of the seventeenth century it was stated that many educated people did not know enough about numbers to enable them, in church, to turn up the chapters and verses of the Bible. In the Scottish Universities the mathematical programme was meagre, including only a little arithmetic and the very elements of geometry; the latter mainly consisting of statements of theorems without proofs. In Andrew Melville's time, 1574-1580, this was taught by the Regents to the second-year students. In the latter part of the seventeenth century pressure of public opinion led to a definite advance in the teaching of arithmetic in the schools: Cocker's *Arithmetic* was published in 1678 and was widely used in Scotland and England.

The early Regents each taught his own set of students throughout their entire course; but in 1577 the charter known as the *Nova Erectio* made provision for three Regents, one to take charge of each of the three years of the Arts course. Arithmetic and Geometry were taught in the second year along with Dialectics, Morals and Politics. These Regents seem frequently to have assumed the title of Professor; and George Sinclar, who was probably in charge of the second year, was referred to as Professor of Philosophy. This arrangement broke down after the Restoration, when the University became decadent, but was revived after the Revolution of 1688, when the University once again prospered.

It would appear that, at some earlier date, there actually was in existence a Chair of Mathematics. It may have been that, if one of the Regents showed a special aptitude for Mathematics, his colleagues were glad to leave such mathematical teaching as was required to him. At any rate, the commission of 1664 recommended the appointment of 'Ane Professor of Mathematickes whiche the Universitie formerlie had, and by the erectione and foundatione aucht to have.' Nothing came of this, however, till after the Revolution, when George Sinclar was appointed to the Chair.

Sinclar, who had been Regent from 1654 to 1666, resigned in the latter year rather than publicly adhere to the Episcopal form of church government. He was reappointed in 1689, and became Professor in 1691. At the beginning of the eighteenth century Divinity and Mathematics were the only Chairs in existence; and they have continued without intermission to the present day.

Sinclar, who came from St. Andrews, where he had been a pedagogue, must have been a very able and versatile man. During his long exile from Glasgow University he turned to civil and mining engineering, developing methods of draining coal mines and, in 1670, superintending the first water supply brought into the city of Edinburgh. His writings on the stratigraphy of the coal measures are highly commended by modern mining engineers and geologists. Using a diving-bell, he assisted in 1655 in the recovery of cannon from the Armada ship, the *Florida,* sunk in Tobermory bay. He seems to have taught Mathematics for a short time in Edinburgh University; an Edinburgh University minute of 1672 states that he received £10 as salary for one year as Professor of Mathematics.

Sinclar wrote treatises on Mathematics, Hydrostatics, Astronomy, Navigation, Coal and Witchcraft. The last, entitled *Satan's Invisible World Discovered,* was received, in those superstitious days, with universal respect. The latest edition of this work was published so recently as 1871. An account of part of it is given in the introduction to Scott's *Woodstock.* His *Tyrocinia Mathematica,* published in 1661 and later in English in 1672, covered the course professed by him in his mathematical lectures. The arithmetical part dealt only with integers: fractions at that time were not of practical importance as the trigonometrical functions were given in terms of semi-chords of circles of radii 10^7 or 10^8, and so were large integers. The geometrical course was very slight.

Sinclar's *Hydrostatics,* published in 1672, was venomously attacked by Professor James Gregory of St. Andrews, later of Edinburgh, before it had been actually published. Gregory was a great mathematician; but his ideas about Hydrostatics were mediæval. In his view Aristotle had said the last word on the subject and it was an impertinence for Sinclar to claim that he could contribute anything new. Probably the virulence of Gregory's attack was exacerbated by the fierce political and ecclesiastical differences of the time. Sinclar had lost his post because he refused to take the Test; Gregory's father, minister of Drumoak in Aberdeenshire, had twice, in 1639 and 1649, been deposed by the Covenanters.

George Sinclar died in 1699 and was succeeded by Robert Sinclair, M.D., who also, from 1704 to 1709, taught Hebrew. The tradition of broad culture rather than high specialisation seems to have persisted long after the days of the Regents. In 1703, when a medical student from England applied to be examined in Medicine for the degree of M.D., the University appointed Robert Sinclair Professor extraordinary of Medicine for the occasion. Robert Sinclair died in 1710 and was succeeded, in the following year, by Robert Simson, the best-known of the Glasgow professors, who held the Chair for fifty years.

Simson was born at West Kilbride, Ayrshire, in 1687, and entered the University in 1701, at the age of fourteen.

He was intended for the ministry; but, having come into possession of a copy of Euclid's *Elements,* was attracted to the study of Mathematics. At the time no lectures on the subject were being given in the University, so that Simson was a self-taught mathematician. He was appointed to the Chair in 1711, at the age of twenty-four, having first spent a year studying in London. His appointment may have been partly due to the fact that his uncle, John Simson, was Professor of Divinity. Undoubtedly family influence counted for much in those days; but Simson justified his appointment. For many years he devoted himself to the study and recovery of the purely geometrical methods of Greek geometry, and he published valuable and influential editions of Euclid and Apollonius. His attempts to solve the mystery of Euclid's lost Porisms are allowed to be the most successful of any made so far.

Simson gave the following definition of a porism.

A porism is a proposition in which it is proposed to demonstrate that some one or more things are given, to which, as also to each of innumerable other things, not indeed given, but which have the same relation to those which are given, it is to be shown that there belongs some common affection described in the proposition.

For 'affection' one would nowadays use the word 'property.'

Simson agrees with the affirmation of Pappus that loci are a species of the porism.

He then gives a number of examples, of which the following are the first two.

Example 1. Given a straight line AB fixed in position and a circle DEF given in position and magnitude, a point E can be found on the circle such that, if PEQ is any line through E meeting AB in P and meeting the circle again in Q, the rectangle PE.EQ is constant in area.

The perpendicular OH from the centre of the circle to AB cuts the circle in E, the thing demonstrated to be given.

PQ is one of the innumerable other things, and PE.EQ= HE.EK, where K is the second intersection of OH with the circle, is the common affection.

Example 2. Having a point given, as also a circle in magnitude and position; if from any point on the circumference a straight line be drawn to the same point, there will be another point to which, if there be drawn from the same point on the circumference a straight line, to which the first drawn straight line shall have a given ratio.

The other point, of course, is the inverse point.

What were formerly called porisms are to-day either well-known geometrical theorems or else rather trivial examples in geometry.

It may be noted that the Greeks used the word porism not only in this sense but also to denote what we would call a corollary.

At this period great progress was being made in mathematical teaching in the schools; and, in the course of the century and in response to the demands of commerce, many new schools, called Academies, of a more modern type than the Grammar schools, were founded. Simson thus came to have good material in his classes, and many able students were attracted by his uncommonly clear and engaging teaching. Among his pupils were James Stirling, Colin Maclaurin, Matthew Stewart, later Professor in Edinburgh, William Trail, his biographer, later Professor in Marishal College, Aberdeen, John Robison, later Professor of Natural Philosophy in Edinburgh, and James Williamson, his own successor. In 1746 he received the honorary degree of M.D. from St. Andrews, where his brother was Professor of Medicine. Many of the stones with Roman inscriptions to be found in the Hunterian Museum were collected by him. Simson, who was a bachelor, seldom left the college grounds, where he had a large garden to walk in. On Saturdays, however, he was in the habit of walking with some friends to the village of Anderston, one mile away, where they had dinner in the local inn. They formed the Anderston Club, Simson being its founder and chairman. Among its members were Adam Smith, Joseph Black, William Cullen and James Watt. Simson retired in 1761, but retained rooms in college till his death in 1768. Adam Smith, who was a pupil and colleague of Simson's, in his *Theory of Moral Sentiments*, said, 'Mathematicians, who may have the most perfect assurance of the truth and of the importance of their discoveries, are frequently very indifferent about the reception which they may meet with from the public. The two greatest mathematicians that I have ever had the honour to be known to, and I believe the two greatest that have lived in my time, Dr. Robert Simson of Glasgow and Dr. Matthew Stewart of Edinburgh, never seemed to feel even the slightest uneasiness from the neglect with which the ignorance of the public received some of their most valuable works.'

On his monument at West Kilbride he is described as 'The Restorer of Grecian Geometry, and by his works the great Promoter of its study in the schools.'

On retiring Simson stipulated that his assistant, James Williamson, should be appointed as his successor. It was during Williamson's time that it was first decided that all candidates for degrees in Arts should be examined in Mathematics by the Professor, whether they had attended his lectures or not. Williamson carried on the work of the Chair till 1789, when his powers began to fail. On his suggestion James Millar, son of the Professor of Law and brother-in-law of James Mylne, later Professor of Moral Philosophy, was appointed assistant and successor; Williamson to retain the house and salary while Millar took the fees. On Williamson's death in 1795 Millar became full professor. As a teacher he was a failure. 'The department of Mathematics,' we are told, 'was presided over by a man so eccentric that his conduct was a dangerous incentive to fun and disorder among the students. The penalty for irregularity was a small fine, and this the delinquents were careful to pay in farthings, so as to afford the greatest merriment to the assembled class. If his back was turned for an instant in drawing or explaining a diagram on the board, there was at once a great uproar, and consequently he regularly presented the curious spectacle of demonstrating his propositions with the figure behind him.' In addition to teaching Mathematics, Millar for a time lectured on English Law. It is interesting to note that William Ramsay, later Professor of Latin, was his assistant, and would probably have succeeded him had not the Chair of Humanity become vacant first. In 1831 Millar retired, retaining his salary, and James Thomson, Professor of Mathematics in the Belfast Institution, now Queen's University, succeeded.

James Thomson was born in 1786 in Ulster, his ancestors having emigrated from Ayrshire in the days of Claverhouse. Being poor he worked as a schoolmaster till he was twenty-four, thus saving enough to enable him to enter the University of Glasgow, which he did in 1810. He graduated M.A. in 1812, and thereafter attended classes in Medicine and Divinity. As the session lasted only for six months it was possible for him, as for many other students, to work during the summer to earn sufficient to cover his expenses while at college. In his first year as professor the salary went to Millar, and he found that he was left with no income at all, for which he had to work very hard. To remedy this he gave lectures on Geography and Astronomy to large and enthusiastic classes of ladies. These lectures he continued for some years till, the mathematical classes having increased in numbers, he was compelled by pressure of work to discontinue them. His most distinguished students were his sons James, afterwards Professor of Engineering, and William, later Lord Kelvin, who entered the University at the ages of twelve and ten respectively. He was a successful and efficient teacher, author of a number of excellent and popular text-books. Probably the proudest day of his life was that on which his young son William was appointed to the Chair of Natural

Philosophy. In the winter of 1848-1849 the city was devastated by cholera, and Thomson succumbed to this dread disease early in 1849.

His successor was Hugh Blackburn, Fellow of Trinity College, Cambridge. Blackburn came of a well-known Glasgow family; indeed, one of his ancestors had been a Regent in 1573. He was educated at Eton and Cambridge, where he became a close friend of William Thomson. His wife, a lady of artistic talents, was a first cousin of James Clerk Maxwell, who for a time resided with them. Unlike his predecessor, who was progressive in politics and in University affairs, Blackburn's outlook was conservative, and he was a strong champion of the rights of the Faculty as against the other professors. Like Professor Millar, he seems to have been quite unable to control his students. During his time attendance on classes in Mathematics became compulsory for candidates for degrees in Arts. He is best known as the inventor of the Blackburn pendulum. Blackburn resigned in 1879 and died on the 9th October, 1909, a month or two after the resignation of his successor, William Jack.

Jack was born at Stewarton, Ayrshire, in 1834, and was educated at Irvine Royal Academy, Glasgow University and St. Peter's College, Cambridge, of which he became a Fellow. He had a remarkably varied career: before coming to Glasgow he had been Inspector of Schools, Professor of Natural Philosophy at Owen's College, Manchester, now the University of Manchester, editor for five years of the *Glasgow Herald,* and publisher with the Macmillans, who in their early days were in business in Irvine. His wife was a daughter of J. P. Nichol, Professor of Astronomy, and sister of John Nichol, first Professor of English: one son, Adolphus Jack, became Professor of English in Aberdeen University. By the institution of higher courses, Professor Jack extended the range and raised the standard of the Honours degree.

George Alexander Gibson, appointed Professor in 1909, was born at Greenlaw, Berwickshire, in 1858, and entered the University in 1874. After graduating he became assistant to Professor Jack in 1883. From 1895 to 1909 he was Professor of Mathematics at the Glasgow and West of Scotland Royal Technical College. At the University he reorganised and raised the level of the teaching, providing tutorial instruction for all the students, and dividing the classes into sections of not more than sixty students. A lecturer in mathematics is at a disadvantage in maintaining discipline in that he has to lecture with his back to the students. Under some of the previous professors the disorder had been notorious, and the reduction in the size of the classes was very helpful. Professor Gibson was one of the early members of the Edinburgh Mathematical Society, of which he was a bulwark in its difficult early days. He wrote a number of widely-used text-books, mainly on the Calculus, and became a recognised authority on certain parts of the history of mathematics; in particular he published a number of valuable papers on the great Scottish Mathematicians. On his retiral in 1927 a fund was raised for the endowment of occasional lectures on the History of Mathematics, to be known as the George A. Gibson Lectures. The first lecturer on this foundation, in 1933, was Albert Einstein. Professor Gibson died in 1930.

We now turn to some distinguished students of Glasgow University.

Colin Maclaurin was born in the manse of Kilmodan, in Glendaruel, Argyllshire, in 1698. His father, the minister of the parish, died when he was six weeks old, and his mother nine years later. The family was, however, taken charge of by an uncle, David Maclaurin, minister of the nearby parish of Kilfinnan, who faithfully discharged his duty to them. At the early age of eleven, Colin was sent to Glasgow University with a view to the ministry; but, like Simson, he fell in with Euclid's *Elements*, and, becoming fascinated by the subject, got into touch with Simson and devoted himself, under his guidance, to the study of Mathematics. In 1717, at the early age of nineteen, after a ten days' competitive examination, he was chosen Professor of Mathematics in Marishal College, Aberdeen. Eight years later, on the recommendation of Isaac Newton, he was appointed to the Chair in Edinburgh.

In 1745 he took a leading part in organising the defences of Edinburgh; but he received little support from the civic authorities; and, on the approach of Prince Charlie, he had to flee to York. His health, never robust, was so much impaired by the hardships endured at this time that he died, in 1746, shortly after his return to Edinburgh.

Maclaurin was one of Scotland's greatest mathematicians. He wrote on Geometry, Curves, Series, Algebra, the Calculus and also on Mathematical Physics. He seems to have been the original discoverer of Pascal's Theorem, on a hexagon inscribed in a conic. Maclaurin's theorem on the connection between an infinite series and an infinite integral is known to all students of convergence of Series. The well-known Maclaurin's Expansion seems to have been discovered earlier by Stirling. In his *Treatise on Fluxions,* written in reply to Berkeley's attack on the method of fluxions, Maclaurin made use of geometrical methods. To this he was driven by the logical difficulties involved in the use of the infinitesimal, a quantity distinct from zero and yet so small that no multiple of it can be of finite length. The result, however, was unfortunate, as it led to the neglect of the fertile methods of analysis by British mathematicians for the best part of a century.

James Stirling was born at Kippen, Stirlingshire, in 1692, so that he was six years older than Maclaurin. His descendants, the Stirlings of Garden, still reside in that parish. Unlike Maclaurin, he was a Jacobite; it is pleasant, however, to know that their political differences did not prevent them from becoming good friends. In 1710, at the age of eighteen, he entered Balliol College, Oxford, with the Snell Exhibition from Glasgow. His name does not appear in the *Glasgow Matriculation Album;* but this signifies nothing, as in those days only such students as intended to graduate were required to matriculate. In order to qualify for the Snell he would necessarily attend classes in the University of Glasgow for at least two years. At Oxford political feeling ran high, and he seems to have taken part in more than one anti-Hanoverian riot. He published his first work, on *Cubic Curves,* in 1717, at the age of twenty-five. Newton, in his *Enumeratio,* had given a summary of theorems on cubic curves; Stirling, in his book, gives proofs of these theorems. In the same year he went to Venice, where he seems to have expected appointment to a Chair. Nothing is known of what happened there, but he was subsequently known as the Venetian. Newton seems to have befriended him, and to have sent him money to bring him home. For some years he taught Applied Mathematics in London; but in 1735 he returned to Scotland to become manager of the Leadhills mines, where he continued till his death in 1770. His most important book, *Methodus Differentialis,* published in 1730, dealt with the Calculus of Finite Differences. Among a wealth of other new results, this book contains his famous asymptotic formula for $n!$

Matthew Stewart was born in 1717 at Rothesay, in Bute, where his father was minister. He was educated at the town Grammar School and entered the University of Glasgow in 1734. There he made great progress in Mathematics under Simson. Later he studied Divinity at Edinburgh and, in 1745, he became minister at Roseneath. Doubtless, while at Edinburgh, he would attend Maclaurin's lectures: for his interests were mathematical; and, in 1746, with a view to the Edinburgh Chair, vacant through the death of Maclaurin, he published a book entitled *Some General Theorems of considerable use in the higher Parts of Mathematics.* These theorems were stated without proof, and include the well-known Stewart's Theorem, which is really due to Simson. [Simson's Line, it may be noted, is now believed to have been discovered by Professor Wallace of Edinburgh.] Regarding this book, it is stated by Chasles that it at once placed Stewart in a distinguished rank among geometers. In 1747 he was elected to the Edinburgh Chair. Like his master Simson, and like Newton in his *Principia,* Stewart preferred the geometrical methods of the Greeks to those of Analysis; and he devoted much skill and energy to finding geometrical proofs of results already obtained by means of the Calculus. Many of these proofs are to be found in his *Tracts, Physical and Mathematical,* published in 1761, and in his *Propositiones Geometricae More Veterum Demonstratae,* published in 1767. His son Dugald Stewart, born in Edinburgh in 1753 and educated at the High School and University there, was sent in 1771 to Glasgow University to continue his studies. In 1772, however, his father's health having given way, he was recalled to Edinburgh to take charge of the Mathematical classes, and in 1775, he was appointed joint-professor. His interests, however, were philosophical; and, in 1785, shortly after the death of his father, he was transferred to the Chair of Moral Philosophy.

During the nineteenth century, many Glasgow graduates proceeded to further study at Cambridge. Among these was William John Steele, Fellow of Peterhouse, who was joint author with Professor P. G. Tait of *A Treatise on the Dynamics of a Particle.* Another was Archibald Smith, of the well-known family of the Smiths of Jordanhill. He was born in Glasgow in 1813, his mother being a daughter of Alexander Wilson, Professor of Astronomy in Glasgow University. He studied at Glasgow and Trinity College, Cambridge, was Senior Wrangler, first Smith's prizeman and Fellow of Trinity. He became a lawyer, but maintained his interest in Mathematics, and founded, with Duncan Farquharson Gregory, the *Cambridge Mathematical Journal.* He became an authority on the magnetic influence of the iron of a ship on the ship's compass. He died in 1872. His eldest son, James Parker Smith, was for a time M.P. for Partick.

We now turn to a mathematician of our own time, Sir Thomas Muir. He was born at Stonebyres, in Lanarkshire, on 25th August, 1844, and entered Glasgow University in 1863, graduating M.A. in 1868. From 1868 to 1871 he was a tutor at College Hall, St. Andrews, and, from 1871 to 1874, Assistant to Professor Blackburn at Glasgow. In the vacations he studied at Berlin and Göttingen. From 1874 to 1892 he was head of the Mathematical Department of Glasgow High School. In 1882, when thirty-eight years of age, he was awarded the degree of LL.D. by his Alma Mater in recognition of his numerous contributions to the theories of Continued Fractions and Determinants. It was as an authority on the theory and history of Determinants that he became famous. The first part of his great history of the subject appeared in 1890, the last part in 1930, when he was eighty-five years of age.

Meanwhile, in 1892, at the age of forty-eight, he was invited by Cecil Rhodes to become Superintendent-General of Education in Cape Colony. In this post he proved himself a great administrator, retiring in 1915. In his intervals of leisure he continued to work at Determinants; but it was not till after his retirement that he was able to devote his full energies to the completion of his magnum opus. He carried on his researches till he was almost ninety, dying on 21st March, 1934.

Finally, mention should be made of three senior living mathematicians who have brought distinction to Glasgow University. They are, in order of seniority: John Dougall, for many years scientific adviser to Blackie & Company, author of many brilliant memoirs on Pure and Applied Mathematics; Horatio S. Carslaw, Lecturer in Glasgow and for many years Professor in Sydney, widely known as the author of treatises on Conduction of Heat and Fourier Series; and Robert J. T. Bell, also Lecturer in Glasgow and later Professor in Dunedin, author of a widely-read treatise on Analytical Geometry of Three Dimensions.

The Chair of Practical Astronomy was founded in 1760. Previously the subject had been taught by the Professor of Natural Philosophy. Alexander Macfarlane, a wealthy Jamaica merchant and a former student of Glasgow University, who was keenly interested in Astronomy, had established an observatory in Jamaica, with the best instruments the times could afford. On his death in 1756 it was found that he had bequeathed these instruments to the University. An observatory, the Macfarlane Observatory, was thereupon erected in the grounds of the old College, and in it the instruments were set up under the supervision of James Watt.

The first professor was Alexander Wilson, a graduate of St. Andrews University and a type-founder, who supplied the Foulis Press with type of artistic beauty. After his appointment his foundry was transferred from Camlachie to a building erected in the College gardens. Wilson seems to have been the first astronomer to realise the nature of sunspots. He also investigated the stability of the stellar universe, and suggested that the stars described vast orbits round an unseen centre of gravitational control; a bold speculation which finds its modern expression in the doctrine of the rotation of the Galaxy.

In 1784 he was succeeded by his son Patrick Wilson, who on his retiral in 1789, endowed the Observatory with a fund for the provision of instruments and books on Astronomy. His successor, William Meikleham, was transferred to the Chair of Natural Philosophy in 1803. James Couper, minister of Baldernock, was next appointed. After a few years he ceased either to lecture or to observe, alleging that the smoke of the town made observing impracticable, and that St. John's Church, built about 1819, obstructed the view.

On Couper's death, in 1836, John Pringle Nichol, an alumnus of King's College, Aberdeen, and a brilliant popular lecturer, succeeded. He was, in his time, the outstanding figure in the University. He wrote and edited numerous works on science, and was responsible for the transference of the observatory to Horslethill, where, with an enlarged stock of instruments, astronomical observing was once again undertaken.

Nichol's successor, Robert Grant, was a noted historian of Astronomy. He published valuable catalogues of stars, from which reliable information about the proper notions of many of them has been obtained. He did much to elucidate the nature of the chromosphere.

Ludwig Becker, appointed in 1893, held the chair for forty-two years. At the time of his appointment the title of the chair was changed to the Regius Chair of Astronomy. A native of Bonn, Professor Becker came to Scotland in 1885 to take charge of the observatory at Dunecht. His researches dealt with the nebulae and with the physical features of the moon. After his retirement the observatory was removed to University Gardens.

LITERATURE
(INCLUDING MODERN LANGUAGES)

by

Peter Alexander

Regius Professor of English Language and Literature

The Chair of English Language and Literature at Glasgow was established by the Universities' Commission of 1858, and on 17th November, 1862, John Nichol, its first occupant, set out in his inaugural address the course of studies he proposed to follow with his students.

In those early days of the academic study of English the course prescribed took its direction more from the interests and temper of the man who was setting it than it would to-day, not merely because he was the first to be commissioned here to teach the subject, but because he had few academic precedents to guide him. Neither Nichol nor his successor, A. C. Bradley, had ever attended a class in what is called English, at least not at a University. They were not, any more than the third in succession, Walter Raleigh, possessors of degrees in the subject. Indeed, when one considers their early education, one might almost conclude that the best preparation for a teacher of English was the reading of the English poets and romancers and essayists for his own pleasure and delight, combined with the academic study of some subject other than English. Nichol and Bradley then, in the absence of any well-established tradition, had to follow their own judgment, and that judgment was inevitably weighted by their earlier studies.

Between Glasgow and Balliol College, Oxford, there are many ties: one of them is to be found in the influence Balliol

exercised through Nichol and Bradley on the direction given
to English studies at Glasgow. The first wave from the South
came with Nichol, though it was perhaps only with Bradley's
appointment that the repercussions within these walls that
were to re-echo throughout the class-rooms of the land
announced that the *fluctus decumanus*—or the ninth wave as
Tennyson will have it,

> *gathering half the deep*
> *And full of voices*—

had reached the Scottish shore. Of course Nichol was in
the first instance a Glasgow man, the son of our Professor
of Astronomy, and a graduate of our University; he had
gone to Balliol as a Snell Exhibitioner. It would be as
foolish as it would be unfilial to underestimate the value of
the education he had received here; his contemporary at
Oxford, James Bryce, later Lord Bryce, the historian of the
Holy Roman Empire and himself known to history as our
ambassador in America, a scholar both ripe and good, who
knew many universities besides Glasgow and Oxford, said
in his later years, in conversation with Professor Gilbert
Murray and others, that the old curriculum at Glasgow
seemed to him to provide the best educational basis of all.
When Nichol went to Balliol that College was entering on
one of its most influential phases, and was about to leave on
the political, religious, philosophical and critical thought of
at least two generations a remarkable impress. Nichol was
fortunate in finding there an intellectual climate so congenial
to his temperament; he continued his classical reading, but
he gave himself whole-heartedly to philosophy, the discipline
in which Balliol for the period excelled. It was not merely
what he got from his tutors that left its mark on him: Nichol,
being slightly older than his fellow-students and having perhaps something of the Scottish genius for dealing with the
natives, gathered round him a very remarkable group of
Oxford men who formed the Old Mortality Club. To it

belonged T. H. Green the philosopher, A. V. Dicey, James Bryce, the poet Swinburne, and others whose scholarship was to contribute so notably to the intellectual life of their time. One may regard it as a circle that circumscribed the many interests of Nichol, whose own position intellectually and as the Club's President was a central one. It would be hard to think of more promising ground in which to find the breadth of interest so necessary to give English studies here a fair start. Nichol was to spend a few years at Oxford, after graduating there, as a most successful coach in Philosophy. He came to the Glasgow Chair when he was twenty-nine and held it for twenty-seven years, retiring in 1889 when he was fifty-six.

Nichol's inaugural address provides us with a summary of his views on the teaching of English in a University, at least the views he held when he first addressed himself to his new task. As might be expected from his training he took no narrow view of his duties, and he set out what he considered the proper procedure under three heads: I. English Composition; II. English Philology; III. English Literature. On the first topic he said:

'The merest utilitarian will not be disposed to undervalue the study of English composition. Unfortunately not a day passes without affording some instance of deficiency in an art which is essential not only to eminence, but, in many cases, to success in life'.

These are truths which need not be stressed to-day. When newsprint was more plentiful in this country than it is at present, and advertising had not yet become the hobby of non-profit making corporations, we used to read almost daily that the greatest handicap to securing or holding down a good position was, next to night starvation, a poor command of English.

The Scottish Universities, however, had not entirely neglected this useful desideratum, even before they resorted to the appointment of Professors of English. They had already revived the old Rhetorical tradition; and, as Grammar, Logic, and Rhetoric, went together in this medieval curriculum, the Professor of Logic, as at Glasgow and Aberdeen, gave instruction in Rhetoric. Just before Nichol's advent as Professor, and at some date after David Murray's first matriculation here, our students were examined in Campbell's *Philosophy of Rhetoric*. Jardine and his successor Buchanan in the Chair of Logic had both given much attention to this topic.

Edinburgh was even more advanced. They already had a Chair of Rhetoric and Belles Lettres, although it had been admitted to the University by what may be called a side door. In 1748-9 Adam Smith had given a public course of lectures on English Literature in Edinburgh. Among his audience was Hugh Blair. Ten years later, in 1759, Blair, by that time one of Edinburgh's most eminent divines, a clergyman whose sermons Dr. Johnson himself had commended, had the idea of following up Adam Smith's example, and so successful did the experiment prove that the university in 1762 provided Blair with the Chair from which he continued to deliver the lectures that he introduced, on his retirement, in 1783, to the reading public with this remark: 'The following lectures were read in the University of Edinburgh for twenty-four years'.

Mr. Stephen Potter, the learned historian of what he calls *Eng. Lit.*, has attempted to account for this Scottish zeal for Rhetorical instruction by supposing that the English tongue must have been to Scotsmen of that time more or less a foreign language. The Scot had set about acquiring in a systematic and business-like way a useful aid to success, and it is notable that it was at Aberdeen that the study was pursued most assiduously under Bain and Minto. But if the spectacle of the laborious Scot is one to raise a smile, the picture of contemporary England is one for tears. As Macaulay in his speech on education in 1847 pointed out, one-third of the males and one-half of the females of marriageable

age in England could not write even their names. Blair and
Bain and Minto were needed even more in England than in
Scotland. The Scottish schools had transformed Scotland
while the bulk of English teaching was in the hands of
those to whom none of us, in Macaulay's words, would
entrust the key of the cellar. Perhaps Scotsmen had been
smit with something more than the love of gain—perhaps
the love of learning, however humble, was stirring in their
hearts, and the Universities were doing something to foster it.

Whatever we may think on these matters it is clear that
Nichol, on his first topic, was speaking to the converted,
and no doubt took advantage of this to pass off on his
approving hearers the less popular features of his design.
The second topic, Philology, had not the same popular
appeal, though it had a strong hold on the academic imagination, especially in England—how strong Nichol himself was to discover some years later.

When Oxford at length decided to establish a Chair of
English Language and Literature, Nichol was persuaded
by his Oxford friends to offer himself as a candidate. There
had been much throwing about of brains at Oxford concerning the rights and wrongs of such an innovation. The
newly entrenched historians were its severest critics. Freeman objected to 'chatter about Harriet', and the thought
that the new History school might be hampered with dilettante teaching, such as the teaching of English Literature,
was abhorrent to Dr. Stubbs. The *Oxford Magazine* of the
time ventured to hope that someone who was both a man
of letters and a scholar would be available, although it
admitted that the man of its choice, Matthew Arnold, could
not be expected to undertake so heavy a task as twenty-four
annual lectures. As a concession to the fears of Freeman
and Stubbs, Oxford appointed to their Chair of English
Language and Literature a young man who had taken a
degree in Natural Science and who had studied early English Dialects at Göttingen. Napier, for he was Oxford's

choice, would be able to teach matter that could at least be tested in examinations. If Nichol did not say much in his inaugural about the place of Philology in an English course, he devoted a pamphlet to it in his later years.

Nichol's third topic was English Literature. We have noted the objections of such learned men as Freeman and Stubbs to this study; but even Professors of English have felt it necessary to advance their subject under cover of some stalking-horse that would not flutter the sedate listeners. University College, London, a foundation in which Glasgow men cannot but take an interest, if only for the reason that it owes its existence largely to the enthusiasm of a Glasgow graduate, the poet Thomas Campbell, had in 1828, two years after its opening, with something of the temerity of youth, set up an English Chair. This was the first English Chair—using the term in its modern sense—to be established in England. Perhaps as a safeguard against further rashness, they appointed as their first Professor the Rev. Henry Dale. In his inaugural he put all fears at rest, and perhaps some hopes too: 'I shall' he said, 'I shall invariably aim to impart moral as well as intellectual instruction . . . I shall esteem it my duty—and I trust I shall find it my delight—to inculcate lessons of virtue.' An excellent account of this chapter in English studies will be found in *Man's Unconquerable Mind*, by R. W. Chambers, in the discourse on *Philologists at University College, London*.

But a Professor of English who spends his time warning his students against reading Byron and Burns might be thought to have missed his vocation. Some of our Rhetoricians had evaded the difficulty Dr. Dale found in dealing with so many authors, by reducing their subject matter to figures of speech or the proportion of Romance and Germanic words in their vocabulary. The intention behind the allegory or irony, the view of the world that moved the author to their use, could be ignored. Nichol fortunately belonged to neither school of exclusionists.

A glimpse of the ills that beset the study in its early years at the University may enable us to appreciate the sanity and robustness of Nichol's treatment at Glasgow. His may seem the obvious regime to-day; but doctors then held very diverse opinions. The only trouble was that Nichol would have needed for its performance the strength of ten, for that is about the number the smallest Universities to-day think necessary, to carry through his programme. Nichol, however, started the study on liberal lines. Professor Ferguson, later Professor of Chemistry here, attended, when an undergraduate, Nichol's course and was struck, he tells us 'by the brilliancy of exposition, and by something which we did not get often, by an amount of humour which completely overbalanced every other quality which he possessed'.

Nichol's humour, his crisp estimate of character, these and other features of his discourse made Ferguson consider him one of the most brilliant lecturers he had ever listened to. Indeed Ferguson in after years, looking round on his colleagues, many of them scholars of real distinction, judged Nichol the nearest to a man of genius of them all.

The memorial window to Nichol in the Bute Hall reminds us of his place in the academic generations in Scotland. This memorial we owe to Professor Jack of Mathematics, who had married Nichol's sister. In the top light is Urania, the heavenly muse; below stand Copernicus, Galileo, Kepler and Newton, to remind us of the studies of Nichol's father; below that again are Bacon, Burns, Byron and Carlyle, the four authors on whose lives and works Nichol had written. Nor did he forget English Composition, and his manual in the series to which Dowden and Stopford Brooke contributed their primers was long in use. Somewhat surprisingly, as it may seem to-day, Nichol published a study of American Literature, but both Nichol and his father had a strong interest in the America of their own day and a faith in its future.

Andrew Cecil Bradley succeeded Nichol in 1889, coming

to Glasgow from Balliol by way of Liverpool University where he had held a Chair for seven years. He was then almost forty. As became the half-brother of G. G. Bradley and the brother of F. H. Bradley, the new Professor was a competent classic and well read in philosophy. His philosophic interests are represented by his early contribution on *Aristotle's Conception of the State* to the collection of essays entitled *Hellenica,* and by his editing of Green's *Prolegomena to Ethics,* which Green, who was Bradley's tutor, had left in manuscript and unfinished at his death. Green, you will remember, was a member of the Old Mortality Club. The same pious duty Bradley later performed for his friend Lewis Nettleship. Bradley, however, by the time he came to Glasgow had already made a reputation for himself and had gained much useful experience as a teacher of English.

To offer any adequate explanation of the remarkable influence Bradley was to exercise on the teaching of his subject or to assess how far that influence, however modified, will continue to be felt is beyond our present purpose. But some well-defined points that would be cardinal in such a survey must be noted if we are to fix Bradley's position at Glasgow.

In the last quarter of the eighteenth century there had been a remarkable revolution in the attitude to literature. In criticism and creation alike the dogmatic opinions of the preceding age were rejected. The new movement seemed in some ways anti-intellectual; poets and critics now sought poetic truth in the imagination rather than in the reason, and claims were made for the imaginative interpretation of life that were not new perhaps but certainly long forgotten. The divine ancestry assigned to the Arts in antiquity had become for good sense a pleasing myth at best, and survived only as a fashionable *façon de parler.* But by 1780 mythology was beginning to interest the learned as more than the creation of pagan ignorance and it was transfigured by the poets. Wordsworth put the new claim for poetry in its most unequivocal form: 'to be incapable of a feeling for poetry, in

82

my sense of the word, is to be without love of human nature and reverence for God'.

By 'poetry in my sense of the word' Wordsworth meant something more than metrical composition. 'Poetry' he said 'is the history or science of feelings.'

It is of course no denial of reason to say that reason must reckon with the whole nature of the mind, or to affirm that the rationalist is the most unreasonable of men. The period from 1780 onwards felt the force of certain elements that the philosophy of its immediate predecessors had not sufficiently allowed for. That feeling found expression in the poetry of England and the Philosophy of Germany. Coleridge is the bridge across which Philosophy and Poetry meet. Modern criticism is the child of this marriage. Behind the modern criticism of literature—the attempt to find some leading principles which will give a coherence and so a validity to its findings—behind that effort lies the great tradition of thought that goes back at least to Plato.

To bring this tradition to bear on the problems of criticism Bradley was admirably equipped by temperament and by education. It was natural then for Bradley in his inaugural lecture here, after touching briefly on the topics set out by Nichol—the history of the language, the theory and practice of composition, and the study of literature proper—to come to what seemed to him the justification of the study as a whole. Poetry was the history or science of feelings—to enter us into that history, to make that science part of our consciousness was his task. That is why he chose as the title for his address *Poetry and Life,* a title that may seem to-day unnecessarily obvious, but justified in its time and place if we consider what had passed at Universities for learned opinion on literary studies.

Most men who make a mark in their own life-time find something in the spirit of the age that co-operates with their efforts, something responsive on which they can work. As the fashions of folly are always changing, so there are epochs of thought in which some aspect of truth needs more emphasis than another. Bradley's lot placed him in a period when his teaching seemed particularly needful. One quotation must suffice as a summary of the situation.

In 1880, when Bradley was contributing his paper on Aristotle to *Hellenica,* Matthew Arnold published his essay *The Study of Poetry* which begins:

'The future of poetry is immense, because in poetry, where it is worthy of its high destinies, our race as time goes on will find an ever surer and surer stay. There is not a creed which is not shaken, not an accredited dogma which is not shown to be questionable, not a received tradition which does not threaten to dissolve. Our religion has materialised itself in the fact, in the supposed fact; it has attached its emotion to the fact, and now the fact is failing it. But for poetry the idea is everything'.

Arnold's words, regarded not as a final analysis of the problem, but as an account of the intellectual difficulties of his generation, provide the setting for Bradley's teaching. The historical and scientific criticism of the century and that before it seemed to threaten the foundations of the moral life itself. And neither science nor history could supply what it threatened to take away. Huxley, in his account of this ingenious piece of mechanism that science had discovered the world to be, a mechanism that we could observe, but only after much laborious investigation, in the very process of piecing itself together, found that the cosmos had come to a point where it contradicted itself. And he had to conclude that it was the duty of moral man to combat the cosmic process. Huxley in his conclusion was only saying what many religious teachers had been saying for centures; they had offered a reason for their conclusions—but Huxley could give none. He had merely taken away the old sanctions from the doctrine he now preached himself—but without authority except his own feelings. And to justify these, to give them some universality, something beyond his own *ipse dixit,* he turns to poetry for the last word:

84

It may be that the gulfs will wash us down,
It may be we shall touch the Happy Isles,
           . . . but something ere the end
Some work of noble note may yet be done.

In 1893, the date of Huxley's *Romanes* lecture, the scientist
is reduced to quoting poetry when he begins to reflect on first
principles. Of course the scientist is usually content to stick
to his particular task and answer the challenge of morality
and religion in his private life by his conduct as a social
being. The wisdom of such an attitude is well illustrated in
the conduct of Faraday. To spend his time examining the
foundations of right and wrong was not his business; as far
as he needed authority here, he was content to accept the
formulæ of the Sandemanians—a simplicity that was past
Matthew Arnold's understanding. But few men can hope
to be so happily inspired as Faraday.

These then were the years in which Bradley was teaching
at Glasgow. The oracles were dumb, or, when they spoke,
the hearers were still full of doubt. But Poetry, as even Huxley
felt, voiced the convictions of the heart; he too took his
question to the shrine

       that has not ceased from speaking.

As Frederick Myers has put it in his essay on *Greek Oracles*
in *Hellenica:* 'poetry is the only thing which every age is
certain to recognise as truth'.

It was as an interpreter of that truth, the truths that every
generation is eager to be instructed in, that Bradley commanded so wide an audience and exercised what has been
described as a magical domination even over his Ordinary
Class at Glasgow. Now Bradley attacked the problem at its
most difficult point, the bastion that towered over all the
outworks as the key to the position. In tragedy the poet
makes no concessions to the weakness or longings of mankind. Here is no wish-fulfilment, here we find something as

85

terrible as life itself. That was why Bradley made Shakespeare the central study of his course—an author as plain to his hearers at the Globe as was Homer reciting to the Delian Maidens—there if anywhere is the open secret, so obvious that it may take a lifetime to discover that there is any mystery at all.

In the notice that appeared on Bradley's death in the minutes of our General Council, he was described as an interpreter rather than a critic of literature. But there is no such thing as criticism without interpretation; for what is your criticism worth if you do not understand the poet's intention; and how can you assess the parts if you do not understand the whole? To teach boys the canons of taste, to instruct them in rules that will enable them to criticise is to maim them for life. 'That born critic,' says Augustine Birrell in one of his essays, with what ironic reservation it is hard to say: 'That born critic, the late Sir George Lewis, had barely completed his tenth year before he was able, in a letter to his mother, to point out to her, the essentially faulty structure of *Hamlet*'.

Boys and men are not in such a hurry to make clever objections to Newton's *Principia* or to the *De Revolutionibus* of Copernicus. Here critics know their place. It was part of Bradley's service to teach his hearers their place when they came to talk about the Poets.

Bradley retired in 1900 when he was fifty; but he later held the Professorship of Poetry at Oxford for five years; and in 1907 he returned to Glasgow to deliver his *Gifford* lectures. Failing health prevented his putting these in order for publication, and it was only in 1940 that the first series was printed from his rough draft. Like everything he wrote they repay study; but it is for his work on the English poets that he will be remembered. There has been of course a reaction to his teaching; that is natural; other apsects of criticism need emphasis. But that there is something central in his teaching, something without which the teaching of literature must lose its full effect, I have no doubt whatever.

Walter Raleigh followed Bradley at Glasgow in 1900, as
he had followed him some eleven years before at Liverpool.
'I regard him' said Raleigh, speaking of Bradley in his
inaugural here, 'I regard him as one appointed by Provi-
dence to make my way in life difficult for me. I am afraid
that this is not a business of which the good-will can be
handed over in a day.

> *The funeral baked meats*
> *Do coldly furnish forth the marriage table.'*

The note had changed, but this too was rich in the overtones
and undertones that give quality and resonance to the discourse. Like Bradley before him and like Macneile Dixon
after him, Raleigh was a son of the manse. They came from
different denominations and the speculative might search in
this sameness and difference for a clue to their very different
treatment of the same task. But the higher psychology is not
our subject; all I would observe is that there was in their
work as in their origin a unity in their differences.

There was nothing of the Hegelian about Raleigh. He
had read History at Cambridge; before that he had been at
University College, London, and had sat under the Professor of English there, Henry Morley, but only on the way
to a pass degree; and I do not think Raleigh was formed in
any way by that hard-working teacher. But although Raleigh
was in training and method a contrast to Bradley, it would be
a mistake to force the contrast. Many of the matters that
Bradley expounded so lucidly to his pupils, Raleigh could
not touch on except in brief and concentrated interpolations,
because these were topics that cannot very well be treated
directly; for their exposition a lecturer requires a machinery,
almost as the dramatist requires his plot and characters,
before he can speak his mind to us. Raleigh's training and
observation of life had given him a different set of plots as
it were from Bradley's. But the comic and the tragic artist
are not fundamentally different; no one supposes that Comedy

is necessarily less serious than Tragedy or that Racine is a more serious author than Molière.

The unwary were often deceived about Raleigh's real feelings; one incident only can be mentioned here to show how and why. Raleigh, when he was leaving Glasgow to found the English School at Oxford, which we left earlier in the evening at its Anglo-Saxon with Napier, was asked by someone what the Oxford school really required; and Raleigh is reported to have replied: 'Tosh and Text, and I shall do the Tosh'. This is not how Dr. Dale would have put it. But Raleigh must be judged by his performance, not by his jests; and there is a remarkable testimony to the quality of Raleigh's teaching from a scholar who combined the highest academic accomplishment with a turn of expression far more disturbing than Raleigh's.

Raleigh, during his tenure of the new Oxford Chair, was invited by the Master and Fellows of Trinity College, Cambridge, to return to his old University as Clark lecturer. There in his audience he encountered a scholar who had also changed his University, only the other way round, an Oxford man who had found as Kennedy Professor of Latin what he gratefully described as an asylum at Cambridge. Housman, for he was Cambridge's new Professor of Latin, had in his own inaugural thought it necessary to warn his audience that he made no pretensions to speak as a literary critic. Many years later, on the same topic, he said:

'I have improved in some respects and deteriorated in others; but I have not so much improved as to become a literary critic, nor so much deteriorated as to fancy I have become one'.

Raleigh's judge might therefore be considered a severe one, and here is his verdict set down in a letter declining the invitation of the Master and Fellows of Trinity to follow Raleigh as Clark lecturer:

'I do regard myself as a connoisseur; I think I can tell good from bad in literature. But literary criticism, referring opinions to principles and setting them forth so as to command assent, is a high and rare accomplishment and quite beyond me. I remember Walter Raleigh's Clark lecture on Landor: it was unpretending, and not adorned or even polished, but I was thinking all the while that I could never have hit the nail on the head like that'.

As an unsolicited testimonial, even from one who was no doubt a better judge of Text than Tosh, few of us would, I think, be displeased with it.

The second ingredient in Raleigh's prescription for Oxford was Text. That was largely the theme of his inaugural here in 1900. Nowhere did he find it written in the bond between a University and its students that it should make them into men of genius. Men who are born to write may begin as they please: indeed a qualification in medicine has here as elsewhere proved no insuperable obstacle to distinction in letters. But a University should direct the reading of its students, and so direct it that if a man of genius does happen to take it seriously he will not find his time squandered. It is in English as in all fields of study. The young Norwegian mathematician Abel asked how he had come so far in so brief a life replied that he had studied the masters. 'Teach me rightly to admire Milton and Keats and I will find my own criticism of living poets. Train me to become a citizen of the Republic of Letters.' That is the demand the teacher has to try to meet. That was the task Raleigh set before himself, and the series of studies he has left us is the evidence of how he discharged it.

There are other views, I believe, in vogue to-day. One must base one's operations, it is said, upon the contemporary poets of one's own social group. The dead poets did not write for us, we are told, though Shakespeare seems to have thought that

> *So long as men can breathe, or eyes can see,*

his verse would have a message; and one hardly supposes

that the lives of local town-councillors would make better reading for the young than Plutarch's *Lives*. If the fashion has indeed changed, then Raleigh was old-fashioned.

Under the heading Text may well fall Raleigh's provision here for the more serious study of the language. Nichol, though interested in philology by Max Muller at Oxford, had not had time to do much if anything on this side of his programme. Bradley himself introduced a short course on the history of the Language, and from about 1895 instruction was given in Anglo-Saxon. Here the Humanity department provided assistance and Daniel Rankine read with the English Honours students select passages from Anglo-Saxon Literature. Rankine was a good scholar, and I am told by one well qualified to judge, one who was also his student, that what Rankine taught he taught well. This teaching was eventually taken over by the English department itself, which was gradually adding to its staff, and now included, as the English lecturer at the newly-established Queen Margaret College, Adolphus Jack, later Professor at Aberdeen. Dr. David Crawford, later one of H.M. Inspectors of Schools, and Mr. Nichol Smith, later Professor at Oxford, were for a period lecturers here. Raleigh, however, decided that Language required the whole attention of a teacher whose main interest lay in Language, and early in 1904, before he had thought of going to Oxford, he made arrangements for Mr. Ritchie Girvan, who had just returned from studying under Sievers and Brugmann at Leipzig, and was working at Oxford with Sir William Craigie and Henry Bradley on the N.E.D., to join his staff, until provision could be made for an independent lectureship in Language. Raleigh, however, left almost as soon as he had made these arrangements, but, before leaving, he urged strongly on the Court the need for a Chair of English Language. In 1907 the Carnegie Trust gave half the sum required for the establishment of such a Chair, and it was hoped that the remainder would be forthcoming at the next Quinquennial reckoning. The lectureship in English Language therefore dates from 1907, although Raleigh's project was realised in its fullness only forty years later in 1947. Fortunately our first lecturer in Language, the scholar who had single-handed made the study of Language here a reality, was still with us to be our first Professor of English Language.

In 1904 Raleigh was persuaded after some demur to go to Oxford, the lighter load of lecturing there being perhaps the deciding factor. He was followed here by William Macneile Dixon from Birmingham. During Macneile Dixon's stay there, Mason College had been transformed into the University of Birmingham, and Macneile Dixon once said that those who wished to read his writings should not open his literary works but study the charter of Birmingham University. There is no doubt that Birmingham owed not a few of the enlightened and truly academic provisions in that early charter to Macneile Dixon; for his capacity for handling men and affairs with firmness and indeed with the utmost resolution was always obvious when the occasion roused him. He did not willingly give himself to what is called business, but he was an ideal exponent of the Platonic precept that the affairs of men are not worthy of great seriousness though we must perforce be serious about them.

A pupil of Dowden's at Trinity College, Dublin, Macneile Dixon also read Philosophy there. During these years he made his first visit to Scotland; the subject for the Chancellor's medal in verse composition one year happened to be *Iona,* and Macneile Dixon decided to get his local colour on the spot. Iona was the first Scottish soil on which he put his foot and there he wished his ashes to rest. He had sailed there in his own yacht, for he was passionately fond of the sea, and in his younger years delighted in the handling of small craft—an interest that found expression in later years in his chronicle of the deeds of the auxiliary craft in the first world war. As Raleigh was the first historian of the part played by the Air Force in that war, so Macneile Dixon was the historian of the men who manned the auxiliary fleet. The debt of this country to its fishermen and yachtsmen, the men who protected the fleet on which our fortunes and liberty depended, has never been better appreciated than in these little volumes.

This attraction the more elemental aspects of living had for Macneile Dixon combined with his literary interests to give the writings and outlook of the Greeks a peculiar hold on his imagination. Macneile Dixon, though not a classical scholar in the technical sense, for he admitted that at Trinity Tyrrell's learned discussion of variant readings in the text of Aeschylus or Sophocles left him admiring the performance but indifferent to the conclusion, was drawn to things Greek, especially its history, its landscape, its art, with what one felt to be an almost atavistic attachment. One of his last adventures took him when he was well over sixty through the mountains of Greece, a journey he recorded in his *Hellas Revisited*. 'To be without interest in Greece,' he wrote there:

'To be without interest in Greece—the fatherland of every thinking soul—as Gregorovius called it—is simply to be without interest in the achievements of the human mind; and although an appreciation of these achievements in art or literature, science or philosophy, unassisted by travel is, indeed, possible, that it should exist unaccompanied by any desire to see Athens or Sparta, Delos or Delphi, is a strange thing, the more strange since to see it is so pleasantly and powerfully to dilate the imagination, and add to the comprehension of a country which became by some divine decree the radiant centre of European thought'.

He offered his record as an introduction to Pausanias whose *Description of Greece,* in Frazer's fine edition, was one of his favourite books. But it was something in himself that found satisfaction in his travels, in his excursion to see with his own eyes the memorial that marks the battlefield of Chaeronea:

A Lion where the lion-hearted lie

or to visit the nearby birthplace of Plutarch and echo the cry 'Plutarch is the man for me'.

His Hellenism coloured all his writing and teaching. That is what drew him to such essayists as Arnold and Pater and why of the German philosophers he preferred Schopenhauer and Nietzsche and why his most characteristic publication is his little book on Tragedy; for like Bradley before him, Macneile Dixon felt that here lay the main problem in literary interpretation. His Hellenism explains too his whole outlook on the Renaissance and his frequent visits to Italy as a halfway house to Greece.

The man to whom these interests were more than second nature could not fail to exercise a deep influence on his students. A wider public felt that influence in his *Gifford Lectures* which he gave on his retirement. They were and are widely read in their published form. At the end, like Bradley and Raleigh, he comes back to the thought on which the teaching of literature must always rest, if literature is to be more than a mere diversion on the long fool's errand to the grave or an industry to provide the bread and butter to enable us to last the course. Having surveyed the human situation from all the vantage points that history, or science, or philosophy, or religion, can afford us he returns to view the features and faculties in man that the poets love and admire, his endurance, his resolution, his heroism, his quixotry—'Yes, the quixotry, the inexplicable preference, even to his own hurt, for the noble and magnanimous, the high and honourable things'.

Whatever you may think of the relative importance of that point of view, you may agree that it is at least a proper one for those whose task it is to comment on the English poets. That was then the ground occupied in turn here by Nichol, Bradley, Raleigh and Macneile Dixon.

If I have spoken at length only of the successive occupants of the Chair of English that is not because I forget the other able teachers and good scholars who have lectured here on our language and literature. I need only add the name of John Semple Smart to those I have mentioned in passing to reassure you about my memory in this matter. In the days, however, before the large increase in the teaching staff and the Professor's appearance as a specialist among specialists the Scots Professor was cast for what was indeed the protagonist's role, and the four men to whom I have directed your attention sustained that traditional part with an authority and acceptance that inevitably made them the centre of our interest.

The Modern Language Chairs have even shorter pedigrees than that of English; for they were created by the generosity of Glasgow citizens only in the present century.

There were, however, as one might expect, in earlier periods, that is before the creation of any language department, occasional teachers here of modern languages. In 1730 the faculty considering that 'it is of considerable advantage to have residing and teaching in this place a native of France who understands and can pronounce his own language accurately', paid someone who seemed to meet these requirements £5 per annum. Later John Anderson, Professor of Oriental Languages, proposed to teach French and Italian; but his own translation to the Chair of Natural Philosophy involved him in other interest and much disputation with his colleagues. He was the founder of Anderson College. But in spite of Anderson's departure from the Arts, French continued to be taught by others for some considerable time.

The French department dates from 1875, that of German from 1899. The Marshall Chair of French was established in 1917, and Charles Martin, at that time head of the department, became Professor in 1919 on his return from service with the French Army. In 1919, too, Dr. Herbert Smith, who had come to us from St. Andrews and Marburg to conduct the German department, became the first William Jack Professor of German.

The Chairs of Italian and Spanish were made possible by the endowment provided by Sir Daniel Stevenson, in

1924. There was already an Italian department dating from 1902, and in 1925 Ernesto Grillo who was responsible for the department, became Professor. In the same year Spanish studies were inaugurated here by Professor William Entwistle.

In 1917, the year in which the French Chair was created, Lord Weir helped to provide for a lectureship in Russian, Mr. Hugh Brennan taking over this new department.

In the last few years the University has undertaken instruction in certain other Slavonic and Eastern European languages.

Although only a Modern Language scholar is entitled to speak to you about Charles Martin and Ernesto Grillo as academic teachers, you will allow me, in spite of my disqualification, to say a few words about the men I knew; but you may fairly expect me to be brief. Charles Martin was a graduate of Paris; but to me he was a Frenchman of the Midi and in many respects a Scotsman's ideal of what a Frenchman should be: a Frenchman so truly devoted to his own country, its customs, and habits, that he could feel and sympathise with, even when he could not or would not always understand, the form our loyalties took. From this devotion and the superrogatory sympathies that such a devotion invariably creates in the generous minded, came one of the benefits of his influence on our students. He made his department the embodiment of the French outlook and way of life; the instruction was in French, the method French, yet it was a department through which no Scot who entered into the spirit of his teaching could pass without coming out a better Scotsman.

Ernesto Grillo was naturally more restricted in his influence, for, as is inevitable here, Italian studies are bound unfortunately to be possible only to a few. He was an enthusiast, perhaps extravagantly so at times, or so it seemed to some, but he put many students in the way of Italian study that would not perhaps have thought of it otherwise; and those of them who continued the study seriously cannot but be grateful for the stimulus he provided.

The Modern Language departments are naturally not content merely to teach the language. Behind every language is the peculiar genius of its people. To quicken in their pupils a sense of that genius is the task of these departments. But as there is in the world a fruitful interchange of influence and thought between peoples and languages, at one moment one language at another another seeming to bring with it a vital influence to a third, so in a University we hope by the cultivation of a suitable range of languages to provide a field in which the same cross-fertilisation, writ so large in the history of languages and cultures, may have a chance to operate in the individual minds of our students. No one can merely by taking thought bring to pass these *callida junctura*— not even genius; they come as a kind of revelation even to genius. Study cannot produce them; but they do not come without study and application. To provide a field in which these happy conjunctions may have the best chance of coming about is part of the contribution which the brotherhood of the languages here can make to that creative work which it is the duty and let us hope the destiny of our University to foster.

My story began in 1862 with no department of English and none of Modern Languages. In those ninety years there has been established here a range of departments and studies in these fields that cannot be called inadequate. It is true that learning and thought, the arts and culture, are carried on by men. Institutions, however well organised, cannot make men with the aptitudes and wisdom necessary for this task. Such men, to use the words of Burke, are the gifts of God. But we have done something as a University in the years I have traversed to make a fuller use, perhaps to show our appreciation, of those gifts which we must trust will yet be abundantly bestowed on Scotland.

PHILOSOPHY

by

C. A. Campbell
Professor of Logic

In the beginning, and for several decades thereafter, the University of Glasgow was in effect a Faculty of Arts. The Faculty of Arts itself, for a still longer time, was not a great deal more than a Faculty of Philosophy. Indeed, even so late as the closing years of the seventeenth century it was still frequently referred to as 'the Faculty of philosophie.' Now this state of affairs confronts the historian of Glasgow philosophy at the outset with something of a problem in procedure. A scrupulous interpretation of his mandate will require him to deal with this early period on a scale which bears some relation to the dominating role which philosophy then played in University studies. On the other hand, he cannot but recognise that, since the story of philosophy in the University during the first two centuries and more is in no small measure the story of the University itself, most of what he will want to say about it will be adequately said elsewhere.

In this dilemma, the sin of disproportion seems to me to be, on the whole, a lesser evil than the sin of duplication. I intend, therefore, to pass very lightly over the long period —well over one-half of the University's life-time—which preceded the final abandonment of the 'Regency' system. The year 1727, in which Regent John Loudon was elected to the Chair of Logic, and Regent Gerschom Carmichael to the Chair of Moral Philosophy, may be said to inaugurate the 'modern era' in Glasgow philosophy, with 'Departments' of Logic and Moral Philosophy in substantially their present

97

form. And it is with the modern era alone that this narrative
will attempt any degree of detail.

THE PERIOD OF THE REGENTS

The brief prologue which must suffice for the period of
the Regents will perhaps be least likely to omit matter of
primary interest to philosophers if it confines itself to answer-
ing three basic questions: (1) What was the *content* of these
early philosophical courses? (2) What were the *methods* of
instruction? (3) What sort of *persons* were those who instructed?

To commence, then, with the question of 'content.'

From the institution of the University right up to the time
of Andrew Melville's Principalship (1574-80), philosophy
in Glasgow—as indeed everywhere else in the Western world
—meant virtually the known works of Aristotle. The staple
subjects of study were Aristotelian texts in Logic, in Metaphysics, and in Psychology. Ethics, rather surprisingly, occupies a somewhat humble place on the periphery of the
curriculum. *Sex Libri Ethicorum* (*sc.* Aristotelis) appears only
in the category of Libri Extraordinarii, *i.e.,* books which might
or might not be included in the course according to the
ad hoc discretion of the Faculty. Doubtless the Church,
which inspired and controlled all educational systems of
the day, took the understandable view that she could very
well impart without secular assistance all the teaching that
was required concerning the principles of good behaviour.

Under the leadership of Melville, however, the some-time
pupil of that arch-enemy of Aristotle, Peter Ramus, the
Aristotelian monopoly was at last broken. Regular instruction is now provided in Ethics and Politics, much prominence is given to the study of Rhetoric, classes in Greek
grammar are instituted for 'Bajanes' and 'Semis'; and while
Aristotle is by no means neglected, many other great names
—among them Plato, the Greek orators, Cicero, Plutarch,
and of course Peter Ramus himself—now figure in the list of

authors of 'prescribed texts.' Melville finds no room in his programme, however, for pure metaphysics; and this, I think, we must place on the debit side of his account—though a prominent school of contemporary philosophers would doubtless hail this as the most signal proof of his genius! But all in all, the reformed curriculum of Andrew Melville is in its breadth and its humanism no unworthy reflection of the sixteenth century Revival of Learning.

From Melville's time until the close of the Regency period one hundred and fifty years later, the Glasgow philosophical curriculum underwent only very minor alterations. Indeed, the spirit of conservatism it manifests is almost a little startling. The seventeenth century is perhaps the greatest age in the history of philosophy. It is the age of Bacon, Hobbes, and Locke in this country, and of Descartes, Leibniz, Spinoza, Geulincx and Malebranche on the Continent. Yet so far as the records show, only Descartes among these philosophers appears to have been studied in any Scottish University. And even this (surely not very reckless) traffic with the Moderns evidently struck alarm in the hearts of the University Commissioners of 1690, who in their Report deplore with some bitterness the attention paid in philosophical curricula to 'Cartesius, Rohault and others of his gang'!

The Glasgow curriculum would certainly have undergone important changes however, had an interesting project first broached by a Universities Commission in 1642, and later revived by Commissions in 1647 and 1690, ever materialised. The proposal was that there should be a uniform *cursus philosophicus* for the four Scottish Universities. Common textbooks were to be printed, embodying courses in logic, ethics, etc., and these were to supersede the 'dyted notes' of the various Regents. The 1690 Commission succeeded in carrying matters a good deal further than its predecessors, and before the turn of the century each University had been charged to devise a draft course on one of the four 'divisions' of philosophy. To Glasgow was allotted 'general and special ethicks,' which included politics and economics. These documents were in fact all completed: but what happened to them thereafter is something of a mystery. We do know that the Glasgow draft, with certain other relevant papers, was sent to Dr. Gilbert Rule, Principal of Edinburgh University, no doubt for that University's observations, and that when Dr. Rule died shortly afterwards, in 1701, the most careful search failed to disclose any trace of them. It may be that the other drafts suffered the same fate. At all events, the disaster seems to have been sufficient to dishearten the apostles of *Gleichschaltung,* and the scheme was dropped for good. As matters turned out, this was perhaps fortunate. Only a quarter of a century later the Regents were to give way to specialist Professors; and it may well be doubted whether any philosophical teacher in a position to concentrate upon the work of a single department would be content to order his teaching by detailed prescription from without.

If Glasgow during the Regency period showed a marked disinclination to 'move with the times' in matters of curriculum (in which respect she differed not at all from other British Universities), we have regretfully to admit, when we turn to look at the *method* rather than the content of its philosophical teaching, that the spirit of adventure is there no more conspicuous. The following description by Veitch applies almost as accurately to the early years of the eighteenth century as to the closing years of the fifteenth:

'Regenting was essentially a method of teaching by means of approved books. The Regent read, expounded, and dictated to the student, who was called upon to write carefully and at full length the *dictata* of the Master. On these he was examined and exercised, chiefly by means of the practice of disputation. This, in its most public form, was known as "determining." It took place in presence of the whole University. The meeting was presided over by one of the Masters, who proposed the questions, in Ethics or Metaphysics. The youthful students of Logic (*juvenes Logicae studiosi*) showed their proficiency in the art by there and then giving their opinions on the question.'

To this we may add that from beginning to end of the Regency period the whole of the teaching was conducted in Latin (in which tongue the students had, of course, to carry on their 'disputations'); and that not until the seventeenth century was well advanced were the Latin translations of prescribed Greek authors at all generally replaced by original texts.

Our third question, 'What sort of persons were the teachers of philosophy?' has already been answered in part. They were, of course, the Regents: that is to say, not philosophical specialists, but the self-same persons who also taught everything else that the University professed to teach. Melville had, indeed, made an effort to put an end to this 'ambulatory' system, according to which each Regent took one year's intake of students through the entire four-year curriculum; but such success as he gained was short-lived. Yet it is hard to see how even the most talented of polymaths could be expected to stand up to the whole teaching programme, particularly after the notable expansion of the curriculum which followed the *Nova Erectio*. Nor must it be forgotten that the Regent was further charged with the supervision of the discipline and the general welfare of his student 'year.' All things considered, we need not wonder that the Roll of Glasgow Regents contains, with the exception of the celebrated jurisprudent James Dalrymple (afterwards the first Viscount Stair), not a single name that has even minor importance in the history of philosophy. The truth seems to be that the 'ambulatory' system could only work at all, in philosophy at any rate, so long as the 'omnibus' duties of the teacher were closely tethered to a few time-honoured texts which could be dealt with as a matter of more or less mechanical routine. Such a manner of filling one's days could hold little attraction for any thinker of spirit or originality.

Let us briefly sum up. The pedagogic scheme we have been describing was not wholly without merits, even for the teaching of philosophy. Methodical and meticulous study of the texts of the great masters must always play an indispensable part in the novitiate of the young philosopher. The practice of disputation, again, has an obvious value in quickening the wits and imparting flexibility to the mind; though where the themes chosen are trivial (as was often the case in the Regency period) there is a danger that the student may come to prize the means rather than the end. But there is no denying that the system as a whole was pretty bad. Exact textual knowledge and subtlety in dialectics are, after all, only the instruments of philosophising. They will remain barren instruments if the true informing spirit be lacking—the urge to seek with all one's resources of mind and soul for some vision of the nature of things that can commend itself to the free and untrammelled intelligence of a rational being. It is just this informing spirit that the philosophical education of the Regency period was quite eminently fitted not to produce. And if it be pleaded that such was not then the aim of a philosophical education; that its aim was, as in the Arts curriculum as a whole, to fit students for the learned professions, like Divinity and Law, and not at all to imbue them with an itch for speculation which, in the eyes of Christian orthodoxy whether Catholic or Protestant, could only endanger their immortal souls; this is indeed all too true. But the conclusion to be drawn is not that philosophy was wisely taught; but simply that, in those days, it was not thought wise to teach philosophy.

OPENING OF THE MODERN ERA— HUTCHESON, ADAM SMITH, AND REID

The abolition of the Regency system in 1727 involved the

institution of two separate philosophical Chairs: the one (Logic) concerned with Logic, Metaphysics, Psychology and Rhetoric, the other (Moral Philosophy) with Ethics, Jurisprudence, Natural Theology and Political Economy. History justified the change dramatically. Well within its first half-century the Glasgow Professoriate was graced by no less than three thinkers of first-rate importance in the annals of British philosophy—Francis Hutcheson, Adam Smith, and Thomas Reid. This flowering of philosophic genius cannot, of course, be accounted for simply by improvements in academic machinery. But nor can it have been mere matter of chance that it followed so closely upon the deliverance of philosophical teachers from the soul-destroying routine of the Regency system.

Before we address ourselves to the achievements of Glasgow's philosophical Triumvirate, a word should be spared for the first incumbent of the Moral Philosophy Chair, Gerschom Carmichael. For Carmichael, who had been a Regent for over thirty years before his appointment to the Chair, was a man of exceptional learning and ability. Had he enjoyed in the vigour of his youth the more favourable working conditions of his Chair he might well have gained a measure of lasting fame. Even as it was, his annotated edition of Puffendorf's *De Officio Hominis et Civis* remained for many years a standard work. There are several indications that Carmichael was more eager than was then deemed altogether decorous in University circles to keep abreast of the currents of contemporary thought. The New Physics in particular fascinated him. In a Report upon the methods and subject-matter of his class instruction as Regent, he writes with the liveliest enthusiasm of 'Ye two great Hinges of Natural Philosophy, or rather ye two constituent parts of it . . . Mathematical Demonstration and Experiment.' Nor should it be forgotten that one of the pupils whom Regent Carmichael guided and instructed was Francis Hutcheson himself.

Francis Hutcheson, a Northern Irishman of Scottish ex-
traction, and a graduate of this University, returned to his
Alma Mater as Professor of Moral Philosophy in 1729 and
occupied the Chair until his death in 1746. Of his quite
remarkable influence not merely as a philosophical teacher
but as an apostle of liberal ideas throughout the whole conduct of life, there can be no two opinions. Scottish culture
in the early part of the eighteenth century was permeated by
many of the less attractive features of Puritanism—harsh
intolerance of opposing ideas, a censorious attitude towards
even the more innocent sensuous enjoyments, contempt for
arts and letters, indifference to most of the graces of civilised
living. To no single person, by common consent, did the
Scottish *Aufklärung* of the late eighteenth century owe so
much as to Francis Hutcheson. In all the manifold spheres
of his activity Hutcheson was the patient, fearless and eloquent
campaigner for enlightened ideas and generous policies: in
the University council chambers; in the pulpit; in extra-
mural lectures to tradesmen and artisans; in public affairs;
in the class-room. Above all, in the class-room. For Hutcheson's greatest gift to his age was, beyond question, the successive generations of students whom he sent out into the world
inspired by his own lofty enthusiasm, and persuaded that the
cultivation of the intellect and the refinement of the feelings,
so far from being at enmity with the good life, is in fact the
one sure safeguard against the degeneration of spiritual fervour
into a crude and ugly bigotry.

When one turns to the question of Hutcheson's rank as an
original philosophical thinker, there is room, perhaps, for
some difference of view. Hutcheson belongs to the school of
so-called 'psychological moralists.' This school, sceptical of
the claims of thinkers like Cudworth and Clarke to be able
to show that moral distinctions are rooted in the nature of
things, was content to show that they are at least rooted in
the nature of man. Hutcheson's *Inquiry into the Original of our
Ideas of Beauty and Virtue,* and his posthumously published

System of Moral Philosophy, have won for him a place of high honour among members of this school: but when one asks 'What was his distinctive contribution to it in point of doctrine?' an answer is not altogether easy. The leading positions one associates with Hutcheson's name are all familiar already from the pages of his acknowledged master, Shaftesbury. This is true of the central doctrine that there is a special 'moral sense' inherent in man whereby he can directly discern the good and the bad in conduct without reflective regard to consequences; of the doctrine that the conduct which the moral sense thus approves is as a matter of fact coincident with the conduct which would best promote the general happiness; of the doctrine—so sharply opposed to the interpretations of human nature made fashionable by Hobbes and Mandeville—that benevolent impulses are as integral a part of the natural constitution of man as are selfish impulses; and of the doctrine that, in the long run, the way of life most conducive to the general happiness is the same as the way of life which will bring to the agent his own greatest happiness. Furthermore, the analogy which Hutcheson is so fond of drawing between our moral and our æsthetic perception is conspicuous in Shaftesbury's writings also. It is true, indeed, that Hutcheson's latest work shows some modification of, and even departure from, positions occupied by Shaftesbury. Hutcheson was a mind responsive to new ideas, and his philosophy by no means remained unaffected by the very vigorous ethical controversies that were a feature of British thought during the last twenty years of his life. But the new elements in his philosophy are in fact assimilated—and somewhat eclectically at that—from the works of other thinkers. To make a case for Hutcheson's originality one is apt to find one's self driven to stressing such trifling innovations as his use of the phrase 'the greatest happiness for the greatest numbers,' which foreshadows the Utilitarian formula; or his proposal of a quasi-mathematical calculus, akin to Bentham's, for computing the relative values of pleasures.

This is not to suggest, however, that Hutcheson is unworthy of the high place which historians of moral philosophy have commonly accorded to him. The influence of his writings upon the subsequent course of ethical thought, both in this country and in Europe (more especially in Germany), has been immense, and Professor Kemp Smith has recently argued with force that it was Hutcheson's presentation of the case for *feeling* as the basis of value-beliefs which directly inspired David Hume's particular brand of 'naturalism,' with its inversion of the traditional roles of 'reason' and 'feeling' in matters of belief generally. Moreover, without minimising Hutcheson's debt to Shaftesbury, one may fairly recognise that Hutcheson's moral philosophy is of broader scope, better knit, and protected with greater skill against critical assault at vital points. It is, in a word, the more professional job of work; and it is, quite properly, to Hutcheson rather than to Shaftesbury that the student of ethics has always tended to turn for the *locus classicus* of the Moral Sense theory.

Even so brief a sketch of Hutcheson's contribution to philosophy must not conclude without at least a mention—no more is here possible—of his achievement in two disciplines with which his name is not so closely associated as with ethics. Hutcheson's *Inquiry* includes the first systematic treatment of philosophical æsthetics in modern times. And in the field of political economy (at that time claimed as part of the terrain of the moral philosopher) the late Professor W. R. Scott has drawn attention to a whole series of interesting parallels between passages in Hutcheson's works and in Adam Smith's *Wealth of Nations* which leave little doubt that even in points of economic doctrine the debt of Hutcheson's greatest pupil to his revered teacher is by no means negligible.

Hutcheson's immediate successor, Thomas Craigie, previously Professor of Hebrew in St. Andrews, held office for too short a time to make much mark. But following his death in 1751 the Moral Philosophy Chair again became a centre of widespread intellectual influence through the translation to it from the Logic Chair (to which he had been elected little more than a year before) of the towering genius of Adam Smith.

Other and more competent hands will deal in this volume with Adam Smith the Economist. But the magnitude of his accomplishment as the founder of modern Political Economy should not be allowed wholly to obscure Adam Smith the Moral Philosopher. Smith's *Theory of the Moral Sentiments* (1759) brought him wide renown as a moral philosopher a good seventeen years before the epoch-making *Wealth of Nations* appeared. It is a work which is still compulsory reading for anyone seriously concerned to follow the development of eighteenth-century ethics through its major ramifications.

Like Hutcheson, Smith approaches ethics by way of empirical psychology. His aim is to elucidate the phenomena of moral approbations and disapprobations by careful scrutiny of the intricate interaction within the human mind of its manifold impulses, passions, feelings and desires. In common too with Hutcheson, he is satisfied that moral phenomena will not admit of explanation in terms of disguised self-love. But in Smith's view we are by no means driven to the alternative of postulating a special moral sense to fulfil the required functions. *Entia non sunt multiplicanda praeter necessitatem;* and Smith is convinced that we can adequately account for our moral judgments without invoking a special faculty for the purpose, if only we pay due regard to the complex manifestations in the human mind of the principle of 'sympathy.'

Smith's whole moral philosophy turns upon the analysis of 'sympathy,' and upon the delineation of its ethically relevant expressions in human nature. It culminates in what is commonly accepted as Smith's distinctive contribution to ethics, the doctrine that our 'conscience' is at bottom sympathy with the feelings of an imaginary spectator, impartial and fully informed, taken to be contemplating our behaviour.

But there is a great deal that is instructive in Smith besides this familiar theory. He was a psychological observer of quite uncommon penetration; and his sensitive descriptions of the motivations of the human heart are not the less persuasive for being set out in a fluent and graceful prose enlivened by singularly felicitous illustrations. It has, indeed, been complained of Smith that he is a somewhat prolix writer; that the principle of economy to which he elsewhere does so much obeisance is not at all noticeable in his own literary style. This is true enough: and the logical structure of Smith's ethical doctrine suffers thereby some loss in clarity. But the rhetorical embellishments dear to his age, in which Smith delighted, hardly if at all impede the communication of his psychological insights. Even the harshest critic would agree that in his *Theory of the Moral Sentiments* Smith has notably illumined our understanding of the subtle interplay of the diverse influences that determine the practical consciousness of man.

A dozen or so years of the Moral Philosophy Chair seem to have convinced Adam Smith that if the children of his teeming brain were to grow to full maturity he must give more time to their nurture than a Glasgow Professorship allows. He resigned his Chair in 1764, returning shortly afterwards to his home town of Kirkcaldy to continue his researches under more leisurely conditions. He was succeeded by Thomas Reid (1764-96)—by common acknowledgment a figure second in importance only to David Hume among modern Scottish philosophers. [Here, and in similar cases elsewhere, the bracketed dates indicate the term of occupancy of the Chair, not the term of life.]

Reid was a native of Kincardineshire, and connected on his mother's side with the Gregorys, which is probably by a wide margin the most brilliant family line in Scotland's (if not in any country's) academic history. Before coming to Glasgow in 1764 he had been for thirteen years Regent in King's College, Aberdeen, and he had already completed his first major work—his *Inquiry into the Human Mind on the Principles of Common Sense*. In 1780 he relinquished his teaching duties (though continuing to discharge the other obligations of his Chair) partly on account of increasing deafness, partly that he might devote his full remaining energies to preparing for the press some of the material of his lecture courses. Two important works speedily followed: the *Essay on the Intellectual Powers* in 1785, and the *Essay on the Active Powers* in 1788. Reid remained mentally alert until extreme old age. His last composition, a paper on *Muscular Motion*, was undertaken in the year of his death at the age of eighty-six, and was inspired by the keen speculative interest with which he observed the progressive deterioration of his own physical capacities—a quaint but rather touching illustration of 'the consolations of philosophy.'

It has long been an agreeable convention in Glasgow that tenancy of one Philosophy Chair rather than the other is to be regarded as more or less a matter of accident, which, while it must with some strictness canalise class-room activities, need by no means dictate the direction of the Professor's private thinking. Reid notably exemplified (and perhaps he initiated) this tradition. He was, it is true, a moral philosopher of real distinction. The ethical theory advanced in his *Essay on the Active Powers* is a very powerful expression of the growing reaction against an ethics of 'feeling' and in favour of a 'rational' intuitionism better fitted to ensure the objectivity of moral principles. Indeed, as judicious a philosopher as Henry Sidgwick, in his *Short History of Ethics,* actually accords to Reid more space than to either Hutcheson or Smith. But there can be no kind of doubt that it is Reid's original contributions in the field of theory of knowledge that constitute by far his strongest claim to enduring memory.

Reid's familiar title of Founder of the 'Common Sense' School of Philosophy is appropriate enough, and he himself would certainly not disclaim it. But it is a title which can easily mislead. If Reid's true merits are to be appreciated, it is important to be clear in just what meaning of the term he can fairly be called a 'Common Sense' philosopher.

In one meaning at least Reid's philosophy is obviously amenable to this description. Among the many beliefs characteristic of Common Sense (or of 'the plain man') are some of a fundamental kind relating to the general nature of the universe in which we find ourselves: *e.g.*, that there exists an external world of relatively permanent things; that events in this external world occur in accordance with causal laws; that each of us is a 'self' which is not the mere flux of our feelings and perceptions, but a relatively permanent entity aware of external events and of its own states and possessing at least some measure of initiative in the field of behaviour. Now Hume had argued, very persuasively, that not one of these Common Sense beliefs is capable of rational justification. But it is of the very essence of the Reidian philosophy to try to rehabilitate them all.

It is another matter when we ask by what *method* Reid attempts their rehabilitation. If Reid's is a Common Sense philosophy in seeking to justify Common Sense beliefs, it is certainly not a Common Sense philosophy in seeking to do so by Common Sense methods. In point of *method* there is and, strictly speaking, can be *no* Common Sense philosophy. For the methods of Common Sense are essentially *un*philosophical. Reid's own method of procedure is—with occasional aberrations—philosophical in the highest degree. Convinced that Hume's formal reasoning is virtually impeccable, he accepts the logical implication that his conclusions can justly be disputed only if some flaw is discoverable in his premises. Scrutiny of the premises does, in Reid's view, disclose serious flaws. The root error lies in the assumption, common to the empiricist tradition since Locke, that what we directly apprehend in perception is always, and only, a 'sensation' or 'impression' which is (*a*) an atomic particular, and (*b*) mental in its nature. Once grant that our original perceptions are of isolated mental sensations and, Reid agrees,

Hume's sceptical conclusions inexorably follow. But a deeper analysis of perception, which Reid conducts with the utmost acuteness, shows, he thinks, that the initial assumption is untenable. The presence of a sensation can never, *per se,* account for even the simplest cognition. In cognition proper —and therefore in perception—the sensation is merely an element in a much more complex experience, which comprises as an integral part of it certain 'judgments.' The most important of these 'judgments' (which Reid is wont to speak of as 'suggested' by the sensations) are the judgment that a sensible quality characterises an existing external thing, and the judgment that there exists a subject or self by which the external thing is being apprehended. These are 'natural judgments,' in the sense that they are 'immediately inspired by our constitution.' The propositions corresponding to them must be accepted by us as true, not because they are logically self-evident (for they are not), nor because they are deducible from the logically self-evident (for as 'first principles' they cannot be deducible from anything else), but simply because the given nature of our minds is such that we find we cannot help affirming them, implicitly if not explicitly. In Reid's view, it is possible by analysis of our original experience, including moral experience, to elicit a considerable number of principles which enjoy this status. Being principles which flow from the very constitution of our minds, and in no sense dependent for their apprehension upon special knowledge or special gifts, they may be said, he thinks, to belong to the 'Common Sense and Reason' of mankind, and hence deserve the title 'Principles of Common Sense.' And with this there comes clearly into view the signification which is perhaps uppermost in Reid's mind when he avows his philosophy to be a philosophy of 'Common Sense.'

There are obvious defects in Thomas Reid's writings which forbid one to claim for him a place among the really great philosophers. Thus, while the credentials of his Principles of Common Sense are in some cases argued with much skill and force, in other cases Reid was far more easily satisfied than he had any right to be. It is not to be denied that Reid did sometimes (as his disciples Beattie and Oswald did constantly) descend to the use of 'popular' arguments whose philosophical value is negligible. Again, Reid puts together his list of Principles with but faint regard to considerations of method. One is entitled to expect, and one does not find, some effort made to ensure that the enumeration he offers is exhaustive. Again, while insisting upon the claim of his Principles to 'necessity,' he can hardly be said to have analysed the nature of this 'necessity' with due thoroughness, or to have brought out clearly how it is to be distinguished from 'logical' necessity. Yet at his best—and he is quite often at his best—the freshness, the robustness, and the perspicacity of Reid's thinking are deeply impressive. His influence upon subsequent philosophy would deserve to be rated high on the score of his critical examination of perception alone, which compelled general reconsideration, even if it did not everywhere procure actual rejection, of the prevailing mentalist and atomistic interpretations. His fame would stand still higher, one may surmise, if the 'Scottish School' of Common Sense philosophers who looked to him as their founder had included any members with sufficient philosophical genius to develop his thought constructively. As it was, even the more eminent members, like Dugald Stewart and Adam Ferguson, did little more than effectively restate his leading positions. Nevertheless, it says much for the vitality of its founder's thought that 'the philosophy of the Scottish School' (as James Seth reminds us) 'became the official philosophy of France and was taught in its colleges from 1816 to 1870.' And Reid's influence across the Atlantic (as Seth further notes) was in the nineteenth century no less potent than his influence across the Channel.

LOGICIANS FROM 1727 TO 1864, AND MORALISTS FROM 1796 TO 1866

It may now seem rather more than time that this sketch took notice of the fact that Glasgow possessed not only a Chair of Moral Philosophy but also a Chair of Logic. But truth to tell, the occupants of the Logic Chair for more than a hundred years did exceedingly little themselves to remind the outside world of their existence. All of them were men of ability and force of character. All of them made their mark in the general administration of the University. But (if for obvious reasons we discount Adam Smith, who held the post for one year) not one of them before the time of Veitch (1864-95) seems even to have attempted, much less accomplished, anything by which he might be remembered by philosophers.

John Loudon, the first occupant of the Chair (1727-51), had been a Regent for more than thirty years previously, and he may be pardoned if he had become a little set in his ways. There is no evidence that the greater concentration of his duties imparted any fresh impetus either to his thinking or to his teaching. But he remained to the end, throughout a stormy period of the University's domestic history, very much a man to be reckoned with in the Council Chamber—usually, it must be confessed, on the side of reaction.

James Clow (1752-74) was particularly prominent in University business. He served as Clerk, and as Dean of Faculty, and was several times Vice-Rector. But it is a sad example of the effect in this age of ecclesiastical inhibitions upon University appointments that the claims of James Clow to the Logic Chair should have been preferred to those of David Hume, who is known now, and was presumably known then, to have been eager for nomination.

George Jardine, elected assistant and successor to Clow, with full teaching responsibility, in 1774, became titular Professor only in 1787, when Clow resigned, but was in virtual or actual charge of the Department for over half a century. From 1781 until his death in 1827 he was also Clerk of Senate. Quite early in his teaching career, Jardine drastically revised the traditional Logic course, which in his view was too abstruse to carry real meaning for the very young lads who formed the bulk of his class, and too remote from the business of life to aid them much in their future careers. How he sought to remedy these defects, and to inculcate in his pupils good habits of thought and of taste is described in his *Outline of Philosophical Education* (1818). This book leaves the impression of a wise, mellow and gracious personality, and it is no surprise to learn that he was, according to his lights, a highly successful teacher. It is easy to ridicule the level upon which, by his own professions, he saw fit to lecture upon the nature and laws of the human mind; but Jardine may well have been right in contending that students who were for the most part in their early 'teens would derive very little profit from a profounder treatment of the subject.

Robert Buchanan, who succeeded Jardine in 1827, seems also to have been a most effective teacher along lines somewhat similar to Jardine's. Lord Bryce, his pupil in 1855, speaks of 'Logic Bob' with affection, and praises his 'admirable skill . . . and freshness' in the *viva voce* examination of students which was a prominent feature of his and Jardine's routine of instruction. 'Freshness,' however, can hardly have been a term applicable to Buchanan's lectures. According to Bryce, 'the only reference the lectures made to any current philosophy was in a passage lately inserted among its leaves yellow with age and which dealt with the quantification of the predicate' (a logical innovation of Sir William Hamilton's). Buchanan's creative energies seem to have found their outlet in the writing of plays, of which he produced several, mostly tragic dramas on Scottish themes. In 1831 he was nominated Vice-Rector by Henry (later Lord) Cockburn, and for a time he served as Senate assessor on the University Court. Buchanan resigned his Chair in 1864, but lived another nine years to the ripe age of eighty-eight.

Unfortunately it must be recorded that, after the time of Thomas Reid until the appointment of Edward Caird in 1866, the moralists were no whit more enterprising as philosophical thinkers than were the logicians; though they too seem to have been diligent in the fulfilment of their duties and active in the general business of the University. Archibald Arthur, who, after a brief spell as College Chaplain, had deputised for Reid in the lecture-room during the last sixteen years of Reid's tenure of the Chair, survived his predecessor by only a year. He was a versatile scholar, and he gave outstanding service to the University as its Librarian for a period of twenty years. In 1791 he completed, in a manner that has been uniformly praised for its care and accuracy, a catalogue of the 20,000 books then in the College Library. James Mylne (1797-1839), who followed, seems to have run wholly true to type. He is described by Campbell Fraser as 'a strong man unknown in philosophical literature.' Like Arthur, he was for a time College Chaplain, and from 1799 he filled the office of Clerk. Mylne was succeeded by William Fleming (1839-64), yet another College Chaplain to become Professor of Moral Philosophy. Fleming had previously (since 1831) been Professor of Oriental Languages, and in 1836 he was appointed Vice-Rector by Sir Robert Peel. 'Moral Will,' as he was known to the irreverent, discharged his duties with a firmness of purpose appropriate to his sobriquet, and Coutts relates several instances of his stout-hearted if lonely dissent from courses approved by his colleagues. Fleming also broke with convention by writing a book. His *Manual of Moral Philosophy* is not a masterpiece; but it secures for him, by a clear margin, the distinction of being the most prolific Glasgow Professor of Philosophy for some generations.

It will be sufficiently obvious that the periods we have just been reviewing—from 1727 to 1864 in Logic and from 1796 to 1866 in Moral Philosophy—are not among the more illustrious in Glasgow's philosophic history. The Professors seem to have been, without exception, good and godly men, and by no means lacking in talents. But it is not always easy to discern what were the strictly philosophical qualifications which weighed with the electors in making appointments to either Chair. Certainly the contribution to the advancement of philosophic thought made by this particular series of incumbents can hardly be underestimated.

MID-NINETEENTH CENTURY RENAISSANCE

With the arrival, however, of John Veitch (1864-95) and Edward Caird (1866-94), the character and standing of Glasgow philosophy take an abrupt and remarkable change for the better. Gone were the days when a student could pass through both philosophy classes and hear scarcely so much as the names of some of the most influential of modern thinkers. The immediate precursors of Veitch and Caird would probably themselves have allowed that, though they were not uninterested in philosophic enquiry, their enthusiasm for it was well under control. Logically as well as chronologically, most of them were clergymen first and philosophers afterwards. Veitch and Caird were also men of genuine piety. But in their case concern for religious truth, so far from inclining them to undervalue the processes of the intellect, seems rather to have led them to attach all the greater importance to independent, resolute, and disciplined thinking about ultimate issues. Not less firmly did they insist with their students upon that sound learning without which even the most powerful minds seldom achieve much. In the new era ushered in by Veitch and Caird, Glasgow's philosophical fame probably stood as high as that of any University in any country. Substantial contributions to the literature of philosophy flowed from Glasgow in a steady stream. But perhaps even more impressive than Glasgow's output of philosophical works was its output of actual philosophers. For fifty years or more Glasgow became a veritable nursery of budding Professors of Philosophy. Pupils of Caird and Jones (1894-1922), and of Veitch, Adamson (1895-1902) and Latta (1902-25) found their way in quite astonishing numbers to Chairs and Lectureships all over the English-speaking world.

Few would wish to dispute that it is to Caird more particularly that credit must go for this resurgence of Glasgow philosophy. As a philosophical teacher he seems to have been superb; equally effective with the small minority gifted with a natural turn for speculation, and with the rank and file who would perhaps never again open a philosophical book but whose intellectual outlook for the rest of their days would be coloured and illumined by what they had heard in the Moral Philosophy class-room. Great numbers of Caird's students in all walks of life have testified to the unique quality of his teaching—at once spiritually nourishing and intellectually astringent. Of Caird it can with truth be said, as of his great predecessor Hutcheson, that his tenancy of the Moral Philosophy Chair lifted the whole cultural level of South-West Scotland.

As a technical philosopher Caird's reputation suffers to-day from the almost total eclipse of the German Idealism to which he gave his allegiance. All of Caird's main works are written from the Hegelian standpoint; not least his monumental *Critical Philosophy of Kant,* which has been called, in virtue of its author's constant practice of correcting Kant by expounding Hegel, the best account of Hegel in the English language! But Caird was very much more than a great Hegelian scholar. Quite as noteworthy, and the secret of the profound impression he made upon the educated public, were the power and freshness with which he applied Hegel's abstract concepts to the interpretation and elucidation of the great movements of thought and history, and to the problems of moral, political and religious life as they presented themselves within the concrete context of his age.

Very similar in character was the intellectual influence exerted by John Caird, brother of Edward, and Principal of the University from 1873 to 1898; and its effect in moulding educated opinion may well have been even greater, for Principal Caird was not only distinguished as a philosopher and University administrator but was, in the opinion of many good judges, the outstanding preacher of his generation. On the strictly philosophical side the works by which he is best known are his monograph on Spinoza in the *Blackwood* series, and his *Introduction to the Philosophy of Religion*. The recrudescence of Glasgow philosophy which we have been chronicling must have owed a substantial debt to a Principal whose periodic orations to his students were so manifestly the expression of a mind for which religion and philosophy are not enemies, but the closest of allies.

When Edward Caird left Glasgow to become Master of Balliol in 1894, he was succeeded by a favourite pupil, Henry Jones. Jones's published works, it must be confessed, have not worn very well; and not entirely because his brand of Idealism is out of fashion. Probably his most satisfying books were two written very early in his career. *Browning as a Philosophical and Religious Teacher* is a searching study of the mind of a poet for whom Jones cherished a life-long admiration, and to whom he was always eager to acknowledge a deep spiritual indebtedness. *The Philosophy of Lotze* is a scholarly and closely argued essay in critical exegesis—almost certainly his most enduring contribution to the literature of philosophy. Latterly Jones fell into a somewhat florid and flamboyant manner of writing. There is distinguished thought in all of his works; but *Idealism as a Practical Creed* and its successors carry too heavy a load of exhortation and rhetoric, and are too imprecise in statement and argument, to appeal to modern taste.

As a teacher, however, Jones was, in his own way, hardly less outstanding than Caird himself. Abundantly, even super-abundantly, endowed with the traditional Celtic attributes of fire and wit and eloquence, a master of the picturesque metaphor, the trenchant phrase, and the scarifying epithet, this colourful and quite unforgettable Welshman had a power to excite and stimulate the mind against which even the most resolutely lethargic student had inadequate defences. In one respect his teaching was perhaps better than he meant it to be. For while the strength of his own convictions sometimes led him to present the case for Idealism in a way which suggested to his hearers that the opponents of that philosophy must be either bad or mad—and were probably both—the very forcefulness of his utterance was apt to provoke in the dour temper of the Lowland Scot a certain suspicion, and even antagonism. The abler students, at any rate, refused to be either daunted or spell-bound. They were goaded into thinking, but into a *critical* thinking which by no means spared the dicta of their Professor. And this was as it should be, whether Jones altogether liked it or not. The real achievement of Jones as a teacher was that it was hardly possible for anyone who sat under him to feel that philosophy didn't matter.

Just how much philosophy mattered to Jones himself, and with what passionate earnestness he regarded his mission as a philosophical mentor, found most moving illustration in the closing years of his life. Stricken by an illness that he knew to be mortal, suffering incessant and at times agonising pain, Jones, until very near the end, would allow himself almost no abatement of his teaching duties; refusing often even the balm of anodynes lest they should impair the full vigour of his faculties. By calling upon his last reserves, he actually contrived to carry to completion the writing and delivery of his final philosophic testament, the *Gifford Lectures* of 1920-21. Jones was ever 'a bonny fechter,' at his best against heavy odds. But the sustained gallantry of his defiance of pain and death in this his last tragic battle bordered on the miraculous. If, inevitably, the body was at length conquered, the spirit was as surely conqueror.

The three logicians who held office during this period did not have Caird's or Jones's exceptional capacity for stirring and kindling the minds of students: but they were able philosophers, held in high respect by their professional brethren, and each is worthy of more than a passing mention in these pages.

Veitch was a pupil of Edinburgh's Sir William Hamilton, and in large measure remained Hamilton's disciple in philosophy. As befitted a pupil of Hamilton, he was a scholar of formidable erudition. No Glasgow Professor of Logic before him could claim anything like his degree of mastery over the whole range of philosophical literature. As a thinker, he was of critical rather than creative temper, and—a little disappointingly in view of the promise of his youth—he did not produce much of significance in constructive philosophy. Of his several books, the volume on Hamilton in the famous 'Blackwood' series is the only one likely to find readers to-day. Had Veitch had anything of an interesting sort to say in philosophy, he would probably have said it surpassingly well; for, like his immediate predecessor, Robert Buchanan, he both delighted in and sedulously practised the art of letters. His love of the poets was exceeded only by his love for his native Border country, and these twin pleasures combined happily to create what is probably his literary masterpiece—his *History and Poetry of the Scottish Border*. The legendary popularity of his class lectures on Rhetoric doubtless owed something to the fact that the alternative before the students was to listen to lectures on Logic; it owed a good deal also to the splendour of the lecturer's declamation of noble passages from literature to illustrate his points; but it probably owed most to the very real marriage of poetry with philosophy in Veitch's own mind. Veitch's Glasgow reputation has naturally been overshadowed by that of his greater contemporary, Caird. But one cannot read the moving memoir by his niece Mary Bryce, nor the appraisement of his thought and personality by his old pupil Professor Mark Wenley, without recognising that Veitch was, both intellectually and spiritually, a man of stature.

Veitch's successor, Robert Adamson, has been described

by Sorley as 'the most learned of contemporary philosophers'. But he was also a very powerful thinker. Though he died at the early age of fifty, just seven years after his translation from the Aberdeen to the Glasgow Chair of Logic, he left a rich, and, as it has proved, a lasting, legacy of writings. To be responsible, as Adamson was, for no less than five works still accepted as profitable reading by philosophers more than half a century after their composition, is to come tolerably near to greatness. The five works are the Shaw Lectures on *Kant;* the 'Blackwood' volume on *Fichte;* the *Short History of Logic* (which is the much expanded version of an article on *Logic* in the ninth edition of the *Encyclopædia Britannica*); and the class lectures and other papers posthumously published under the titles *Development of Greek Philosophy* and *Development of Modern Philosophy.* The last-named, which is in two volumes, includes matter of peculiar interest. Adamson's mind was very much 'on the march' in his closing years, and the *Development of Modern Philosophy* shows him moving fast from his early Idealistic standpoint in the direction of a Realism better able, as he believed, to do justice to all the empirical material. Adamson's untimely death while engaged in working out his positive theory may well have deprived the world of a major philosophic classic.

Robert Latta also came to the Glasgow Chair by way of Aberdeen, where he had been Professor of Moral Philosophy since 1900. Although not outstanding as an original thinker, he maintained admirably the growing reputation of the Logic Chair for exact scholarship. His volume on Leibniz—a translation of some of Leibniz's chief works with introductory essays and very valuable notes and appendices—was for some time recognised as the standard English book on this philosopher. A premature failure of health, accentuated by his labours in the first World War, interfered with later literary projects. As a teacher, Latta had not the gifts that make popular appeal. His lectures contrasted sharply with the lively entertainment provided across the Quadrangle by the brilliant and ebullient Jones. But if the manner of delivery was not inspiring, the abler and more serious students soon came to appreciate that in content Latta's Logic lectures (and indeed his lectures on Psychology likewise) had outstanding merits—always beautifully organised, phrased with precision and lucidity, and scrupulously fair in the presentation and appraisal of rival theories.

In Latta's time, Psychology was still regarded as part of the province of the Department of Logic: though in 1908 the University showed its prescience of the direction in which this science was moving by instituting a special Lectureship in Experimental Psychology and appointing to it a distinguished pioneer in the laboratory investigation of sensory processes, Dr. H. J. Watt. In 1926, however, a full-fledged Department of Psychology was created under an independent Lecturer, Dr. R. H. Thouless; and a Chair of Psychology (not yet tenanted) was founded in 1947. This evolution towards autonomy has been closely paralleled by two other of Philosophy's offspring: Political Economy, in which a Lectureship was founded in 1892 and raised to the status of a Chair in 1896, and Political Philosophy, in which Dr. R. A. Duff (a fine Spinozistic scholar and notable University administrator) was appointed special lecturer in 1901, and which has recently, under the title of Political Science, achieved full independence as a Department qualifying for graduation.

THE RECENT PAST—A. A. BOWMAN

We have now passed in rapid review Glasgow philosophy and philosophers during all but twenty-five of the University's five hundred years. It will not be expected, and indeed would not be fitting, that there should be any attempt to deal in like manner with the quarter-century that is still fresh in our minds. Save in a single case, where there is obvious reason for making exception, it must suffice merely to name, for the sake of completing the record, the eight Professors who have occupied the Philosophy Chairs since Jones and Latta.

The Professors of Logic have been Archibald A. Bowman (1926-27), later Professor of Moral Philosophy; Herbert J. Paton (1927-37), now White's Professor of Moral Philosophy in the University of Oxford; and the present writer (1938—   ). The Professors of Moral Philosophy have been Alexander D. Lindsay (1922-24), later Lord Lindsay of Birker, Master of Balliol from 1924-49, and now Principal of the new University College of North Staffordshire; (Sir) Hector Hetherington (1924-27), later Vice-Chancellor of Liverpool University and since 1936 Principal and Vice-Chancellor of this University; Archibald A. Bowman (1927-36); (Sir) Oliver Franks (1936-45), later Provost of Queen's College, Oxford, and since 1948 H.M. Ambassador to the U.S.A.; and William G. Maclagan (1946—   ).

Archibald Bowman, as the only one of these eight not now living, may fairly be regarded as belonging to history, and of him it will be in place to say something more. A brief account of this very remarkable man must bring our long story to its close.

Born at Beith in 1883, schooled at the local Academy and Spier's School, a student of this University from 1901 to 1905, Bowman received his first appointment, following a post-graduate year of Continental study, as Assistant and Lecturer in Logic at Glasgow in 1906. Six years later he became Professor of Logic at Princeton. In 1915 he obtained release to take his part, as a combatant officer with the H.L.I., in the struggle with Germany. A few months before the end of the War he was taken prisoner. Returning to Princeton in 1919, he remained there, with a rapidly increasing fame, for seven years. In 1925 he accepted a recall to Glasgow, to take effect from October, 1926. In the first session he occupied the Logic Chair, and thereafter, until his lamentably early death in 1936, the Chair of Moral Philosophy.

Two large-scale works, neither in a finished state but both

the fruit of long meditation, were published posthumously: *Studies in the Philosophy of Religion,* the earlier in order of composition, and the nearer to completion; and *The Sacramental Universe,* based upon the *Vanuxem* Lectures which Bowman delivered at Princeton in 1934. Bowman also contributed fairly frequently to philosophical and other journals, and he wrote a considerable amount of verse, some of the best of which, written in captivity, he published under the title *Sonnets from a Prison Camp.* But it is by his posthumous works that his ultimate philosophical reputation must stand or fall.

A personal judgment, unsupported by the evidence which it is here impossible to produce, cannot be of great account. But the present writer would wish to put on record his firm conviction, for what it is worth, that the eight chapters of Part One of *The Sacramental Universe,* comprising the first half of the *Vanuxem* Lectures (the only part which the author found opportunity to make ready for publication) contain some of the finest philosophical writing of recent times. Not that there is not also a great deal that is of high value in the *Studies.* But Bowman's mind was in constant growth, both in the range of its assimilated material and in the technique of manipulation, and it is to the later work, I think, that one must turn to find his powers at their zenith. The general purpose of these chapters is to prepare the way for a constructive metaphysic by examining the nature and inter-relations of the physical and spiritual modes of being. The sustained vitality, rigour and penetration of the argument seem to me wholly remarkable. Particularly impressive are the handling of the implications for philosophy of recent advances in the physical sciences; the criticism—searching, but always fair-minded and always constructive—of the naturalistic trend in contemporary metaphysics, as exemplified particularly in the systems of Santayana, Whitehead and Alexander; and the original and delicate analyses, through three long and close-packed chapters, of the notions of subjectivity, self-hood, and self-consciousness—this last the high-light, as I think, of the whole book. The unprejudiced reader of these chapters cannot fail to realise that he is in contact with a mind of the rarest philosophical quality. The deplorable thing is that, partly because of its unfinished state, partly because of the outbreak of the Second World War, but chiefly, I think, because of the unfriendly *Zeitgeist* (already casting its shadow, as Bowman well knew, while his book was being written), few if any philosophic works of comparable importance within the last twenty years have been so little read. It seems scarcely credible that philosophers will continue indefinitely to ignore the ripest thoughts of a mind so superbly equipped as Archibald Bowman's.

Upon those who knew Bowman through the medium of the spoken word, the impression he created was at once profound and indelible. What trans-Atlantic alchemy transformed the rather halting and diffident Bowman who left Scotland in 1912 into the golden-voiced orator who returned to these shores fourteen years later—a consummate master of language whose eloquence achieved at times an almost lapidary splendour—it is hard to say. But the miracle did occur. And many high causes greatly gained thereby; for Bowman had a missionary zeal for the things in which he believed, and spent himself in their service with a prodigality that caused in his friends alarm that was only too well founded.

Within the precincts of Gilmorehill, and above all, of course, in the class-room, Bowman's influence upon the student mind cannot often have been surpassed in the annals of the University. His impact upon his students was, notoriously, as much spiritual as strictly philosophical. And it is possible that, from the point of view of the potential Honours student, the spiritual side predominated over-much. A beginner in philosophy, following the seemingly faultless course of Bowman's dialectic to its conclusion in the triumphant vindication of a religious interpretation of the Cosmos, could easily feel that the great issues of life had been to all intents and purposes finally closed; and all the more so when his revered teacher was himself so patently afire with religious conviction. It is perhaps not without significance that relatively few of Bowman's huge Pass class proceeded to advanced study in philosophy. But in the company of philosophers, formal or informal, Bowman was, in a different way, hardly less impressive. Then it was the sheer intellectual force of the thinker, backed by a learning prodigious in its range and variety, that commanded admiration; and, above all, his extraordinary fertility in the construction of possible, and even probable, theories (often apparently *ad hoc*) to meet literally any problem with which he might be confronted. Bowman had that rarity of rarities, a naturally creative mind. And if his admirers were often tempted to apply to him the term 'genius,' this particular historian at any rate, who was once his colleague, is not prepared to say that they were wrong.

NOTE ON THE GROWTH OF
POLITICAL ECONOMY

by

A. L. Macfie

Professor of Political Economy

Lectures on Political Economy have been delivered in Glasgow University at least as long as the Moral Philosophy Chair has existed. Adam Smith's indebtedness in Economics to the lectures he heard from 'the never-to-be-forgotten Francis Hutcheson' is certainly greater than a mere reference to sources can show. Even the puzzling order of his argument in Book I of the *Wealth of Nations* has been identified as that in Hutcheson's lectures, and in his *System*. Again, Hutcheson's several variations on the theme of 'the greatest happiness of the greatest number' were probably one source from which Priestley drew; and Bentham has told us, 'Priestley was the first (unless it was Beccaria) who taught my mouth to pronounce this sacred truth.' Thus, as utility remains the main highway for our teaching of economic theory, the early philosophers of this University certainly assisted in the building of this highway.

The more metaphysical mind of Reid was not so interested in economic issues. And it is not surprising that economic instruction appears prominently once more only on the arrival of the neo-Hegelians. It was Edward Caird who found comment on economic interest at once necessary and for him probably rather harassing. And it was Caird who, finding among his Honours students one who in his judgment could teach the subject, arranged that William Smart would lecture on Political Economy as his substitute within the Moral Philosophy Department. This provision naturally blossomed into an independent lectureship instituted by the University in 1892. In 1896 Mr. Andrew Stewart, a Glasgow iron-master, fulfilled an ambition traditionally conceived when visiting Adam Smith's house in Kirkcaldy, and provided the endowment for the Adam Smith Chair of Political Economy. The University Court, with one representative from each of the Merchants' House of Glasgow, the Trades House of Glasgow and the Chamber of Commerce, acts as Patron.

Until 1898 there was only a first year, or 'Ordinary,' Class; but in that year the Honours Class began. Until 1940 this Honours Class met as one unit, the subject of study being mainly Public Finance. In 1940 it was split into First Year and Second Year sections, dealing also with theory of value, international trade, and fluctuations in output and employment. In 1907 Mr. Thomas Jones (whose later career in the public life of the country has been so distinguished) became the first Assistant in the Department and also the first lecturer in the sub-department of Social Economics. In 1911 a lecturer in Economic History was added. This equipment sufficed till after the First War. Modern wars, however, at least stimulate interest in Economics. The larger numbers after 1918 appeared especially in the first year class, necessitating additional lecturers. After 1945 it was especially the Honours classes that filled out with ex-Service students (of ideal quality) whose interest seemed usually to have been lit by the cultural education they received in the Forces. To-day, along with the Professor in the Political Economy Department there are three lecturers and one assistant; two lecturers in Social Economics and two lectureships in Economic History. A significant departure in 1946 was the institution of a Department of Social and Economic Research. This Department has its own staff, and co-operates for suitable research purposes with the staffs of other departments. In 1949 the University Court instituted a new Chair in Applied Economics, the incumbent of which will also be the Director of Social and Economic Research. The primary aim of the Department is to survey the social and economic structure of the South-west of Scotland and deal with the various problems that arise in such a developing area.

In view of its sources, it is not surprising that the Political Economy Department has always professed a widely humane interpretation of its discipline. Since it became independent, its philosophic sympathies have in no way diminished. In fact, the spirit of its illustrious progenitors has in the last fifty years settled into a living departmental tradition and atmosphere which all who have served in it appreciate. This has been the special achievement of the two men who have led the department. William Smart and William Robert Scott were before all else humane, widely experienced scholars. Each of them served actively in business, as directors of manufacturing concerns. Each of them had the firmest grasp of and respect for facts, human as well as industrial. Their sense of history and its constant relevance to any finally valuable economic theory is worthy of the master who was their continual joy and inspiration. And their active part in the affairs of a great industrial city was as inevitable as his. In each of them is found that energetic growth from the core of hard facts to their deeper philosophic meanings which was Adam Smith's most shining gift. And each of them contributed his thinking to the direct service of the State on many commissions and committees, just as did Adam Smith in the more personal, less official manner of his day.

William Smart was a native of our district. Between 1870 and 1880 he worked in the Mile End Thread Works of James Clark, Junr., and Company, of which his father was the manager. On his father's retirement, he became a partner in the firm until the business was sold in 1884. This allowed him to give his full energies to the University. There, his special enthusiasms developed in teaching, writing, official committee work, and social work in Glasgow. The hallmark of his writing is the high altruism, the selfless spirit of service which always inspired it. The early *Introduction to the Theory of Value* and *The Distribution of Income* were written to help young students, and well they have done so everywhere. The faithful labour that went into his translations of Böhm-Bawerk's *Capital and Interest* and *The Positive Theory of Capital* has earned the gratitude of a host of readers all over the world. Looking back, one can now realise what a unique service to British and American economic schools these renderings of the rich Austrian classics have afforded. His final labour of Sisyphus was also the service of a supremely generous man. *The Economic Annals of the Nineteenth Century* was intended to collect into convenient form the more important knowledge embedded in the mass of Hansard and of Official Reports generally. The modest sense of duty behind such toil is beyond praise. In his final book, *Second Thoughts of an Economist,* Smart gave expression to gathering personal worries as to whether the analytic theory of his day considered adequately the actual distribution of incomes and wealth. The swing in our interest to-day shows how prescient his doubts were. His labours on the Poor Law Commission were equally toilsome and self-effacing. He certainly had his reward in the affection and high respect of his friends, students and colleagues in Britain.

William Robert Scott was also by remote derivation a Scot, from the Border family. His forbears, however, settled in Northern Ireland about 1720. They were from 1847 the leading millers in County Tyrone, W. R. Scott being chairman of directors of this family firm for over forty years. Like his predecessors at the University, Scott graduated in philosophy, in his case from Trinity College, Dublin. In 1896 he was appointed assistant to the Professor of Moral Philosophy at St. Andrews, where he remained until in 1915 he became the second Adam Smith Professor of Political Economy in Glasgow.

While Scott commanded all the virtues of the scholar, there is little doubt that his special genius lay in historical research. He once remarked of one of his students that 'he has the nose'; and certainly his own capacity to pick out a faint trail was only matched by his tenacity in exhausting it. His philosophic aptitude stimulated his historical adventures by supplying imaginative hypotheses and by cutting clear lines of approach through very tangled country. These qualities shine in all his work, especially in the *Francis Hutcheson* (1900), *The Records of a Scottish Cloth Manufactory at New Mills, Haddingtonshire, 1681-1703* (1905), *The Constitution and Finance of English, Scottish and Irish Joint Stock Companies to 1700* (1910-12), and *Adam Smith as Student and Professor* (1937). Of these, the *Joint Stock Companies* is unique, definitive and classic. It is a model of that utterly trustworthy scholarship which only the ampler air of pre-war days could nourish. Of equally lasting and magisterial value was his demonstration that the main immediate source of Smith's work is found in the Scottish School and not, as had usually been assumed, in the French Physiocrats. Here perhaps we see his personal flair. His tracking of evidence has all the excitement as well as the practical ingenuity of a story in detection.

Scott did much more than his share of official committee work. But it is the man that his students most remember. He had indeed reached that highest peak, the ability to be a scholar on almost any subject at any time, without being for a moment either a pedant or a bore. Academic people well know how difficult this is to achieve. One root of his strength lay in the sweetness of his temper and his complete command of it. He was genuinely kind in the practical way of taking thought for the future of his students. And his selfless labour in the service of his adopted city and university at once strengthened the tradition created by his predecessor and fortified a department shaken, as all was, by the impacts of war.

The inspiration is bearing fruit. Nourished by official help and nursed by the University authorities, the Social Sciences are showing vigorous growth in Glasgow. They fall heir to a sound generous tradition from the older Philosophy and Political Economy departments. They are fortunate in a steady flow of excellent students who do realise the necessity for hard work. And they have a uniquely rich and unexplored area for field work at their door. If they keep courageously to their furrow, the harvest should be rich.

ORIENTAL AND
OLD TESTAMENT STUDIES

by

C. J. Mullo Weir

Professor of Hebrew and Semitic Languages

Oriental languages, or, more specifically, Hebrew, Aramaic and Syriac, were, with Latin and Greek, the first languages taught in the University, but, while Latin was used as the spoken language for University teaching until early in the eighteenth century, the other languages were almost or entirely neglected until the Reformation. Even on the Continent, students of these languages ran the risk of being suspected of heresy, although, in a few Continental centres, Hebrew and Arabic had been introduced more than two centuries earlier, chiefly in order to train missionaries for the conversion of Jews and Moslems. The admission of Hebrew and Greek into University curricula at the Reformation was due not so much to an interest in literature and philology as to their being the languages of the Bible and of its earliest translations; and although the Oriental languages, like Greek, soon came to be loved and studied for their own sake they have continued to the present day to be closely connected with Biblical, especially Old Testament, studies.

The teaching of Oriental languages at Glasgow falls into three periods. First, the sixty-eight years from 1574 to 1642, when they were taught by the Principals, usually assisted by a regent with the honorary title of professor; second, the sixty-seven years from 1642 to 1709, when they were the responsibility of the Chair of Divinity, though for more than the latter half of the period they were in fact relegated to a regent styled professor of Hebrew; and third, the long period of two

133

hundred and forty-two years from 1709 to the present day, when they have been taught by a succession of fifteen regular professors of Hebrew and Oriental, or, more recently, Hebrew and Semitic, languages.

That Hebrew was not ignored in Scotland in pre-Reformation times is proved by the statutes of Aberdeen Grammar School of 1553 which prescribe, somewhat naïvely, that the languages which the scholars may speak are Latin, Greek, Hebrew, French and Gaelic. More significantly, in 1540, twenty years before the Reformation, Archibald Hay, afterwards Provost of St. Mary's College, St. Andrews, in a panegyric to Cardinal Beaton, wrote concerning the newly-founded college: 'It will be of far more consequence to procure teachers capable of interesting youth in the three learned languages than to endow a rich but illiterate college; if it should be thought proper to add teachers of Chaldee and Arabic I shall strongly approve.'

By 1560, John Row, minister of Perth, who had studied Hebrew in Italy, was teaching it at Perth Grammar School, and in his house, where sons of the nobility were boarded, Scripture lessons from the Old Testament were always read in Hebrew, while his son John, afterwards minister of Carnock, could read the Hebrew alphabet at the age of four, and a chapter of the Hebrew Bible by the age of seven.

In the same year a plan was drawn up in the First Book of Discipline for the reorganization of the Universities. Its framers, some of whom had learned Hebrew on the Continent, enjoined that at St. Andrews, which was to be a model for the other Universities, there should be a theological college with a principal and with readers in Divinity, Hebrew and Greek. The grammar of the languages was to be taught for half of the first year and the rest of the year was to be devoted to exegesis of a book of Moses, the Prophets or the Psalms. A more moderate plan in 1563 provided for only a principal, a reader in Hebrew and a reader in Law, and although, owing to the disturbed times, even this project could not be realised in all the Universities, Hebrew was being taught in St. Andrews University by 1567 or 1568 by James Lawson, who had studied it on the Continent. When, however, in 1569, he became sub-principal of King's College, Aberdeen, the teaching of Hebrew at St. Andrews lapsed and it is not known if he taught it at Aberdeen. James Melville, who studied at St. Andrews in 1571, complains 'I wald haiff gladly been at the Greik and Hebrew toungs because I red in our Bible that it was translated out of Hebrew and Greik, bot the languages war not to be gottine in the land.'

Three years after this, however, in 1574, not only Hebrew but also Chaldee (*i.e.,* Aramaic) and Syriac were being taught in the University of Glasgow by its Principal, Andrew Melville, who introduced there the scheme which was shortly to rule in all the Scottish universities.

Melville had begun the study of Hebrew, on which he had been, it is said, 'speciallie set', ten years earlier in the University of Paris, under the tuition of Jean Cinq-Arbres, who had published a Hebrew grammar, and the even more celebrated Jean Mercier, author of Hebrew and Aramaic grammars and commentaries on Old Testament books. After two years as regent in the University of Poitiers, Melville 'tuk journey to Genev, leaving buikis and all ther and caried na thing with him bot a little Hebrew Byble in his belt.' At Geneva, while Professor of Humanity, he continued his Oriental studies, including Syriac, under Cornelius Bertram, who, in 1574, published a book on the comparative study of Hebrew and Aramaic; he also attended lectures on Muhammadan jurisprudence.

On Melville's return to Scotland in 1574 he acted as tutor to his nephew, James, who writes: 'and last, entering to the Hebrew, I gat the reiding declynations and pronons, and sum also of the conjugations out of Martinius' Grammer, quhilk he haid with him, and schew me the use of the Dictionair also, quhilk he haid of Reuclius with him.' The grammar referred to, that of Martinez, was published at Paris in 1548 and re-issued at Salamanca in 1571; the dictionary may be the grammar and lexicon published by Johann von Reuchlin at Pforzheim in 1506, but is more probably Anthony Reuchlin's Hebrew lexicon published at Basle in 1554 and in an abridged form at Basle by Lucas Osiander in 1569.

Entering on the Principalship of Glasgow University in autumn, 1574, Andrew Melville quickly made it the greatest of the Scottish universities, and a noted centre for languages. In the first year he himself undertook all the teaching, including, presumably, Hebrew. In the following year, 1575, his nephew, James Melville, became a regent at Glasgow but tells us: 'all the tyme I could get, by my ordinar calling, I employed to the studie of the Hebrew toung and theologie.'

In his third year Principal Melville assigned specified subjects to each regent, reserving for himself theology and the Oriental languages. 'By and attoure his awin ordinar profession, the holy tonges and theologie,' writes James Melville, 'he teachit the Hebrew grammar, first schortlie, and syne mor accuratlie; thairefter the Caldaic and Syriac dialects, with the practise thairof in the Psalms and warks of Solomon, David, Ezra and Epistle to the Galates.' This means that parts of Galatians were read in Syriac, parts of Ezra in Aramaic, and parts of the Psalms and of some other books in Hebrew.

The New Foundation of 1577 which confirmed these arrangements declares that the Principal must be 'qualified to expound the hidden treasures of Holy Scripture, and be versed and skilled in languages, especially in Hebrew and Syriac of which we appoint him the professor, for we are desirous, as is most fitting, to promote the Holy Tongue among those set under us, that they may open up aright the sources and mysteries.'

It soon became customary to appoint one of the regents professor of Hebrew to assist the Principal, but for nearly a century the Principals seem to have done most of the Oriental teaching themselves. Accordingly, when in 1580 Andrew Melville was called to be Principal at St. Andrews, his

nephew James, who accompanied him, was appointed professor of Oriental Languages there, but Andrew continued
to lecture on Biblical and Rabbinical Hebrew, Aramaic and
Syriac. Among Principal Melville's published works is a
commentary on Deuteronomy, chapter xxxii, and Job, chapter iii, issued at Basle in 1574; there is also in Dublin a MS.
dealing with one of the Aramaic chapters (ch. iv) of Daniel.

Melville's successor in the Principalship at Glasgow,
Thomas Smeaton, was, we are told, 'a man learned in
both Latin and Greek . . . also thoroughly skilled in the
Sacred, that is, the Hebrew Language.' His knowledge of
Hebrew is shown in his *Responsio* to Archibald Hamilton's
Dialogus. He was assisted in his teaching by one of the
regents, Patrick Melville, another nephew of Andrew, who
was appointed professor of Hebrew at Glasgow and afterwards at St. Andrews. Smeaton died after only three years
of office, in 1583.

The range of Oriental studies in Scotland had by this time
increased if we are to judge from an Act of Parliament of
1579 which prescribed that at St. Andrews parts of Psalms,
Proverbs, Job, the Pentateuch and the Prophets should be
read in Hebrew, with the Aramaic chapters of Daniel and
Ezra and readings from the Targums and the Syriac New
Testament. No details are known, however, of the Oriental
teaching of Smeaton and the next two principals, Patrick
Sharpe, who officiated for twenty-eight years (1586-1615),
and Robert Boyd of Trochrigg, who held the post for the
next six (1615-21), though both were competent scholars.
One of Sharpe's students, Zachary Boyd, afterwards, between
1635 and 1646, while minister of the Barony, Glasgow, wrote
a series of metrical paraphrases of parts of the Old Testament,
but these are quaint rather than scholarly. During Robert
Boyd's Principalship the University Library acquired Buxtorf's Rabbinical Bible, published in 1618-19, containing the
Aramaic Targum and some Rabbinical commentaries. Other
Library acquisitions at this time were two Hebrew Bibles (one

unpointed), the Hebrew grammars of Buxtorf, Bellarmine, and Cancellarius, several Old Testament commentaries, the works of Philo, a Qur'an (in Latin) and a History of the Turks.

The next Principal, John Cameron, had been a student of Sharpe's and had, in 1618, won the examination for the Divinity Chair at Saumur, which included an examination in Hebrew. He is said to have written 'a Collation of the Original Tongues in one volume' and to have 'translated several Hebrew writers into Latin in one volume' and although no such writings can be traced among his extant works, the former was presumably a comparison of Hebrew and Greek Biblical passages with the ancient Versions and the latter a translation of chapters of the Hebrew Bible into Latin. Robert Baillie, one of his pupils, speaks in high terms of the enthusiasm Cameron excited in his students for the study of Hebrew, Aramaic and other languages.

Demitting office after only one year to become Professor of Divinity at Montauban, Cameron was succeeded by John Strang, who remained Principal for twenty-four years (1626-50). He is recorded to have 'taught Hebrew assiduously to the students,' and his pupil Robert Baillie writes enthusiastically of his diligence and accuracy. In 1640, however, he was relieved of part of his teaching duties by the institution of a new Chair of Divinity, whose first holder, David Dickson, shortly afterwards published in three volumes a commentary on the Psalms. In 1642 an additional Divinity Chair was created for the teaching of 'the controversies, oriental languages and chronology'; its first occupant, Robert Baillie, continued his task for twenty years from 1642 until his death in 1662 and had, it is said, a knowledge of thirteen languages (including Arabic and Ethiopic). He had studied under Principals Cameron and Strang before becoming a regent in 1625 and had in 1629 written a panegyric, still preserved in manuscript in the University Library, in praise of the Hebrew tongue. By 1639 he was writing a series of letters to his cousin in Holland, urging him to persuade Dutch printers to publish text-books for students of Oriental languages, including a pocket Hebrew Bible with Syriac New Testament, a pocket Septuagint with Greek New Testament, manual editions of the Talmud tractates and of the Targums, with Latin translations and vowel-points, an edition of the Massorah and Bibles in Arabic and Syriac. Not until the late nineteenth century, however, had so enlightened a programme any hope of being fulfilled.

Baillie's *Letters* throw much light on his work as an Oriental teacher. In January, 1643, a few months after his appointment to his Chair, he wrote: 'I hope to dait [*i.e.*, dictate] before June, a little compend of the chief controversies, and much more Hebrew, I meane of the text, than was ever before.' In summer of the same year he wrote: 'I am but yet a meer novice . . . yet I have taught Hebrew everie Mononday afternoon. I have gone through Buxtorfe's Epitome, and dytes [dyted(?)] notes on the texts in his end, triple more already than ever was taught in Scotland. I hope, before the end of the second year, to close my Hebrew notes, so that my third year allwayes may be for the Chaldaick, Syriack and Rabbinick. I have little of these, bot I hope to learn with my scholars.' Baillie also mentions that Professor Dickson was proposing to give the students an analytical commentary on the text of Job, Psalms, Proverbs, Isaiah and the rest of the Prophets, and to lecture on Chronology.

University statutes of this time show that Hebrew was studied not only in the Divinity course but also in Third Year Arts, as a preparation for Divinity. A Commission of Visitation in 1644 ordained that the Principal and the theological professors should ensure that their students were not only proficient in Hebrew but also had 'some touch of Chaldee and Syriac.' In the same year the first two Scottish books to use Hebrew type were published in Glasgow for an Aberdeen minister, John Row, grandson of the Reformer who had taught Hebrew at Perth in 1560. One of these, a grammar entitled *Hebraeae Linguae Institutiones,* had been com-

piled several years earlier when Row was Rector of Perth
Grammar School. The other, termed Χιλιας *Hebraica,* was
a lexicon containing 1,000 Hebrew words and an alphabetical index of Hebrew proper names. In 1646 the General
Assembly recommended the grammar for general use, but
Glasgow seems to have continued to use Buxtorf's *Epitome,*
issued at Basle in many editions, and in 1653 Baillie published in Edinburgh a supplement to it, called *Appendix
Practica ad Joannis Buxtorfii Epitomen Grammaticae Hebraeae.* Of
its two parts the earlier, reproducing his class lectures for the
year 1650, gives a grammatical analysis of the text of eighteen
Psalms and of passages from Genesis, Exodus, Deuteronomy,
Job, Isaiah, Jeremiah and Daniel, while the latter, in six
Quaestiones, or critical discussions, of passages from Genesis
and Psalms, compares the Hebrew text with the Targum,
the Septuagint and versions in Latin, English, French, Italian
and Flemish.

In his Preface, Baillie gives interesting sidelights on the
teaching conditions of his day. 'Students daily,' he complains,
'in all the Universities waste most lamentably the greater part
of the precious hours in useless and criminal writing. They
spend more time writing that would abundantly suffice for
learning thoroughly what is being written; let alone that
many write the dictates so crassly and wrongly that with the
best intention they could scarcely decipher again with pleasure or much profit what they had written.' Baillie deplores
the neglect of Oriental languages in the Scottish universities.
'A crass ignorance,' he remarks, 'was tolerated not merely of
Arabic, Syriac and Rabbinic but even of the original text of
Holy Scripture. . . . As regards texts, some teachers transmit
their lectures only orally; these disappear from the minds of
their hearers . . . as if written in water. Those who, to obviate
this, try to dictate their lectures go so slowly, every letter and
single point having to be dictated, that the students are nau-
seated and soon forget all they have learned.' In offering to
his students (such as cared to purchase it) an authentic copy

of his own lectures, Baillie commends similar works by Bellarmine and Keckermann and expresses the wish that the younger Buxtorf would produce similar manuals on the text of the Hebrew Bible, the Targums and the Syriac New Testament and that Golius, author of a recent Arabic lexicon, would do the same for Arabic. Baillie presented a copy of his work to Professors Voet of Utrecht, Golius of Leyden, and Buxtorf of Basle; Voet, in his letter of thanks and appreciation, recommended recent Continental books on Rabbinics, Aramaic, Syriac, Samaritan, Arabic and Ethiopic.

When, in 1651, Baillie succeeded to Dickson's Chair he continued to teach his former subjects, reading Hebrew on Thursdays, and in 1655 he wrote: ' I got leave to bring all the schollars twice a-week to my Hebrew lessons and discourses on the Catechise; whereof I was very glad, for linguistic students we have very few. . . . Mr. Patrick, before the end of the year, dyted two or three hours something on the first of Ezechiel.' The reference is to the regent, Patrick Young, one of Baillie's former pupils. Baillie also taught 'Chronology,' *i.e.,* Church History, including Old Testament history, and published his lectures under the title *Operis Historii et Chronologii Libri Duo* which was still used in 1701 by the Presbytery of Kirkcudbright in its trials for Licence.

In 1660, Baillie became Principal of the University, and after his death in 1662, interest in Oriental studies waned at Glasgow, and Hebrew was probably not taught there during the next seven years, while the University was settling down after the Restoration; but a manuscript notebook, dated 1665 and belonging to a Scottish (probably a St. Andrews) student named Robert Melville, which is in the National Library of Scotland contains lectures on Chronology and on the Oriental languages, including Hebrew, Aramaic, Syriac, Samaritan, Ethiopic and Arabic, besides original compositions in Hebrew comprising letters, poems and a dialogue, and it gives a very favourable impression of the range and quality of Oriental teaching in Scotland at this time.

The standard was, however, shortly afterwards to decline for a time in all the Universities.

In 1669 Gilbert Burnet, an Aberdeen graduate who had learned Hebrew in Rotterdam from a Jew, was called to the Divinity Chair at Glasgow and lectured on Hebrew on alternate Thursdays, reading 'a Psalm in Hebrew, comparing it with the 70 [Septuagint] the Vulgar [Vulgate] and our version [of 1611],' but he does not appear to have taught Aramaic or Syriac and he was the last Professor of Divinity to teach Hebrew, for, after his departure to England five years later, in 1674, to become Bishop of Salisbury, the teaching passed into the hands of a regent until, thirty-five years afterwards, the Chair of Oriental Languages was founded.

It is known that James Wodrow, Professor of Divinity from 1692 to 1707, revised annually his knowledge of Hebrew and read the Bible (including presumably the Old Testament) in the original to his classes, but the Hebrew grammar was taught to Arts and Divinity students by the regent, John Tran, for thirty years, from 1674 until his death in 1704, apart for three years when it was in the care of Thomas Gordon.

Gordon, a younger regent, was, while visiting London in 1686, presented by King James VII to a Regius Professorship of Oriental Languages in the University to be endowed out of the University's vacant stipends, but the University, which had not been consulted, claimed that their funds were insufficient and refused to make any available. Their action was approved by the Privy Council, but they were required to induct Gordon to the Chair without a stipend, which they did in 1687. The following year witnessed the Revolution and the fall of King James, and the University undertook, unsuccessfully, a suit for scandal against Gordon. He resigned, however, from his regentship while retaining his title to the Chair, and in 1690 claimed as his salary for teaching Hebrew for the previous three and a half years 600 marks, part of which had been promised. The University offered him 1,000 marks if he would resign his Chair and upon his accepting this the Professorship was regarded as lapsed and the regent Tran resumed his interrupted duties.

In 1696, the General Assembly, deploring the denial of 'the certainty and authority of the Scripture revelation,' declared that they, 'considering how necessary it is that they who declare the oracles of God to others should themselves understand them in the original languages, do require that none be licensed to preach, or ordained to the ministry, unless they give good proof of their understanding of the Greek and Hebrew; and the General Assembly recommend to all candidates for the ministry, also the other Oriental languages, especially the Chaldaic and Syriac, so far as they can.'

After Tran's death, in 1704, the University, finding 'that the profession of Hebrew was vacant,' and that there was none in the College who could 'allow so much time for the teaching of the Hebrew as that language would require, except Dr. Sinclare [Robert Sinclair, M.D.], professor of Mathematicks,' relegated the duty to him at the same salary as Tran had enjoyed. Four years later, however, in 1708, Queen Anne allotted an annual grant of forty pounds to the Professor of Oriental Languages and in 1709 the University nominated Charles Morthland, a country schoolmaster, to the Chair, allowing him leave of absence to prepare for his 'trials.' Morthland, after a few months' study of the Oriental languages under the tuition of Professor Adrian Reland of the University of Utrecht, submitted a testimonial from him, and the University prescribed 'an analytical and critical discourse on the original text of Jeremiah, 10th chapter, verses 10, 11 and 12,' verse 11 being in Aramaic. The University was 'well satisfied' with the discourse and, after several members had 'conversed with Mr. Morthland to their satisfaction,' they inducted him with exceptional ceremony. The stipend of the Chair was afterwards augmented by Queen Anne and renewed by George II.

Morthland has left an account, written in 1717, of his lecture programme. After completing in a month or less an exposition of Reland's *Compendium* of Jakob Alting's *Fundamentum Punctationis* he examined the students in this and then read, interpreted and analysed an historical portion of the Bible and some thirty or forty Psalms, revising in the process the grammar. In the second year, after ten days or less of grammar revision, parts of the Prophets were read and Aramaic grammar was begun; then, from January onwards, Morthland read and analysed all the Aramaic parts of the Old Testament, taught Syriac grammar and read eight or ten chapters in Syriac, presumably from the New Testament. Only one student had studied Arabic and little progress had been made with other Oriental subjects, but Morthland had given fortnightly public lectures on important topics and intended to do this more frequently. His teaching, however, was mainly confined to Divinity students, for he writes: 'As for the students of philosophy, the dyets being so short and the meetings so few in a year, all I can gett done with them is to initiate them in the Hebrew Grammar, and read two or three Psalms in a year with them.' In 1721, Morthland published at Glasgow a small Hebrew and Aramaic Grammar, entitled *Brevis Introductio ad Grammaticam Hebraicam et Chaldaicam in usum Academiorum Glasguensium* which, as he states in the Preface, is virtually a third edition of Reland's *Compendium*.

When Morthland died, in 1744, he had held his Chair for thirty-five years; during the following sixteen it was to have no fewer than seven occupants, most of whom, though eminent in other fields, contributed little to Oriental scholarship. The Lord Advocate, on the ground that the Chair was a royal foundation, had wished to appoint Morthland's successor, but the University vindicated its right and chose Alexander Dunlop, son of the Professor of Greek and grandson of a former Principal. As he was abroad, tutoring, his induction was postponed for a year, his salary being meantime used to equip the new Chemistry department. Dunlop died after five years and his successor, William Rouat, son of the minister of Jedburgh, taught Oriental

Languages for only two years before moving, in 1752, to the Chair of Ecclesiastical History. The next incumbent, George Muirhead, minister of Dysart, was transferred only just over one year later to the Humanity Chair, the Muirhead Prizes being afterwards founded in his honour.

Muirhead's successor, the versatile but eccentric John Anderson, son of the minister of Rosneath, was tutoring in France so did not undertake his teaching duties until the following session, when he combined them with instruction in French and English, and only two years elapsed before he demitted his post on appointment to the Chair of Natural Philosophy, becoming later the founder of the rival academic institution afterwards known as Anderson's College. James Buchanan, who followed Anderson, died after four years and was succeeded by Robert Trail (D.D. St. Andrews, 1760), the distinguished and scholarly minister of Banff, but after a tenure of only three months—the shortest in the history of the Chair—he was made Professor of Divinity, subsequently attaining to the Moderatorship of the General Assembly.

Paradoxically, his successor, Patrick Cumin (LL.D., 1803), occupied the Chair for the record number of fifty-nine years, until his death in 1820, although for the last six he was relieved of teaching duties. A son of the Professor of Ecclesiastical History at Edinburgh, he was a good linguist and, though teaching Hebrew only two days a week, lectured also for thirty years on French and Italian. On the occasion of his jubilee the University gave a dinner in his honour. The irregularity of attendance on all the Divinity classes was at this time a scandal, and to remedy this the regular payment of a class fee (already customary in Arts classes) was introduced from 1800 onwards for Hebrew and Ecclesiastical History, presumably on the ground that people value what they have to pay for.

A distinguished student of the period, William Rae Wilson (LL.D., 1844), who became a solicitor and an Oriental traveller, wrote *Travels in the Holy Land* and other

books and was joint-founder of the Cleland and Rae Wilson
Medals, one of which is awarded annually in the Senior
Hebrew Class. Another graduate, John Reid (M.D., 1808),
a minister and afterwards, in Glasgow, a surgeon and a
teacher of Oriental languages, numbered among his publications a Hebrew lexicon. One of the founders of Old
Testament Higher Criticism, Dr. Alexander Geddes, of
London, a native of Banffshire, obtained leave from the
University about this time to collate its valuable Clementine
Septuagint manuscript for his new translation of the Bible
to which the University became a subscriber. Class Prize-
lists, preserved from 1787 onwards, furnish useful information on the teaching of the period, prizes being awarded for
exercises on the Hebrew pronoun or verb, while open University prize subjects included a commentary on the Hebrew
text of the Song of Moses (in Exodus, ch. xv.) and essays
on various periods of Old Testament history.

In 1813, Professor Cumin obtained leave to employ as his
assistant James Couper (D.D., 1800), the Professor of Astro-
nomy, who in the following year published in Glasgow a
Hebrew grammar abridged from that of Professor Wilson of
St. Andrews. At the end of the session, however, the Uni-
versity appointed as Assistant and Successor to Cumin
Gavin Gibb (D.D., 1804), a distinguished Churchman
who had been Dean of Faculties and was afterwards Vice-
Rector of the University and Moderator of the General
Assembly. Gibb continued to function also as minister of
St. Andrew's Church, Glasgow, even after Cumin's death
in 1820. Gibb's First Year Hebrew class met five days weekly
to study grammar and read the Hebrew Bible, while the
Second Year class, twice weekly, studied the text critically
with special attention to the meaning of particular words,
such as *berakh, shama', berith, nephesh, she'ol* and the various
terms for deity. Hebrew poetry, syntax, and prose composition, including original composition, were also included in
the curriculum, and Aramaic grammar was probaly taught,

but no texts were read, on the ground that an Aramaic dictionary was not available for students though all had to possess a Hebrew lexicon. Lectures on Arabic and Persian grammar were occasionally given but much of Old Testament exegesis, as well as style of Scripture and history of the text, continued, as hitherto, to be part of the Divinity Class work. Notable *alumni* of the period include George Gilfillan, author of *Bards of the Bible;* Robert S. Candlish (D.D., Princeton), writer of a commentary on Genesis, Professor of Biblical Criticism at Edinburgh University and afterwards Principal of New College, Edinburgh; John Gemmill (D.D., 1881), minister of Fairlie and composer of a long poem on the Hebrew accents, entitled *The Tiberiad;* and Micaiah Smith, a minister who went to Tangier and became a noted Arabist. Two future Indologists also attended the University, one of whom, John Muir (C.I.E., D.C.L. Oxon., LL.D. Edin.), wrote many books on India, while the other, Robert C. Mather (LL.D., 1862), a missionary, edited the *Hindustani Reference Bible.* William Bell Macdonald, another *alumnus,* became a surgeon and an eminent Coptic scholar.

From 1828 Professor Gibb suffered from ill-health and employed as his assistant Josiah Walker, son of the Professor of Humanity, but on Gibb's death, three years later, in 1831, the University appointed as his successor William Fleming (D.D., 1829), minister of Old Kilpatrick, who had at one time been Assistant Librarian and College Chaplain. During his eight years in the Chair, Fleming acted for two as Vice-Rector and published a substantial encyclopædic work, in two volumes, entitled *The Scripture Gazetteer* and containing an alphabetic dictionary of Biblical geography, history and natural history, with maps, a bibliography, and an essay on 'the importance and advantages of sacred geography.' In 1838, Fleming was transferred to the Chair of Moral Philosophy. Among alumni of this period was the future Sir William Muir (K.C.S.I., LL.D., 1866, D.C.L. Oxon., Ph.D. Bologna, LL.D. Edin.), Principal of Edinburgh

University and author of works, still standard, on Arabic and Islamic history.

Fleming's successor, inducted in 1839, was George Gray (D.D. Edin.), minister of Maybole, who combined his professorial duties for a time with those of University Chaplain. He continued in office until his death eleven years later and, besides teaching Hebrew and Aramaic, gave occasional lectures on Biblical geography and antiquities, subjects which were beginning to attract widespread attention in the light of nineteenth century exploration and discovery and which greatly added to the interest of Oriental studies. One of Gray's students, John McGill (LL.D., 1869), became Professor of Oriental Languages at St. Andrews.

Gray was succeeded, in 1850, by Duncan Harkness Weir (D.D., 1864), minister of the Scots Church in Manchester and a native of Greenock, who had studied under Fleming and had in 1849 published a notable article on the Hebrew verb. In his first year, he taught, in addition, Ecclesiastical History, and for twenty-one years acted also as Clerk of Senate. Though modest and shy, he was an exacting and able teacher with an enthusiasm for his subject and as early as 1854 obtained permission to hold a more advanced class in Oriental languages; he was also prominent in urging the resuscitation of the B.D. degree. Classes were held in Aramaic, Syriac and Arabic, and the most advanced results of nineteenth century research were made available with the aid of Gesenius' Hebrew Grammar and Lexicon of which English translations had recently appeared, while the extensive publication of new text-books on Oriental languages enabled the range of reading to be widely extended. The Higher Criticism of the Pentateuch was beginning to disturb the Churches and in 1871 the General Assembly ordained that 'whereas it is desirable that young men studying for Ministry of the Church, should acquire such knowledge of the Hebrew language, previous to entering the Divinity Hall, as is necessary to prepare them for the systematic study of the Hebrew Scriptures, as a souce of theology, and for the investigation of the important questions relating to the origin and interpretation of these Scriptures which have emerged especially in recent times—in and after the year 1872 the elements of Hebrew grammar shall be included among the subjects of Examination for students about to enter the Divinity Hall.' It is indicative of the new light being thrown at this time by archæology upon the Bible and the Near East that in 1875 the Essay subject prescribed by the University for the Ewing Medal was 'The History of Assyria.'

New Bible dictionaries and journals were a feature of the period; Weir's literary output included articles in the *Imperial Bible Dictionary*, the *Journal of Sacred Literature* and the *Academy*, and his unpublished notes on the text of Isaiah were commended by Professor Cheyne of Oxford in his commentary on that book. Weir was also one of those appointed to prepare the Revised Version of the Old Testament.

A distinguished student of Weir's was E. J. W. Gibb, who, besides attending the Arabic Class, privately studied Persian and Turkish and eventually became an authority on Turkish literature on which he wrote several important works, among them a six-volume *History of Ottoman Poetry*. Other eminent alumni of the time included J. E. H. Thomson (D.D. St. Andrews), missionary in Palestine and afterwards minister of St. Boswells, joint-editor of the *Temple Dictionary of the Bible* and author of a commentary on Daniel and works on the Samaritans and on the Apocrypha and Pseudepigrapha; James Orr (D.D., 1885), Professor in the United Free Church College, Glasgow, and author of *The Problem of the Old Testament;* and Buchanan Blake (D.D., 1919), Professor in Wilson College, Bombay, and author of several books on Old Testament subjects. Weir's son, who became afterwards Lecturer in Arabic in the University, was another of his pupils.

On Weir's death, in 1876, the Hebrew Chair was entrusted to an Aberdeen and St. Andrews graduate, James Robertson (LL.D., 1910, D.D. Aberdeen, LL.D. St. Andrews), minister of Mayfield, Edinburgh, who, as a former missionary in Constantinople and Beirut, had first-hand knowledge of the Near East. A man of enterprise, vigour and enthusiasm, he was loved and revered by his students, and as early as 1880 he founded Glasgow University Oriental Society, which, meeting at first in the Professor's house, soon grew to include members from all the Scottish universities, including many living outside Scotland. Professor Robertson was a learned and painstaking teacher and a devout Old Testament scholar. He kept aloof from the Biblical controversies of his day, adopting a cautious but open-minded attitude toward the Higher Criticism. His interest in Hebrew grammar led to his translating and editing Müller's *Hebrew Syntax,* while his important writings in the Old Testament field included Baird Lectures on *The Early Religion of Israel,* Croal Lectures on *The Poetry and Religion of the Psalms,* an introduction to the Books of Kings (*Temple Bible*), a popular introduction to the Old Testament and many articles in encyclopædias and elsewhere. On the occasion of his eightieth birthday in 1920 the Oriental Society issued a volume of Semitic studies in his honour. He died later in that year.

Considerable developments took place in the Oriental department under Robertson's régime. Following upon decisions of the Universities' Commission in 1889, the title of the Chair was altered in 1893 to 'Hebrew and Semitic Languages' and Hebrew and Arabic were included among subjects for the Ordinary M.A. Degree. Aramaic and Syriac classes grew larger, Syriac being taught on an advanced as well as an elementary standard, and in 1902 a full-time Lecturer in Arabic was appointed, making possible the institution in 1903 of an Honours degree in Semitic Languages by which the scope of the teaching in non-Biblical Oriental studies was vastly expanded.

The new Arabic Lectureship was committed to Thomas

Hunter Weir (D.D. Aberdeen), the son of Robertson's predecessor in the Oriental Chair. He had been Assistant in Hebrew and Semitic Languages since 1895 and had in 1899 published a *Short History of the Hebrew Text of the Old Testament.* His numerous subsequent works included *The Shaikhs of Morocco in the Twelfth Century, Arabic Prose Composition, Omar Khayyám the Poet,* and editions of Sir William Muir's histories of Muhammad and the Caliphate, besides catalogues of the Arabic, Syriac, Hebrew, Persian and Turkish manuscripts in the Hunterian Library. Weir also instituted the Class of Modern Arabic and for two years taught Persian. After his death in 1928 the Oriental Society founded the Weir Memorial Prize to his memory.

Among Professor Robertson's many distinguished students were A. R. S. Kennedy (D.D., 1893, D.D. St. Andrews, LL.D. Edin.), Professor of Oriental Languages at Aberdeen and afterwards at Edinburgh, author of commentaries on several Old Testament books, translator (from German) of a number of Oriental grammars and compiler of a long succession of encyclopædia articles; D. B. Macdonald (D.D., 1920, D.H.L.), Professor of Semitic Languages in Hartford Theological Seminary, U.S.A., a prolific writer on Arabic and Islamic subjects and author of notable works on the Hebrew literary and philosophical genius; and A. C. Baird (D.D., 1926), Professor of Divinity and Biblical Criticism at Aberdeen, who had been Assistant in Hebrew in the University and had in 1909-10 delivered there a course of lectures on the Assyrian and Babylonian civilisations.

Distinguished graduates of the time who completed their studies elsewhere include John Murphy (D.D., 1932, D.Litt.), Professor of Comparative Religion in the University of Manchester and writer on Oriental religions; James Moffatt (D.D. 1943, D.Litt., D.D. Oxon. and St. Andrews), Professor in Mansfield College, Oxford, the Free Church College, Glasgow, and the Union Theological Seminary, New York, and author of a well-known translation of the Bible; and

William Ewing (D.D., 1913), missionary in Palestine, joint-author and -editor of the *Temple Dictionary of the Bible* and writer of several books on the Near East.

Graduates who became missionaries in India and wrote important books on Indian subjects or in Indian languages were Robert Kilgour (D.D., 1909), joint author of a *Nepali Dictionary,* a translation of the Old Testament into Nepali and an *Introduction to Ginsburg's Hebrew Old Testament;* Robert B. Douglas (D.D., 1936), author of an exposition of the Book of Job in Marathi and one of the revisers of the Marathi translation of the Bible; and Nicol MacNicol (D.D., 1928, D.Litt.), author of *Indian Theism, Psalms of Marathi Saints* and other works on Indian subjects. William Hastie (D.D. Edin.), the Professor of Divinity at this time (1895-1903), was also a good linguist and in 1903 he published a translation of a long Persian poem by Jalaluddin together with a scholarly introduction on the *Rubaiyat of Omar Khayyám.*

When Professor Robertson retired in 1907, after a professoriate of thirty years, the University found a worthy successor in William Barron Stevenson (LL.D., 1938, D.D. Edin. and Wales, D.Litt.), who officiated until his retirement in 1937, thirty years later. He had already for nine years held the Chair of Hebrew and Old Testament at Bala Theological College and, besides translating Dillmann's commentary on Genesis and editing with valuable appendixes Young's *Concordance to the Bible,* had published a Hebrew grammar, a commentary on some of the books of the Apocrypha and numerous encyclopædia and other articles. His subsequent writings have included works on the Crusades, on which he is an authority, an official Government handbook on *The Jewish Colonies of Palestine,* a *Grammar of Palestinian Jewish Aramaic,* an introductory manual on *Isaiah, Jeremiah and Ezekiel,* Schweich Lectures on *The Poem of Job* and numerous articles on a variety of subjects; he is still an active researcher, lecturer and writer.

The Arabic Lectureship which became vacant in 1928

was filled by the appointment of James Robson (D.D. St. Andrews, D.Litt.), minister of Shandon, a former pupil of Dr. Stevenson, and missionary for a time in India and South Arabia. He was designated Reader in Arabic in 1948 and, when called to the Chair of Arabic at Manchester in the following year, he had already published important transla- tions of Arabic manuscripts besides compiling a catalogue of the Oriental manuscripts in the University Library.

In 1934, following the Union of the Church of Scotland and the United Free Church, the University had been en- riched by the transference to it of the Chair of Old Testament Language and Literature in Trinity College, Glasgow, which had been instituted in 1856. Among its distinguished occupants had been George (afterwards Sir George) Adam Smith (D.D., 1931, Litt.D., LL.D.), one of the foremost Old Testament scholars of his generation, who later became Principal of Aberdeen University, and John Edgar McFad- yen (D.D., 1911), writer of many notable books in the Old Testament field. This acquisition enabled a wide choice of advanced courses to be offered annually.

The Union of the Churches more than doubled the size of the classes. Glasgow has for long trained the greater (often the overwhelming) proportion of the Divinity students of Scotland, besides providing tuition for what is one of the largest Jewish communities in the British Isles whose interest in Hebrew grew rapidly with the Jewish colonisation of Pales- tine. Both ordinary and advanced classes have been, accord- ingly, well attended. In almost every presbytery in Scotland to-day, as well as in the mission-fields, there are former stu- dents whose Hebrew studies here, in spite of the hard work they entailed, are remembered with gratitude and pleasure. Of the more advanced students, several now hold university chairs or lectureships in Semitic or Old Testament studies, while others occupy key positions in museum-work and -administration, Colonial government or Jewish education. Several have gained Doctorates of this or other universities in the subjects of the Oriental departments. Special mention falls to be made of Henry George Farmer (D.Mus. Edin., D.Litt.), author of more than twenty works on Oriental music, on which he is an authority, including several translations of Arabic manuscripts.

The Oriental Society had, by the time of Professor Stevenson's retirement in 1937, published seven volumes of *Transactions* and has now published thirteen. The University Library, already enriched by the gift of Dr. A. B. McGrigor's valuable collection of books on Palestine, was further enhanced by the donation of Professor Robertson's Oriental library and afterwards by that of Professor Stevenson. On the occasion of Professor Stevenson's seventy-fifth birthday, in 1944, the Oriental Society published in his honour a volume of Semitic studies by several of his former students.

In the long period of three hundred and seventy-seven years the Oriental school at Glasgow has had a variety of teachers, some better than others; but, on the whole, both the University and the Church have been well served. The training of candidates for the Christian ministry has always been the primary interest. Many generations of Divinity students have had a window opened for them on the unfamiliar, but fascinating and many-sided, world of Oriental lands and peoples and customs and ideas. The study of the Scriptures in the original languages has cultivated in our ministers the accuracy of observation so essential to the scholar and the habit of careful analysis, comparison and inference so important for the seeker after truth. The history, literature and religion of the Bible have been expounded to them in the light of other contemporary civilisations and, while they have been taught to love and enjoy the Old Testament, to understand its peculiar idioms and to interpret it aright, a first-hand knowledge of the idiosyncrasies of the Hebrew text has proved for them the surest safeguard from the ignorant, obscurantist bibliolatry against which the Church must perpetually be on guard. In the wider field also of Oriental Studies the

University has long played, and is likely to continue to play, a leading part both in the dissemination of knowledge and in the prosecution of research.

LAW

by

Andrew Dewar Gibb
Regius Professor of Law

On surveying the syllabus of lectures and realising that only one of them is to be devoted to the Faculty of Law, I am conscious both of my inability to do justice to all the great and important fields of law represented in our teaching, and of the honour which I enjoy of speaking for the Faculty as a whole.

He would be a bold critic who claimed that in modern times the teaching of law was a foremost purpose of the University of Glasgow. Yet it would be inaccurate to deny that this was indeed a foremost purpose of those responsible for the foundation of the University. For the Bull of Pope Nicolas directed the foundation of a *studium generale,* not only for the cultivation of the humane arts but also for the study of the Civil and Canon Law, that is to say, of the law of the Roman Empire and the law of the Roman Church. It is easy to recognise the appropriateness of the latter. The Canon Law played a large part in the lives (and the deaths) of men and women, whether through the laws affecting marriage, paternity or succession. But the utility of a *studium* for the purposes of the Civil Law at that time is less clear. This indeed was to come, but to provide for it in 1451 suggests either that the words of the Bull were merely formal or that they embodied a highly intelligent guess as to the future and what it must hold for the law of the country, which is not a very probable idea. It was almost certainly less for the advantage of legal practitioners that instruction in these subjects was required than for the enlightenment of those who sought high place in the service of Church or State.

The great University of Bologna was to be in some sort the pattern of the new *studium* of Glasgow, as it was of many other European Universities. Bologna was a great school of both the Civil and the Canon Law. It attracted to itself not a few Scotsmen, amongst whom one at least, Peter Bissat, even became a professor. Indeed the early Italian Universities as a whole seem to have been primarily concerned with law. Even to-day the published Statute and Regulations of the University begin by stating that '*La Regia Università di Bologna comprende le Facoltà di Giurisprudenza, di Lettere . . . di Medicina*' and so on. The Faculty of Law is on every occasion given the first place. The student of our own University history will look either wryly or complacently, according to his profession, at the disparity of emphasis in the mother and daughter universities.

Law and Legal Institutions in 1451. What was the state of the law and legal institutions in Scotland in the year 1451? We do not know a great deal with certainty. Jurisdiction was shared between the King's judges central and local, and the local judges who operated in the private jurisdictions of the nobles, a state of matters which was to endure for three hundred years longer. That there was a system of law in being we know: the *Regiam Maiestatem* (surely the most resoundingly named of all legal works) had probably been for long in existence. And there was legislation to add to and correct the existing law. In 1451 James II was on the throne and the legislation of the year was almost entirely taken up with questions of the currency. Nor must it be forgotten that the Parliament showed serious concern for the proper education in law of the nobility, for by an Act of 1496, it provided that all barons and freeholders should send their sons to the grammar schools until they acquired a perfect knowledge of Latin and that then they should be sent to the Universities in order that they might be qualified to administer the law in their jurisdictions.

Law Teaching. There is very little material available for an assessment of the teaching of law in the earliest times at Glasgow. The historians of the University have recorded little, and I can here only echo them in saying that apparently from an early period lectures were delivered at least occasionally on the law. In 1460 lectures were delivered in Civil and Canon Law and the name of the lecturer is known. But, on the whole, we to-day are scarcely in a position to dissent from the view of that distinguished scholar Dr. David Murray, that although law was one of the original subjects and we know that *some* lectures were given, for some two hundred years there was really no law school in the University. The same writer, however, reminds us that Gavin Dunbar was an undergraduate at Glasgow and distinguished himself in law. It is not easy to reconcile these two views.

Dunbar, who ultimately became Chancellor of Scotland, holding office from 1528 to 1543, was at one time tutor to King James V, and it appears to have been his advice which led the King to inaugurate the Court of Session. However ambiguous the motive which prompted James to this course, the story, if true, records a deeply interesting connection between a distinguished son of Glasgow and the foundation of the Supreme Civil Court in Scotland. It reminds us too that the Court of Session came into being eighty years after our own University.

Coutts, in his *History* of the University, mentions traces of teaching and of the granting of degrees in law during this period. He points out that bachelors' degrees *utriusque iuris* or *in utroque iure: in decretis:* licences *in legibus* or *in utroque iure* and even a doctorate *decretorum* were conferred so that at various epochs there was presumably some teaching, though he concludes that, by the time of the Reformation, teaching was nearly dormant. This is borne out by the fact that on the occasion of the reorganisation of the University known as the *Nova Erectio,* in 1577, no special provision for teaching law was made, though for my own part I find it hard to understand how the recognised needs of one generation could simply cease to be supplied in succeeding generations. But the whole conceptions and purpose of law teaching were so different four hundred years ago that we can scarcely apply to the question the reasoning of to-day.

Lord Stair. In this period, however, one great fact stands out. In the year 1635, James Dalrymple of Stair entered as an undergraduate in our University, and in 1641, as Coutts puts it, he came forward as a young captain attired in his 'military uniform of buff and scarlet to dispute for the office of regent then vacant in the University and carried the appointment against several competitors.' Between that year and 1647 or 1648, when he was called to the Bar, Stair taught philosophy at Glasgow. It has been suggested that the general part of his great *Institutions of the Law of Scotland* was based upon the lectures on jurisprudence which he delivered as part of his course on Ethics. However that may be, by this work the former Regent or Professor in the University of Glasgow constituted himself the supreme exponent and master of the law of Scotland. If the University which gave nurture to an eminent man is entitled to any share in the bright light of his fame, then the great name of Stair is certainly one in which our University may well rejoice. I make the observation with regret that the University has never publicly rendered to him the homage which he has so richly deserved, not only at the hands of lawyers but at the hands of all who are able to appreciate the virtues of our great and enlightened system of law.

1713. We have seen that the *Nova Erectio* was not concerned with the exposition of law. And indeed nothing appears to be known with certainty as to instruction in law until we come to a date about a century and a half later, when a step was taken which may be said in some sort to have inaugurated a new era. Already in 1664 we find Commissioners of Visitation recommending the institution of a Chair of Civil and Canon Law. I am bound to say that the year 1664 seems a little late for the latter part of this recommendation. The important thing is that opinion was evidently stirring. But it was nearly fifty years before a definite step forward was taken. In the year 1713, £90 a year was given for a new Regius Chair of Civil Law. In the same year, £40 was given for a new Chair of Medicine. To us to-day these figures seem to be in a strange proportion one to the other. In the last year for which I have figures, the Chair of Medicine and the teaching of Medicine cost the University £169,000, whilst the Chair of Law (which corresponds with that of 1713) and the Faculty cost about £10,000. But by 1713, law was an ancient craft and branch of learning and study, whose principles had won acceptance for centuries, whilst medicine was still dabbling in the most extraordinary theories, such as that, for example, of nervous fluids, and its practitioners had not so very long before taken in their barbers' poles.

From 1713 onwards there has never been a break in the teaching of law, though there have been many changes and considerable growth. It will perhaps be convenient to say a few words first about the more important of the men who taught law between 1713 and the present day.

Professors of Law. The first professor to be appointed to the Regius Chair was William Forbes, advocate. Forbes deserved well of the University. He held the Chair from the beginning of the year 1714 until the year 1745. Besides lecturing both on Civil Law and on the Law of Scotland, he was the author of authoritative works on Bills and on Church Lands and Teinds. But his most important work was his *Institutes of the Law of Scotland* published in two volumes in 1722 and 1730. This was an abridgement of a greater work, which exists to-day only in manuscript in the University Library. But Forbes' smaller work is meritorious, and had the greater edition been published, it might not have yielded the field even to Erskine. As it is, the *Institutes* is a work which might well have been perpetuated in further editions, as it is comprehensive, convenient in form and lucid in style. It is scarcely fair to fasten on Forbes a belief in witchcraft, as if such a belief were exclusively his. It was not until the 9 Geo. ii cap. 5 (in 1735) that prosecutions for witchcraft were forbidden by law. In purely University affairs, we find Forbes breaking a lance for his Faculty in claiming for it the order of precedence and place second only to that of Theology, a place which has now been usurped by the Faculty of Arts.

After Forbes' death, one William Cross, or Crosse, an advocate, was appointed to the Chair of Law. This was in 1746. In 1750 Cross, who had become Sheriff of Lanarkshire in 1748, resigned his Chair after having for four years, on one shabby pretext or another, avoided lecturing at all in the University of Glasgow. This extremely unworthy professor was succeeded by the person who had acted as his deputy during these four years, namely, Hercules Lindesay. Perhaps the most noteworthy feature of Lindesay's tenure was that he gave up the practice, thitherto followed, of lecturing on Justinian in Latin. The Faculty of Advocates protested, but to no purpose. His name, therefore, is linked with what must on the whole be regarded as a disservice to scholarship. In our day there are undergraduates in the Faculty of Law whose attainments in the language of Justinian are indicated simply by their possession of a qualification in what is well styled 'Lower Latin.' Lindesay died in 1761 without having enriched the literature of the Law of Scotland by a single line, so far as I have discovered.

It is in the person of John Millar, his successor, who held office from 1761 to 1801 that we discover the most remarkable occupant of the Regius Chair. Millar did for the teaching of law in Glasgow what nobody before or since has ever done for it. He drew students hither from all parts of this island. On page 222 of Dr. Murray's *Memoirs* the author's industry has collected many names of the most eminent amongst Millar's students, and they are by no means all

Scotsmen. The following account of his teaching is to be found in the account of the University published in 1891 with the sanction of the Senate (page 96):

'Millar was a man of liberal culture and varied attainments; ardent, energetic and enthusiastic in study and in teaching; clear and subtle in exposition and argument. Lecturing always merely from notes, he has full scope for his faculty of ready suggestion and illustration. He was not content with prelecting merely on the *Institutes* and *Pandects* of Justinian. His courses included, besides Jurisprudence, the theory of government, Scots Law and latterly English law.' Perhaps a further eulogy, this time by the poet Campbell, may be quoted:

'Such was the truth, cheerfulness and courage that seemed to give erectness to his shapely bust, he might have stood to the statuary [sculptor] for a Roman orator: but he was too much in earnest with his duty, too manly to affect the orator, but keeping close to his subject he gave it a seriousness that was never tiresome. . . . His students were always in the class before him waiting as for a treat.'

Dr. Murray informs us that the bust referred to by the poet is reproduced on the east side of the Library of the Royal Faculty of Procurators.

Sets of Millar's lectures exist, and there is one in the Murray collection which I have seen. It was made by Robert Ferguson of Raith. I am bound to say that if Millar indeed lectured extempore as is recorded, the lectures are remarkably polished and finished. Most of them could be printed as they stand and they would have formed an excellent introductory text-book of that day. The lectures on Jurisprudence cast a surprisingly wide net in point of subject-matter, though they are undoubtedly impregnated with the rules and examples of the law of Rome.

In politics Millar was a noted radical, and this was the only point of criticism made against him as a public man. As an author he was responsible for two works, neither of a purely legal nature. One is the *Origin of the Distinction of Ranks,* published in 1771, and the other an *Historical View of the English Government from the Settlement of the Saxons in Britain to the Accession of the House of Stewart,* published in 1787. I have glanced at them, but it is scarcely for me in this context to comment on them. The latter work is concerned almost wholly with English government, as its name indicates, with here and there a side-glance at Scottish institutions. Thus on page 441 the author makes the interesting, if rather doubtful, suggestion that the Court of Session with its fifteen members, the number of a Scottish jury, was meant to supersede the use of jury trial in Scotland.

In a general sense it must be said that Millar was the most outstanding man who has held the Chair of Law at Glasgow even although he made no real published contribution to the *corpus* of our law. His influence appears to have been considerable and at one or more periods it may have had a beneficial effect upon the fortunes of the University. One of his pupils was the Earl of Lauderdale who, perhaps through his connection with Millar, was a great encomiast of the French Revolution. He was amongst the last of the peers, other than eminent lawyers, to take an active part in the judicial business of the House of Lords, his sole qualification being that he was an advocate.

Millar's immediate successor was Robert Davidson, son of a Principal of the University, who occupied the Chair for no less than forty years, dying in 1841. His was apparently a modest talent, and law students no longer resorted to Glasgow from all over the country as in his predecessor's time. He confined himself to lecuring on the law of Scotland and that to an audience of some thirty hearers. He wrote a small treatise on the Scottish poor law.

On Davidson's death, Allan Maconochie, a son of Lord Meadowbank, was appointed to the Chair. There are several points about his tenure which seem to me to be worthy of mention. The first is that Maconochie, although given the

Commission of Professor of Civil Law, agreed with the Lord Advocate of the day that he would lecture on the Law of Scotland. It was coming to be recognised, and surely not before time, that our own system of law in the growing community of Scotland called for exposition by a man who should devote all his time to the task. From this time onwards the work of the senior professor in the Faculty of Law was recognised as being the delivery of a course of lectures on the law of Scotland. The other point of interest was the securing by Maconochie for the Universary Library of a copy of all printed papers in Court of Session proceedings, together with a valuable 'back set,' as the librarians call it. Unhappily this most valuable collection was left to moulder unbound in the vaults of the Library, and when attention was drawn to the fact in the 1930s the Library Committee, having for some obscure reason sought the opinion of Lord President Normand, decided to dispense with it in future and to hand over the whole collection to the Faculty of Procurators, a poor sequel to the enlightened enterprise of Maconochie.

Coutts, the historian of the University, tells of the firm stand made by Maconochie when he found himself at a loss for works on the law of Scotland which he was expected by the government to teach. He declined to go on with his teaching until the matter was put right, and very soon a grant of £200 was made towards an extension of the law library. Another point worthy of mention is that Maconochie had sufficient enlightenment to favour and help with the inauguration of the *Law Debating Society* the fore-runner of other legal clubs of which the present *Law Society* is not the least admirable. Professor Maconochie resigned in 1855. So far as can be discovered he wrote nothing. Nor did his successor, George Skene, unless we are to commemorate here that a Professor of Law was the compiler of a *Chronology of the Old Testament*. One of the most interesting features of Skene's professorship was that for the first time an appointment 'to the sole profession of law' was made, and Skene was accordingly the first 'Professor of *Law*' in the history of the University. Another point of interest is that according to Murray, Skene taught Scots Law and Conveyancing in alternate sessions, which strikes me as being an inconceivably inconvenient arrangement. He retired in 1867 and took up a post in the Register House.

There remain three names between Skene's and that of the present occupant of the Chair of Law. Of the first two I will say little. Robert Berry was Professor of Law from 1867 to 1887: acted as Secretary to two University Commissions and in 1887 became Sheriff of Lanarkshire. I believe, *ex relatione* of a late Sheriff-Clerk of Lanarkshire, that his appointment to this post was commonly regarded as illegal, since he was not supposed to comply with the requirement that the person appointed should be a practising advocate. He was succeeded in 1887 by Alexander Moody Stuart, and on his retiral in 1905 William Murray Gloag was appointed.

Professor Gloag, whom very many lawyers alive to-day will well remember, was the son of a judge of the Court of Session, Lord Kincairney. To the distinguished memory of the latter, it is no disrespect to say that his fame has been eclipsed by that of his son. Gloag was an outstanding jurisprudent. In lecturing, his rather dry, nervous style was mordant and memorable. He was a master of elegant and accurate compression. His lectures and he himself were most popular. There were some excellent lecturers amongst the lawyers in my undergraduate days, but Gloag was easily the best. Fortunately his fame rests on more than the evanescent word of mouth. His great treatise on the Law of Contract, which is a classic, is the finest text-book on a single subject which has ever been added to the literature of our law. It seems to me to yield at no point even to such a masterpiece as Pollock's work on the English Law of Contract. And the *Contract* was not Gloag's only work. His two collaborations, one in the *Law of Rights in Security* and the other in his *Introduction to the Law of Scotland* are notable, the latter having actually ousted Bell and the 'little Erskine' from the field as students' text-books. I regard Gloag as beyond all question the most remarkable legal scholar who has ever held this Chair, and the University ought to be proud of him.

Expansion; Conveyancing. We have now followed a tenuous thread of the history of law teaching from the earliest times to the year 1934. We have seen a great ideal prove incapable of being realized; then prolonged darkness followed by a faint spark which developed into a steady illumination. Before any appraisement of the system is attempted it may be well to finish the story of how the teaching of law developed—how the spark which was lit in 1714 gradually broadened so that in the end the steady candle flame grew to need a candelabrum. In other words it has to be shown how the University was forced gradually to add subject after subject to the radical topic or topics dealt with by the Professor of Law, the agglomeration of subjects technically known as Scots Law.

It has already been remarked how Davidson alternated in his lectures between Scots Law and Conveyancing. Obviously it had now come to be recognised that the formidable subject of the Scots feudal law was one which called for exposition at length. Indeed in 1817 the Faculty of Procurators in Glasgow had already inaugurated lectures and appointed their own lecturer. And that body in 1861, by providing a salary, enabled the Commissioners to set up a Chair of Conveyancing, the patronage of which remains to this day in the hands of the Faculty. The first man to be appointed was Anderson Kirkwood, a Glasgow writer, who held the Chair for some half-dozen years only. His successor, Sir James Roberton, a distinguished Glasgow writer, was professor until 1889. Both were apparently acceptable as lecturers, but neither of them has left a line to enrich our knowledge of his subject. It appears indeed that one man, unless he has extraordinary qualities, can scarcely expound this subject, write books about it and conduct the work of a busy solicitor. And lest it be said that this illustrates a weakness in the mode of teaching law in our University, it is pertinent to quote here the words of Dr. David Murray. In his *Memories* at page 236, he says:

'To set a man to teach Conveyancing who is not engaged in large practice and who only knows the subject from books or historically is like making a man professor of surgery who has only read about it and who never performed an operation.'

The logic is not intact, but the passage does enshrine a broad truth about all law teaching which reformers will disregard at their peril.

The next holder of the Chair was James Moir, a very learned feudal lawyer. So occupied (and rightly) was Moir with the history of his subject that his students used to complain that it was with difficulty, if at all, that he took them past the Conveyancing Act of 1874 in any one session. An enormous man, ponderous and slow of gait and speech with a sardonic sense of humour, Moir certainly drove home the principles of his subject in an unforgettable manner. A short tenure of the Chair by the eminent constitutional lawyer, William McKechnie (who was never quite at home in it), was followed by the appointment of John Girvan, an excellent teacher who contrived to combine the theoretical and practical in a manner unusually satisfying. His death in 1946 was very deeply regretted.

With the inauguration of teaching in Conveyancing the workaday subjects of instruction in law may be considered as covered *tant bien que mal*. The subjects lectured on by the Professor of Law were at least by the middle nineteenth century very much as they are to-day, with the outstanding exception of the Criminal Law. In his evidence before the University Commission in 1827, Davidson said that no teaching in criminal law was given. Even in my day, Gloag gave not more than two lectures to the subject. Criminal law has usually seemed to the Scots lawyer to be something rather beneath his notice, an extremely foolish notion.

But much was still wanting to make Glasgow even remotely resemble a school of law.

The matter of law teaching was somewhat faintly discussed by and before the Commission of 1826, and the Commission suggested that more lectures should be given, without however suggesting new topics. (Incidentally the Senate represented that if the recommendation were accepted it would be too much for the students, almost all apprenticed clerks, who would probably not attend. To-day this is still being said, though now rather by the profession than by the Senate.) The Commissioners made themselves responsible for the unfortunate statement that only in Edinburgh could a full course in law be established! But the Commissioners under the Universities Act of 1858 did make a change, when they introduced the teaching of Forensic Medicine into the Faculty of Law. The same body was responsible for the foundation of the new Chair of Conveyancing already mentioned.

It is with the advent of the Royal Commission on the Scottish Universities of 1878 that progress towards the broadening of the course really begins. For the Commissioners obtained Ordinances which were the foundation of the modern curricula for the degrees of Bachelor of Laws and of Laws. The former degree was to be attainable by graduates in Arts who studied Scots Law, Civil Law, Conveyancing, Public Law, Constitutional Law and History, and Forensic Medicine in a three-years' course. This was a great advance, and effect was ultimately given to these paper changes by the institution of the necessary new lectureships inaugurated, and to-day we are on the verge of the appointment of a Professor of Civil Law. Thus the years 1451 and 1712 saw the creation of Chairs of Civil Law whose holders ultimately ceased to teach the law they were appointed to teach and now, centuries later, a new Chair of Civil Law comes into being, to co-exist with the Chair of Law whose holders, nominally civilians, were compelled by circumstances to throw over the teaching of the law which gave their Chair its very name. Parker Walton, Irvine and Dr. Hugh Buchanan have been amongst the distinguished holders of the lectureship.

It is necessary to press on and to concentrate the remainder of the story into rather shorter compass. An Ordinance of 1894 created an eight-subject course for the degree of Bachelor of Laws and is in force to-day. In addition to changes already adverted to this ordinance belatedly introduced the subject of Jurisprudence into the degree, as also Mercantile Law, Accountancy, Administrative Law and Political Economy. Evidence and Procedure was to be added later. In Mercantile Law a Chair was founded in 1920, and in 1925 a Chair of Accountancy.

The modern degree, despite all its shortcomings, is, by reason of the long course and the very high standard required, one which it is not easy to obtain. For the past fifteen years a movement has been on foot for a thorough overhaul of it and a new and more enlightened ordinance may be expected soon. In pressing for change, Glasgow has taken a leading part.

Degrees in Law. I have been with imperfect accuracy speaking of the Law degree in the singular, having in mind the degree of Bachelor of Laws which, in the opinion of many, should be the single and sufficient baccalaureate. But it will be well to pause here for a moment to consider the degrees in law which have throughout its history been given by the University of Glasgow. The story is difficult to tell, and it is far from easy to fit the known facts into a coherent narrative, revealing a rational and consistent policy and purpose.

I have already referred to the glittering variety apparently available in pre-Reformation days, but how much of this was mere window-dressing I am unable to say. A Commission of 1664 makes the very modest statement that before the Reformation, Bachelors of Law were created. Dr. Murray records (*Memories,* page 306) that the only degrees given in his undergraduate days in Divinity and Law were honorary. But this, if Coutts is correct, had not always been so, for according to him, in the eighteenth century, the LL.D. degree was sometimes obtained by passing an examination and propounding and defending a thesis. In 1775 the Senate prescribed rules plainly recognising the existence of a degree of Bachelor of Laws which might be followed by a Doctorate. But in the main, despite some attempts to alter the practice, and despite a brave defence of the Doctorate after examination by Sheriff Vary Campbell in his evidence before the University Commissioners in 1878, the degree of Doctor of Laws has been given purely *honoris causa*. There are examples of the same use of LL.B. and even D.C.L. It is at least reasonably clear that in the early nineteenth century a baccalaureate of laws was being given after examination, and during the century it became customary to give the degree of Doctor only as an honour. The debasement of the degree of LL.D. in the Scottish Universities has been disadvantageous to legal scholarship. In the 1940s the Senate even saw fit to withdraw from the Dean of the Faculty of Law the right to present to the honorary degree in Law. Until the end of the century graduates in law were a rarity.

In 1874 the University, following the example of Edinburgh, created a degree of Bachelor of Law, which was and is obtainable by undergraduates who have taken no degree in Arts. The degree, like the LL.B. but with less reason, exempts from two years of a writer's apprenticeship and has become all too popular. The University Commissioners, under the Act of 1889, had some hesitation in continuing it, but continued it was and, despite much disapproval, it will probably survive all contemporary reforms, the main reason—a very bad one—being that the six years' period required for the LL.B. is felt to make too great demands on time and money. Those who think that the adequate training of our lawyers is a function no less important than the training of our doctors will find it impossible to agree.

Mode of Lecturing. There remain to be dealt with two other matters of fact: one, the method of lecturing employed by the teachers of law, and the other the relation of University teaching and qualification to the needs of the professional bodies.

The method of teaching followed to-day in the Faculty is the method of the formal lecture. This has attracted a great deal of criticism but, although in the hands of a dull and unimaginative lecturer it is probably worse than the intelligent study of a good text-book, it has much to commend it when competently handled. No student of Gloag's, for example, could have wished for anything better than his fluent, precise and interesting lectures: nobody grudged the slight labour of writing them down. The result was most valuable and the law, as he expounded it, tended to fix itself upon the memory of the student. A good many Scottish legal works are the finished and perfected lectures of University professors. There are, however, certain statements on record which suggest that different methods were at one time employed. Here, for example, is a description of Millar's style taken from Murray's *Memories* at p. 558 (though his source is obscure) 'The Professor asked questions, encouraged questions in return and the freest conversation and argument . . . he checked no inquiry; no speculation was too daring . . .' Then at a later date we have the *ipsissima verba* of Davidson giving evidence before the Commissioners in the year 1827.

In answer to the question (at p. 145 of the *Minutes of Evidence*) 'Have you examinations in your class?' the witness said (I compress a little): 'I do not pretend to examine minutely upon the substance of my lectures of the preceding day: but I point out at the end of the lecture the passages in the *Abridgement* of Erskine and the sections that relate to the lecture of that day and upon these . . . I *examine minutely* (my italics) next morning . . . in the course of the session I go over the greatest part of Erskine's *Abridgement* with my students and examine minutely upon it.' Then in answer to the question: 'Do you follow the same course in regard to Heineccius on the

Civil Roman Law?' the answer 'Yes' was given. At this time five lectures on Scots Law were given each week and three lectures on Civil Law. Students were not numerous. It is difficult to see how the Professor could expound the law at length as, say, Forbes and Millar did, and yet examine minutely from day to day. Davidson's method may have savoured more of the tutorial class and the small numbers might just have made it feasible, but it is not really easy to understand how it worked. It will be difficult to disturb the traditional mode of lecturing. After all it is less the method adopted than the ability of the lecturer which counts, and so far no method of ensuring the possession by lecturers of adequate ability has been discovered. Some approach to a tutorial system and publication of a syllabus may make for alleviation, but so long as there is a dearth of good students' text-books in Scotland so long will and must the present method persist as the sheet-anchor of the public teacher of law in Scotland.

Relations with Professional Bodies. Let us turn now for a few minutes to the relationship of the law-school in the University with the principal professional bodies.

Like other professional societies the Faculty of Advocates itself originally prescribed the qualifications which it demanded of its *Intrants*. These varied from period to period, and it would be equally difficult and otiose to follow the changes here. Attendance upon University lectures in Scots and Civil Law was long a requirement. Thus in the year 1817 we find mention of the 'long-established practice of producing certificates' of attendance at classes in these subjects. As late as 1854 we find that candidates were being examined simply on Justinian and on Erskine's *Principles*. A Latin thesis, probably then as great a farce as it is now, was also required, as well as attendance at classes for two years. By 1862 knowledge of a much wider range of subjects was being demanded, viz.: Civil Law, Scots Law, Conveyancing, Public Law (*i.e.,* Public International Law and Conflict of Laws) and Forensic Medicine. How strange is this last requirement, which still appears in the Faculty's rules and haunts the counsels of those who try to reform law ordinances. No doubt advocates have not infrequently to deal with the lay topic of medicine and medical questions. But to elevate this small field of lay knowledge into an examination subject competing in importance with vital legal topics (as in the B.L. ordinance where it is actually an alternative to juris-prudence), is to do a signal disservice to legal education. In 1854 a Committee of the Faculty of Advocates recommended that a knowledge of the subject should be made a condition of entry, although the Committee had had evidence that of six other countries (including England) only Germany required knowledge of it. The Faculty's insistence on it undoubtedly stands in the way of reform. The truth is that neither ac-countancy nor forensic medicine is a legal topic and the intrusion of these into the law faculties of Scottish universities is an anomaly.

In 1866 another Committee of the Faculty of Advocates reported against accepting a law degree in lieu of the Faculty examination. Yet eight years later, in 1874, the Faculty examiners were 'empowered to accept the degree of LL.B. granted by a Scottish University as sufficient evidence of qualification in law for admission to the Bar without further examination.' To-day most of those who are called to the Bar avail themselves of the privilege of offering the law degree of a Scottish University in lieu of a pass in the Bar examina-tion.

Up to the year 1873 the various societies of solicitors in Scotland made their own varying demands upon students in the matter of their qualifications. But by the Law Agents (Scotland) Act of 1873 one, and only one, set of minimum qualifications was imposed upon all who sought to become solicitors. Attendance at law classes in a Scottish University was one of their requirements. By an Act of Sederunt of 1878 it was for the first time prescribed that an applicant for admission who held the degree of LL.B. or B.L. need not undergo an examination in law, except in procedure.

It is plain, therefore, that there is a long-standing connection between the University and the legal professional bodies through the requirement of attendance upon classes, while in the last seventy years or so the law degree has been accepted by these bodies in lieu of a pass in their own special examinations. To-day by far the larger proportion of men entering the profession does so by way of the Universities. So far, the Bar in England has declined to accept a University degree as exempting from its examination. As Sheriff Vary Campbell said in his evidence before the Commissioners in 1878, in a sense unknown in England the qualifications for legal practice in this country are linked up with the University.

University Jurisdiction. In conclusion it is tempting and perhaps proper to mention one feature of the life of the University which, even if it proves on inquiry to have little real connection with the Faculty of Law, does suggest a connection with it. For the University is not merely a school of law: it is a body which is possessed of jurisdiction. That jurisdiction has been mainly criminal and exercised by a varying body which has consisted usually of the Rector, the Principal and certain regents or professors, and sometimes of the whole Senate. On one occasion John Satcher was confined in the steeple by the Principal for insolence, and T. Yates was later fined £18 for attempting to rescue him. Other offences which have been charged ranged in seriousness from handing in derisively the name of a fellow student to be prayed for in church, cutting a 'condisciple's' gown, drinking in an alehouse after eleven, speaking English, and wearing a sword, to stark murder. As for the murder case the verdict was 'Not Guilty,' which in view of the doubt current as to the jurisdiction was only common sense. It is amusing to see that the Bedellus sometimes acted as public prosecutor, though in the murder trial a solicitor from the town was brought in.

The whole story of the jurisdiction is so vague and incomplete that it is impossible to deal with it in small compass. We learn that even in the fifteenth century the University was apprehensive about the maintenance of the jurisdiction, but as late as the Second World War the Senate was, without a formal hearing, imposing swingeing fines on students who failed to do fire-watching. However, further mention of this feature of University life is scarcely to the present purpose, since, so far as can be discerned, no special duties were assigned to the Faculty of Law.

Conclusion. A few words by way of summing up the story of the Glasgow law-school may now be in place.

The five hundred years have seen an intermittent course of teaching, beginning with instruction in the Civil and Canon Law and ending with the wide and varied curriculum which is in force to-day. In 1451 the students were probably in the main clerics and officials: in the last two centuries they have been embryo practitioners. To-day, however, we may be seeing again the gradual return of the student-official: I hope not, unless, indeed, our curriculum can succeed in humanising the species. Yet it is remarkable that a student of 1951 could have understood not badly the lectures given in 1451, for Law is an ancient lore and Scotland owes much to that very system which was old and revered and civilised when its teaching was introduced to Glasgow in 1451. In a year when the doctor's formula might have been 'take two drachms of the spittle of an adder . . . ' and when the scientist was ploughing the infertile fields of alchemy and astrology, the Glasgow law student was quietly studying the learning of Gaius and coming to appreciate how men and nations could learn to live side by side in civilised happiness if only they would bend their stubborn necks to what their descendants were to call the 'rule of law.'

And if as a law-school we have scarcely succeeded in living up to the reputation of Bologna, our model, we can claim to have given to this island many notable lawyers. Here are the names of a few. First and foremost comes Stair, of whom up to date Glasgow has shown herself less than adequately proud. And his connection with the University, where he was both student and regent, was, amongst the great lawyers, uniquely close and prolonged. But there were many others. In Alexander Wedderburn, later Earl of Rosslyn, Glasgow produced her only Lord Chancellor. Henry Erskine was here, a far finer though less successful man than Wedderburn. Francis Jeffrey, judge and man of letters, was a Glasgow student. Lord President Miller (Lord Glenlee) an outstanding lawyer, was one of several Presidents who studied at Glasgow. Others were Ilay Campbell, David Boyle and John Inglis (the greatest of Scots judges after Stair), all three of whom were later Rectors of the University. Glasgow had two great legal antiquaries in Thomas Thomson and Cosmo Innes, even if but a share in the latter. Watson, the eminent Lord of Appeal, was also of Glasgow provenance. In modern times Strathclyde and Scott Dickson (who, as we have seen, once lectured in the University on Constitutional Law) were at the same time Lord President and Lord Justice-Clerk. Besides these men the College of Justice has for the last two hundred years always had a large number of Glasgow men amongst its members. It is impossible to read of this without realizing that our University, through its Law Faculty, has for long exerted a remarkable civilizing and humanizing effect upon the nation.

It is not really for me here to speculate upon the future of the Faculty. The way is not easy. In his evidence before the University Commissioners in 1878, Lorimer made a striking comparison of the place of law in a Scottish and a German University. At page 363 of the third volume of the Report of the Proceedings he said:

'The real reason for the pre-eminence of the Faculty of Law in a German University is that [it] embraces not only those who are to practise law, but it embraces the wide circle of those who are to exercise the public functions of the State: those who are to go into diplomacy: those who are to go into all the public offices of the government in Berlin and the other political centres: those who are to hold all the local civil employment . . . and in my opinion that is what accounts for the grand position which a German Faculty of Law holds both relatively to ours and relatively to the other faculties in the German Universities.' In an age when it seems as though science alone counted in our Universities and when the scientists with their vast demands for expenditure have forced the Scottish Universities to become partially parasitic on the State, the Faculty of Law, with its modest needs and small numbers tends to be passed over and neglected. Such claims as we make are not universally applauded. 'Unto him that hath . . . ' was never and nowhere truer than in the University to-day. This attitude on the part of our 'administrators' must be resisted if the Law Faculty is to do its work in the threatening circumstances of the hour. Somehow or other the questions which have long been agitating us—the length of the course, the clash of vocational and cultural (an absurd antithesis), the question whether the teacher shall be active in the forum or dwell in an ivory tower, the question whether the student shall also be articled, the abuse of the doctorate and the abolition of the dual baccalaureate, all these questions must be resolved if the Faculty is to flourish. And to-day the health of the Faculty of Law in all Universities is of more importance for the nation than the health of any other, since never did the rule of law stand in greater peril from the assaults of the ignorant and the unscrupulous. The calm and wise detachment of the law can be nowhere better appreciated and inculcated than in a great University, with a long tradition of honourable and disinterested teaching such as we possess. I will conclude by saying that I believe that all the public teachers of law in the University fully realize the outstanding importance of their task in the circumstances of the modern world.

MEDICINE

by

Sir John McNee

Regius Professor of Practice of Medicine

This lecture deals with the beginnings and developments of 'Medicine' in our University, a knowledge of which in the early days was simply accepted as part of a general education. The degree of M.D. in fact, generally acquired at one of the older Universities in Europe, might easily be held by a classical scholar or a bishop. Medicine, when the first Chair was founded in 1637, then included all the appropriate special knowledge or pure hypothesis of interest for a University training, and it was not considered necessary for the teacher to practice the healing art among patients at all. Surgery began as a craft, practised early in this country by the Barber Surgeons, and refined largely among the wounded on the battlefields in the era of cold steel. Surgery thus came into University teaching as a branch of 'Medicine' much later (1815), and the Obstetricians, who developed as 'men-midwives,' only a little earlier (1792). Chairs in both of these subjects were established in 1815.

Thus, in this lecture, Medicine in the early University of Glasgow includes the whole of Medicine, and the commencement and separation of a number of branches now taught separately will be briefly commented upon. Some separated from the main body of Medicine very early, others much more recently. In the later parts of this lecture Medicine will therefore be dealt with in the more restricted sense.

When the teaching of Medicine began in our University in 1637, what we would now term the scientific subjects, which form the basis of Medicine, were all in a primitive state. One man could no doubt easily be found to teach most of what was known or believed about all of them, and the University teaching was therefore inextricably mixed up. For instance, Botany and Anatomy were for long united, and since a herb-garden was essential for Materia Medica, that subject was closely allied to Botany. Materia Medica was the earliest to break away in teaching from the parent stem of Medicine, and a note on its development has been contributed by our present Regius Professor, and appears later. Chemistry in our early days was also closely related to Medicine, and in fact was the jumping-off ground of three of our most distinguished Professors of Medicine—William Cullen, James Black and Thomas Charles Hope. All three returned to Chemistry, as will be seen, to the great loss of Medicine in our University at an early and critical stage.

It is interesting here to describe how what we now term Physiology became an off-shoot of Medicine. Its first name was Theory of Physic, later changed to Institutes of Medicine and finally to Physiology. It began when Charles Badham in 1832 could not combine teaching of the theory of Physic with the more lucrative practice of Medicine in Glasgow. He chose the latter, and the writer is the Regius Professor of Practice of Medicine, a terminology not used in any other British University. Harry Rainy, as will be described in another lecture of this series, thus began to teach the Theory of Physic (Physiology) in 1832.

Other branches of Medicine, now included in University teaching and subsequently described in this lecture, have all broken off within the last hundred years, and some of them only lately.

It will be seen from the foregoing introductory remarks that it is not easy to describe the development of Medicine in our University. At the beginning Medicine included the whole—later it separated into many parts, many of them described in other lectures of this series. The same difficulty in words remains—a man enters the profession of Medicine, in the old general sense. He need not, however, remain a Physician, with the development of whose University training my lecture in its later parts must chiefly be concerned.

FOUNDATION OF THE CHAIR OF MEDICINE

The Chair of Medicine appears to be the oldest named Professorship in the University of Glasgow, Robert Mayne being appointed Professor of Medicine in 1637 to 'teache ane publict lecture of medicine in the same Colledge once or twyce everie weik, except in the ordinar tyme of vacance.' It must be pointed out, however, that at that period and dating from the foundation of the University, all business and teaching was in the hands of the Principal and three Regents. The Principal dealt mainly with Theology, but the Regents may properly be regarded as super-professors, for they each taught in turn a variety of academic subjects and not a single one. Robert Mayne became a Regent in 1635, and, because of his appointment to the Chair of Medicine in 1637, it is generally assumed that he possessed the degree of M.D. The place of his early education is unknown, but if he followed the usual course of study abroad, it may be that some day his name will be discovered on the graduate roll of one of the ancient continental universities.

In relation to what follows in connection with the history of the Chair of Medicine, and to avoid confusion, something must be said here quite briefly about the terms University, College and Faculty. A University grants Degrees, a College is a society of scholars incorporated within a University, while a Faculty may mean (and essentially does mean in Glasgow) more than one thing. The University of Glasgow had only one College from the outset, and the two terms are often used loosely in the early days with practically the same implication. Moreover, the University had only one Faculty, namely Arts, which embraced the whole body of the College. Only much later were Faculties of Theology, Law, Medicine, and still later others, developed to meet the advancing specialisation of knowledge. Robert Mayne, when appointed Professor of Medicine in 1637, did not start a new Faculty—he remained as before in the Faculty of Arts.

There was, however, another Faculty in Glasgow, nothing to do with the University or College, but in its origin a type of Trade Guild. This was the Faculty of Physicians and Surgeons of Glasgow, founded in 1599 by a Charter of James VI, and thus long ante-dating the early developments of Medicine and the Chair of Medicine within the University. This Faculty did not grant Degrees or interest itself in teaching; its general duties, rigidly upheld even against the University as will be seen, were to control the practice of medicine and surgery in the West of Scotland.

When the University was founded no plans for the teaching of Medicine or for the granting of Medical Degrees were envisaged, but it was not long before Medicine began to knock at the door. There is uncertainty about the doings of Andreas de Garlais, noted in the University Records as M.D. in 1469, and of William Manderstoun (later Rector of St. Andrews University) noted as M.D. in 1506. We must leave these two men as somewhat mysterious, but what is quite certain is that an Englishman, Samuel Benion, had the audacity to apply to be examined for M.D. in 1703. By this time the first Professor of Medicine was long dead (Robert Mayne, 1637-1646), and the Chair of Medicine had lapsed because of lack of funds. The University, however, was equal to the occasion, since fortunately one of the Regents, Robert Sinclair, who taught Mathematics, held the Degree of M.D. from some unknown University, probably abroad. He was appointed a sort of Professor Extraordinary for the occasion, and Samuel Benion duly graduated M.D., Glasgow.

In 1711 the same thing occurred again. Robert Houstoun, a well-known local surgeon, wanted the M.D. of Glasgow, and was duly examined by two Doctors of Medicine in the area, Johnstoun (later our second Professor of Medicine) and Montgomerie. To sustain the dignity of the University, the Dean of Faculty, then a clergyman, acted as Assessor and Houstoun got his M.D.

These events undoubtedly helped to hasten plans for the development of Medicine within the University which had been simmering for some time. When William and Mary came to the throne of the United Kingdom in 1689, more tranquil times came to Scotland after the great religious troubles around 1666 and 1679; and Principal William Dunlop, in 1691, went to London, to plead with the new King on behalf of the now impoverished University. He was instructed to take with him the Report of the Committee of Visitation of 1664, which stated both the parlous financial state and the other needs of the University. Among the needs referred to was the revival of the lapsed Chair of Medicine.

It was only in 1712, however, that the University began to be really interested in Medicine again, but about finance first and about a Professor afterwards. In January, 1712, probably shaken by Benion's M.D. in 1703, and Houstoun's quite recent M.D. in 1711, they decided that each candidate for the Degree of M.D. should pay a fee of £10 sterling, half to go to the Library and half to the Examiners, with twenty shillings extra to the servants. In November, 1712, the University Regents resolved that 'the professions of Law and Medicine should be revived,' and application was made to Queen Anne for a grant of funds. She was fortunately agreeable, and in December, 1713, she assigned £90 per annum as salary for a Professor of Law, but only £40 for a Professor of Medicine. The precedence of Chairs was then firmly fixed in the dignity of the University—Divinity comes first, Law second, and Medicine third.

A point of historical interest is that the University itself made its own first appointment to the revived Chair of Medicine, but ever since then the presentation to the Chair has remained firmly a prerogative of the Crown, and the Chair is thus a Regius Chair. On 1st June, 1714, Dt. John Johnstoun, M.D., Utrecht, five years previously, was appointed the second holder of the Chair of Medicine; and the present holder is the sixteenth in line.

In 1727 the Regents disappear from the University scene, and from that year onwards there were in action what are often termed the 'thirteen original Chairs' of the University, among them the Chair of Medicine.

Once the Chair of Medicine was firmly re-established in 1714, natural developments soon began to follow the gradual extension of knowledge. The separate teaching of Anatomy began in 1720, but for a whole century was combined as a Chair with Botany. The first real breakaway of a subject, still closely related to Medicine, involved Materia Medica, in which a Lectureship was established in 1766 and a Chair in 1831. Physiology (Theory of Physic) separated, as has been mentioned in the introduction, in 1832; and since then, at irregular intervals a whole series of new Chairs and Lectureships have been created which may be said properly to belong, in modern description, to the 'Division of Medicine' (in contrast, for example, to the Division of Surgery) in our University.

FACTORS INFLUENCING THE EARLY DEVELOPMENT OF MEDICINE IN GLASGOW AND GLASGOW UNIVERSITY

It is of some interest to describe the condition of Glasgow at the time the University was founded in 1451 and during the interval until Robert Mayne was named the first Professor of Medicine in 1637. In 1450 Glasgow was one of the very small townships in Scotland, with a population estimated at about 2,000. By 1560 the estimated figure was only 4,500, in which year the population of Edinburgh was about 30,000. In 1755 (Dr. Webster's unofficial census) Glasgow still had less than half the population of Edinburgh (Glasgow 23,546, Edinburgh 57,195); and it was only in the early days of the industrial era, between the National Census of 1801 and that of 1811 that Glasgow passed Edinburgh in the number of its inhabitants (1811, Glasgow 110,460; Edinburgh 102,987).

The smallness of Glasgow in these early days influenced the development of Medicine in the West of Scotland in three different ways. First, it no doubt delayed the recognition of Medicine in the University; second, it led to the formation of the Trade Guild known as the Faculty of Physicians and Surgeons; and third, it tempted away to the capital and much larger centre of Edinburgh, with its great social, intellectual and other advantages, the two real founders (Cullen and Black) of our Medical School in Glasgow University.

The manner in which the Chair of Medicine began in 1637 and its revival in 1714 after a lapse of nearly eighty years, have already been described.

Prior to either of these events, however, the Faculty of Physicians and Surgeons had been founded in 1599 by Charter of James VI in the following circumstances. Glasgow was small and poor, with a population around 7,000, and in 1600 it is stated that there were only six 'surgeons' and one physician in the town, and two midwives. The attractions for good practitioners were in fact so poor that the Town Council was compelled to subsidize, by payment, doctors to work in the town. Thus in 1599, when the early University was not at all interested in Medicine, the Town Council entered into an agreement with Maister Peter Lowe, a surgeon who had just returned from a long practical experience on the battlefields of Europe. Lowe founded the Faculty of Physicians and Surgeons almost immediately after coming to Glasgow, not to develop teaching except through the apprentice system, but to control medical and surgical practice in the district. The dispute between this Faculty (which became a Royal Faculty in 1910) and the University must be referred to later.

The loss of the real founders of Medicine in Glasgow University by their transference to the much larger capital city of Edinburgh is discussed when dealing with the Professors themselves.

A point of interest, quoted from Cowan, is the dates of foundation of Chairs of Medicine in other Universities. King's College, Aberdeen, 1505; Cambridge, 1540; Oxford, 1546; Dublin, 1618; Glasgow, 1637; Edinburgh, 1685; Marischal College, Aberdeen, 1700; St. Andrews, 1721.

SOME PROFESSORS OF MEDICINE
IN THE UNIVERSITY

It is natural, on an occasion such as this and with strict limits of time and space, to speak more of the earlier occupants of the Chair and of the notable ones. Two at least of the sixteen have been described as 'inert'; others had their peculiarities, as will be seen.

Robert Mayne (1637-1646) has the distinction of being first in line. His name is noted as one of the Regents in 1635, and no doubt he taught other subjects in addition to discoursing on the aphorisms of Hippocrates once or twice a week in term time. It is presumed that he must have held the degree of M.D. as part of his education abroad, but he certainly never practised Medicine in Glasgow. It is amusing to note that a Visitation from the General Assembly to the University in 1642 decided that the profession of medicine was 'not ncessar for the Colledge in all tyme coming.' Mayne was not disturbed in his Chair, which however at his death was allowed to lapse for nearly seventy years (Comrie). On his tombstone he is described as philosopher, orator, poet and physician—it seems unknown which of these excellencies he pursued most of all.

John Johnstoun (1714-1750), second in line after the long gap, had taken his M.D. at Utrecht in 1709, and at first may actually have practised medicine. He held the Chair for thirty-six years, but it was stated that 'he teaches little and prelects none.' In 1750 he came to an arrangement with his distinguished successor and agreed to resign so long as he was allowed to retain his house in the College for life. It seems clear that at this, and even at much later times, a house in the College was a privilege much sought after.

William Cullen (1750-1756) was appointed when forty years of age, and had previously had a remarkable education for his time. He first attended classes at Glasgow University, and then was apprenticed, as was the custom, to John Paisley, a well-known Glasgow surgeon, an anatomist and possessor of a good medical library. Thereafter Cullen went to London, and after a voyage to the West Indies with his cousin, a ship's captain, he became an apothecary. He returned to Scotland in 1731, when twenty-one years old, and spent two years 'in practice' (we might call it unqualified nowadays) at Shotts, Lanarkshire. He inherited a small legacy, and decided to better his medical knowledge; but since Glasgow could not compete at the time (Professor Johnstoun did no work), Cullen went to the active medical school in Edinburgh from 1724 to 1726. He then practised in Hamilton, where the famous William Hunter (brother of the still more famous John) was his apprentice. Cullen graduated M.D. Glasgow, in 1740, at the late age of thirty, and intended to move to Glasgow at once. He was dissuaded at first by the Duke of Hamilton (Cullen's father had been the Duke's land-agent or factor) who knew his interest in Chemistry and offered to provide both a private laboratory and a physic garden. On the Duke's death, Cullen moved to Glasgow in 1744 and at once began to teach Medicine since, as already stated, Professor Johnstoun was inert. In 1748 he also taught Materia Medica and Botany, and in 1747 Chemistry. It must be admitted that although Cullen was appointed Professor of Medicine in 1751, his real love was obviously Chemistry, and in 1755 he moved to the larger city of Edinburgh as Professor of Chemistry.

With Cullen really began the Glasgow University School

of Medicine, and his influence in Glasgow between 1744 and 1755 was profound.

Joseph Black (1757-1766) did not immediately succeed Cullen, but Robert Hamilton died three months after his appointment to the Chair. Black was, of course, Cullen's most distinguished pupil, and perhaps as famous a chemist as his teacher. He lectured both in Medicine and Chemistry, and attracted pupils from far and wide, so that the accommodation for Chemistry soon proved hopelessly inadequate. In 1766 he succeeded Cullen as Professor of Chemistry in Edinburgh, Cullen having transferred to the Chair of Institutes of Medicine (*i.e.,* Physiology). Black's influence in Glasgow was also great, and it is related that, when he left, most of his many students followed him to Edinburgh.

Various less distinguished occupants of the Chair of Medicine followed, and only a few items concerning them are of interest. Thomas Charles Hope (1789-1796) was also a well-known chemist, and he too went to Edinburgh to succeed Joseph Black in 1795. Robert Freer (1796-1827) had an adventurous career when young and was present at the Battle of Bunker Hill (1755) in the American War. He retained the Chair for thirty-one years, until his death at eighty-two. Charles Badham (1827-1841), an Englishman appointed by the Crown and unknown in Glasgow, must have been an interesting character, and was certainly a fine classical scholar (as was his son), with no fear of University authority. He soon quarrelled with the University about examination fees and refused to examine. Subsequently he was a frequent absentee from duty, and in 1841 without informing the University he sent his resignation to the Home Secretary, making the remarkable arrangement that his successor in the Chair should pay him £300 a year for life. This astonishing bargain was actually carried out, although it is known that the emoluments of the Chair of Medicine in 1861, twenty years later, were only £410 sterling. This of course did not include the fees from students, and it seems evident that the Chair of Medicine was a good financial proposition in those days.

Sir William Tennant Gairdner (1862-1900) held the Chair for thirty-eight years and lived for seven years after his voluntary retirement at the age of seventy-six. He is certainly the most distinguished practising physician to have held the Chair, and his clinical work and teaching were equally matched by his interest in Public Health. He was the first Health Officer for Glasgow (1863-1872), at a time when epidemic disease and especially typhoid and typhus fevers and smallpox were rampant. He was a contemporary of Lord Lister (Professor of Surgery 1860-1869), and the presence of these two men together in the Glasgow School of Medicine must have had an extraordinary effect. G. A. Gibson of Edinburgh, who wrote *The Life of Gairdner* in 1912, claims that Gairdner had no superior anywhere as a systematic teacher in the second half of the nineteenth century.

Samson Gemmell (1908-1913) was another great character whose sayings have been remembered to this day, although his only published work was a section of a composite book. His forte was teaching, his vocabulary enormous and pungent, and his influence on the students of his time, many of them still alive, is unlikely to be forgotten.

THE FACULTY (LATER ROYAL FACULTY) OF PHYSICIANS AND SURGEONS OF GLASGOW. ITS IMPACT ON MEDICINE IN GLASGOW AND ITS DISPUTES WITH THE UNIVERSITY

Different from London, Edinburgh and Dublin, the Glasgow physicians and surgeons always were and continue to be united in one Faculty, founded in 1599 by Maister Peter Lowe, to foster and also to control professional practice. It was a very early step for Glasgow, and the Royal College of Physicians of London, founded in 1518, is the only similar corporation which preceded it. The Royal Col-

lege of Physicians in Edinburgh began only in 1681. Gradually the Glasgow Faculty increased its power as a Trade
Guild, and it was often in conflict with the Town Council.
In 1800 it was also attacking the University, which still had
no Chair of Surgery, for the Faculty claimed that the University M.D. only allowed the graduate to practice as a pure
physician. He could not practice surgery or be in general
practice (which involved surgery) in the area, without the
licence of the Faculty. Some University graduates, holding
the M.D. degree but not the licence began general practice
in Glasgow, and in 1815 the Faculty raised an action against
them in the Court of Session, and easily won their case. In
the same year the University founded a Chair of Surgery,
and its first occupant, John Burns, had a bright idea. Why
should the University not institute a Degree in Surgery
(C.M.—Master of Surgery) as well as the Degree in Medicine
(M.D.) and thus defeat the Faculty? This was done, and
when in 1826 there were already twenty-three men holding
both University Degrees practising in the neighbourhood of
Glasgow, the Faculty raised action against the lot. The fat
was then in the fire between the University, which was
finally accepted as 'defendant' in the case, and the Faculty,
and legal action dragged on for fourteen weary years. The
case, as expected, finally went to the House of Lords, and
judgment was given in favour of the Faculty in August,
1840. It has often been stated that the Medical Act of 1858
finally deprived the Faculty of its local monopoly in regard
to the practice of Surgery. This is not correct, for in 1850
(see Duncan—Appendix VI) the Faculty applied for and
obtained a new Act for better regulating their privileges and
amending their Charter of Incorporation. The Faculty, after
long and costly litigation, was clearly in difficulties about its
Widows' and Children Fund, which was now legally
wound up. At the same time they agreed in the Act to
relax their privileges so that 'all Persons found qualified and
licenced to practice Surgery by any Corporation authorised

by law to grant such licences might have Right to practice within the said District.'

The effects of the long dispute between the University and the Faculty weakened the Glasgow School of Medicine in more than one way. First, as Dr. Alexander Duncan, historian of the Faculty, has written, 'For half a century, indeed, this lawsuit cast a chilling blight on the relations of two neighbours under obligation to live together in peace and harmony as they were working together for a common end.' Second, although the Faculty won their case, the legal expenses over fourteen years were so heavy that its financial strength has since always remained below that of the Sister Corporations (Royal College of Physicians, Royal College of Surgeons) in Edinburgh. Fortunately the long quarrel is now forgotten and the University and the Faculty (created a Royal Faculty in 1910) are now on the best of terms, and completely combine in furthering all the interests of the Glasgow Medical School.

CLINICAL TEACHING OF MEDICINE

At first, as has been indicated, the teaching of Medicine in Glasgow was entirely by lectures in the University. The history of clinical teaching naturally begins with the opening of the first *suitable* hospital—not of course by any means the first town hospital. The Royal Infirmary was opened, for 150 patients, in 1794, and the two physicians appointed were Dr. Thomas Charles Hope (later Regius Professor of Medicine in the University) and Dr. Robert Cleghorn (Lecturer in Materia Medica in the University from 1788-91, and in Chemistry 1791-1818). Hope and Cleghorn from the very outset applied for and were given permission to give lectures on medical cases, and the teaching of clinical medicine at the bedside has never since been interrupted. When the Royal Infirmary began, Glasgow was just beginning to grow rapidly in size—by 1801 its population was about 83,000 and in 1831 it was 200,000. Overcrowding and pestilences were rampant, and in 1837 it is noted (Cowan) that 74.81 per cent. of the patients admitted to the Royal Infirmary were sufferers from 'fevers'—undoubtedly a mixture of typhus and typhoid fevers, which were only identified as separate diseases a few years later. In 1851 it is recorded that 163 cases of small-pox were admitted. Clinical teaching, already firmly established, developed still more with the arrival of Sir William Gairdner in 1862, for he was not only physician to the Infirmary but the first Health Officer for Glasgow.

A great upheaval occurred in 1870 when, as is described in other lectures, the whole University moved from the East End to the West End at Gilmorehill. The Western Infirmary, designed from the outset as a Teaching Hospital close to the University, was completed in 1874; and in its Charter special provision was made that facilities for clinical teaching should always be available there for the Regius Professors of Medicine and Surgery. This change and the transfer of the two Regius Professors naturally adversely affected the prestige of the much older and larger Royal Infirmary, and this was added to by the foundation in 1874 by the University Court of Chairs of Clinical Medicine (and Clinical Surgery) also placed at the Western Infirmary. The two Professors of Clinical Medicine (McCall Anderson and Gemmell) both in turn succeeded to the Regius Chair, and the Clinical Chairs were suppressed in 1911. In the same year the balance at the Royal Infirmary was restored by the establishment of the Muirhead Chair of Medicine and the St. Mungo Chair of Surgery.

The Victoria Infirmary, opened in 1890, has never been so actively engaged in the teaching of clinical medicine to students of our University.

THE GLASGOW EXTRA-MURAL SCHOOLS OF MEDICINE

John Anderson, at first Professor of Oriental Languages but later (1757-96) Professor of Natural Philosophy, had, as Coutts states in his History of the University, a stormy and combative career. This seems odd, for his portrait apparently depicts a stout, cheerful, rather benevolent-looking man. He clearly had exceptional teaching and administrative abilities, and a strong hold on the good-will of the ordinary citizens of Glasgow; but he quarrelled bitterly with most of his University colleagues. He died in 1796, and left nearly the whole of his property to establish what was clearly to be a rival University in Glasgow, and was boldly named Anderson's University. 'Never,' says Dr. Alexander Duncan, 'was there probably an instance of wider disparity between the magnificence of the intentions of the founder of an institution and the narrowness of the means left to carry them into effect,' for the total sum available, not disclosed until years afterwards, was about £1,000. Anderson confidently envisaged four Faculties, of Arts, Medicine, Law and Divinity, and even himself nominated the first occupants of the thirty-six Chairs. The extraordinary thing is that the scheme, if never complete, worked and flourished! Some of the Faculties amalgamated with the Technical College of Glasgow in 1886, but the Medical Faculty remained until, following the recommendations of the Goodenough Report on Medical Education, it was taken over by the University in 1947. The Chair of Medicine at Anderson's University (later less grandly known as Anderson's College) gave excellent opportunities to young and aspiring teachers, two of whom later became Regius Professors of Medicine in the University. Many University students attended these lectures, for Anderson's College was close to the Western Infirmary, in addition to the extra-mural medical student working for the Triple Qualification of the Royal Colleges and Faculty. The best-known medical student of Anderson's College, who took the Licence of the Faculty only, was certainly David Livingstone, the famous missionery and explorer of Africa. He also attended some University classes in 1835-37, and the University acknowledged this by conferring on him the degree of LL.D., *in absentia,* in 1854.

St. Mungo's College, also taken over by the University

in 1947, dates from 1870, and was founded as a Medical School at the Royal Infirmary when the University departed to Gilmorehill. Its teachers of medicine were all physicians to the Royal Infirmary.

There is no doubt that, in their day, these two extra-mural Schools had a very definite effect on Medicine in Glasgow, for most of their teachers were young, vigorous and bent on making a name in the Glasgow School.

THE DEPARTMENT OF MEDICINE IN GLASGOW UNIVERSITY

Until 1938 there was no real Department of Medicine in the University, but only a lecture room and a small retiring room for the Professor. The science departments naturally developed laboratories first, the basic sciences of medicine next, and the clinical subjects last of all. Surgery, under Sir William Macewen, was far ahead of Medicine in this advance.

In the old College in High Street, the class-room of Medicine was entered by the eastern turret-stair, and was just above the reading-room. When Sir William Gairdner was appointed he was able to envelop the reading-room as well. At Gilmorehill the lecture room for Medicine remains, as from the beginning in 1870, and is also entered by a turret-stair in the east quadrangle. It is plain and austere, too small for the large number of students, and a constant pain to the Professor who must hasten from his wards at the Western Infirmary to give his lectures. Times have rapidly changed, and in 1938 a complete department, the Gardiner Institute of Medicine, containing research beds and ample laboratories, was built in the grounds of the Western Infirmary. It is hoped that before long a new and modern lecture and demonstration theatre may be built at the Western Infirmary for the various clinical subjects.

THE BRANCHES OF MEDICINE

It has already been explained how, as knowledge advanced,

many branches of Medicine were gradually compelled to break away from the parent stem.

These must now be referred to in turn, the description being modified for reasons of space from information kindly supplied by the Professors and Lecturers themselves.

MATERIA MEDICA

It is scarcely possible to give systematic instruction in Medicine without dealing also with Materia Medica and Therapeutics. Thus it seems certain that Cullen, while Professor of Medicine at Glasgow, taught Materia Medica —even though the subject 'was regarded as falling within the encyclopædic scope of the Chair of Anatomy and Botany as Surgery and Midwifery continued to be for a much longer time.' (Coutts). About the middle of the eighteenth century there was evidently a demand for a separate course of lectures in Materia Medica. Hamilton, in the Chair of Anatomy, was too busy to give it, and so the University, with Hamilton's concurrence, permitted William Irvine to teach a class. This was in 1765, and a Lectureship in the subject was created in the following year—when Irvine graduated Doctor of Medicine.

In the period of almost two hundred years of teaching of Materia Medica in Glasgow, three phases are apparent: at the beginning and at the end the teaching was guided by men of conspicuous originality and energy—Irvine, Hope and Richard Millar (our first Professor of Materia Medica, 1831) in the earlier period, and Stockman and Morris in the later one. They were separated by Couper, Easton, Cowan and Charteris, a succession of Professors whose chief interest was in private practice. In this group Robert Cleghorn, Lecturer from 1788-1791, should also be included. Before Stockman's appointment in 1897, the Professor had merely his own room and the use of a lecture theatre, and assistance was provided on a meagre scale. Such circumstances would not be considered inimical to the prosecution of research, yet it will be seen from the brief biographical notes which follow that important advances in scientific and medical knowledge were made by men who were thus handicapped.

That William Irvine (1743-1787) should have taken the initiative in teaching Materia Medica before his lectures were officially recognised by the University is highly significant of the character of the man. Irvine was a pupil of Joseph Black, the eminent chemist, and took some part in Black's classic experiments. His Lectureship in Materia Medica dated from 1765-66, and in 1769 he also became Lecturer in Chemistry. Primarily a physicist and chemist, he took a keen interest in the scientific aspects of manufacturing processes in Glasgow. The scope of his interest is revealed in the titles of some of his essays: on the Nature of Heat; on Some Principal Discoveries made by Help of the Thermometer; on Rain; on the Fertility of Soils; on Cements; on Latent Heat.

Robert Cleghorn (1755-1821) was a man of different stamp from his erudite predecessor. He was first and foremost a practitioner and one of the two earliest physicians of the Royal Infirmary. Raeburn's portrait of Cleghorn, which hangs in the Royal Glasgow Mental Hospital, depicts a handsome head and a benign expression difficult to reconcile with the character of 'Dr. Wormwood,' of whom he is reputed to be the original in 'Northern Sketches.'

Thomas Charles Hope (1766-1844) held the double lectureship in Chemistry and Materia Medica for only two years (1787-1789) before he succeeded his uncle, Alexander Stevenson, as Professor of Medicine. Although he joined the staff of Glasgow Royal Infirmary he was primarily a research worker in Chemistry, and for a time was a pupil of Dalton and Lavoisier. Hope's title to fame rests on his discovery of the element strontium and on his classical observations on the density of water.

Richard Millar (1791-1833) was Lecturer in Materia Medica for forty years, and in 1831, two years before he died, he became the first Regius Professor. He too was an active practitioner, but found time to indulge his taste for classical literature and anthropology; and in addition he was a successful teacher. In 1833 the Senate was surprised to receive Dr. John Couper's Royal Commission assigning to him the Regius Chair of Materia Medica. It then emerged that Professor Millar had resigned in a letter addressed to the Home Secretary, but the Principal of the University had not been informed. In these inauspicious circumstances Couper was admitted. Almost immediately he applied to the Faculty for a salary (no provision having been made by the Crown when the Regius Chair was created) and for an allowance of £60 to provide apparatus, but without success. Possibly soured by disappointment in the academic sphere, his writings were few and stereotyped.

John Alexander Easton (1807-1865) taught Materia Medica at Anderson's College for fifteen years before his translation to the University Chair in 1840. He was also a physician at the Royal Infirmary and acquired a large practice in the Partick district. As a man of learning, a fine teacher and an outstanding practitioner, Easton has a triple claim to be remembered in a historical review of the Glasgow School of Medicine, but in the eyes of the lay public his intellectual achievements were eclipsed by what was in a fact a trifling incident in his life—the compounding of the famous 'tonic' known as Easton's Syrup.

John Black Cowan (1829-1896) and Matthew Charteris (1840-1897) between them complete the series of practitioner-professors of Materia Medica in the latter part of the nineteenth century. After serving in the Crimea, Cowan returned to a Lectureship in Materia Medica at Anderson's College and eight years later became Lecturer in the Practice of Medicine there. In 1865 he was appointed Regius Professor of Materia Medica, but by this time he had an extensive practice and was adviser to several insurance societies.

Charteris, like his predecessor, served first at the Anderson College where he taught Medicine for a few years before his appointment to the University Chair of Materia Medica in 1880. His time was increasingly devoted to private practice and thought he professed a keen interest in the teaching of practical therapeutics he had no hospital appointment.

Stockman will always be remembered as one of the remarkable men associated with Glasgow University. He possessed many of the attributes which make for greatness in any walk of life—a fine intellect, general culture and wide experience, and independence amounting almost to austerity. His philosophy emerges clearly in a masterly historical essay on James Lind—a man very much after his own heart; his outlook was eclectic and there were few things he valued more highly than originality.

In 1897 he came from Edinburgh to the Chair of Materia Medica in Glasgow and remained for nearly half a century. The original department in the main building at Gilmorehill was poorly equipped, but it is recorded that 'a retiring room was immediately fitted up as a laboratory and research was set on foot at once; the beginning of a museum was made in a store-room.' Stockman was also soon appointed Physician to the Western Infirmary, an incident which at the time created very lively local controversy. With this new commitment and his academic duties he combined a considerable consulting practice, but still continued to carry out original research. His early papers include reports on the pharmacology of nicotine, iodides, bromides, arsenic, phosphorus and certain heavy metals. Out of his extensive experience of rheumatic diseases he published his well-known book 'Rheumatism and Arthritis' and numerous papers on the salicylates; and at the end of his clinical appointment he spent the last few years of his professional career in the investigation of lathyrism and kindred diseases.

When Noah Morris succeeded Stockman in 1936, decisions of far-reaching importance were made. The Professorship became a full-time appointment and a clinical unit was made available at Stobhill Hospital by arrangement between the

University and the Corporation of Glasgow; thus the practice of combining the teaching of pharmacology and therapeutics with clinical medicine, begun forty years before, was allowed to continue. Morris was by training a physiologist and bio-chemist with a lively interest in the application of laboratory techniques to the investigation of clinical problems. Unlike his predecessor, he was convinced that animal experimental pharmacology should be developed in the Department, and a senior lectureship in experimental pharmacology was created by the University Court in 1949.

MENTAL DISEASES

Until the beginning of the nineteenth century all mentally afflicted persons in the Glasgow area were confined in cells in the Town's Hospital, which had been opened in 1740 on the bank of the Clyde just west of the present Stockwell Bridge. This hospital, it is recorded (see Cowan), contained 'six vaulted cells for mad people, the first of that kind in North Britain, well suited for their purpose.' These cells were on the ground floor, sometimes inundated by water and always damp. Concerned at this state of affairs, a director of the hospital, Robert McNair, the Dean of Guild, appealed for funds to improve the accommodation of these patients. The response was sufficient to provide a new Asylum for the Insane to the north of Parliamentary Road on a site now occupied by Buchanan Street Station Goods Yard. One of the original physicians was Robert Cleghorn (1755-1821), already mentioned as Lecturer in Materia Medica at the Uni-versity, and physician not only to the Town's Hospital but also one of the first appointed to the new Royal Infirmary in 1794. This asylum was opened with great ceremony in 1814 and its rules show that very humane treatment was employed from the outset. The activity of this hospital, which became a Royal Asylum by Charter in 1824, continued unabated until the opening of the present building in extensive grounds at Gartnavel in 1843.

The University first became interested in the teaching of mental diseases to its students in 1880, when a lectureship was created and held until 1905 by Dr. David Yellowlees, the Physician Superintendent of the Glasgow Royal Asylum. At first the attendance of students was voluntary, but the class was made compulsory in 1892. Since then two further lectureships have been instituted, and in 1948 a full-time Chair of Psychological Medicine was established by the University Court, with Dr. T. Ferguson Rodger as the first Professor.

DISEASES OF CHILDREN

In 1882 the first Hospital for Sick Children in Glasgow began in a small way in two converted private houses at 45 Scott Street, Garnethill. It was staffed mainly by physicians and surgeons from the Western Infirmary and in 1888 a dispensary for out-patients was opened nearby in West Graham Street. At this time Diseases of Children was not regarded as a special branch of Medicine, and even at Great Ormond Street Hospital, London, the staff were almost all clinicians in charge of wards at adult teaching hospitals. The recognition of Diseases of Children as a speciality only really came about in Glasgow, as indicated below, in 1919.

Work is still carried on at the Dispensary at the present time, but in 1914 the old hospital in Scott Street was closed and the newly built Royal Hospital for Sick Children at Yorkhill opened. Here there was accommodation for two hundred and eighty children and the hospital was at that time, with one exception, the largest children's hospital in Britain.

Some instruction to medical students had been given at the original hospital since 1888, and in 1914 this became compulsory. After the First World War in 1919 instruction for medical students was put on a firmer basis by the appointment of Dr. Leonard Findlay to a newly-founded Lectureship in Medical Pædiatrics, endowed by Mr. Leonard Gow, a Glasgow shipowner. In 1924 the Samson Gemmell Chair of Medical Pædiatrics (renamed Child Health in 1947) was established with Findlay as the first Professor.

DERMATOLOGY

One of the main clinical interests of Sir Thomas McCall Anderson, Regius Professor of Practice of Medicine from 1900 to 1908, was the study of diseases of the skin. On his death the directors of the Glasgow Hospital for Skin Diseases founded a University Lectureship in his memory, while at the same time the whole work of the hospital was ended and transferred to the Western Infirmary, where wards with a distinctive entrance and an out-patient department were provided. The first Lecturer appointed, in 1909, was Dr. Wyllie Nicol.

INFECTIOUS DISEASES

Glasgow has always had a high incidence of the epidemic disease, and severe outbreaks of plague, cholera, typhus and relapsing fever are found in its history. A century ago typhus and cholera were still major diseases, the last epidemic of cholera occurring in 1866. Smallpox was so common that absence of the characteristic scarring of the face was unusual among Glasgow citizens. The city was fortunate in its early pioneers in Public Health, for, as has been mentioned, Sir William Gairdner combined the offices of Regius Professor of Medicine and first Health Officer for the city. He was succeeded in 1872 by Dr. James Burn Russell who held the post of Medical Officer of Health until 1898. It is not too much to say that Russell's work in Glasgow was both astonishing and outstanding. Under him the special Fever Hospitals of Glasgow rapidly developed, and both their work and the men who worked in them have always had a high reputation throughout the whole of Britain. Of past physicians and teachers in the Fever Hospitals of Glasgow the name of Dr. John Brownlee, first of Belvidere and later of Ruchill Fever Hospital, must not be forgotten, and will never be forgotten by his students and house physicians.

The teaching on acute infective fevers was for long quite loosely organised. It was compulsory, but the student could attend any approved Fever Hospital and obtain a Certificate of Attendance. In 1946 a Lectureship in Infectious Diseases was founded by the Court, the first occupant being Dr. Thomas Anderson.

EPILOGUE

I have tried, in this Lecture, to give an account of the development of Medicine in our University both in a broad and in a restricted sense. When the first Chair of Medicine was created in 1637, it was 'everything'; but since then Medicine has given birth to a large number of University children, all grown up and flourishing, and some of them even with children of their own in University Chairs and Lectureships.

The old and original Chair remains, but some may doubt, in this age of specialism, whether after three hundred years it may have more to do than gracefully expire. Personally, I do not think so, and hope that the Regius Chair of Practice of Medicine will attract in future men just as distinguished as some of my predecessors.

I have also tried to tell of the impact of the Royal Faculty of Physicians and Surgeons of Glasgow, and of the Extra-Mural Schools (Anderson's and St. Mungo's Colleges) on our medical development, since the influence of both was profound.

Finally, with the help of colleagues in Chairs and Lectureships, which I gratefully acknowledge, I have briefly sketched the history of some of the subjects which belong essentially to practical medicine.

I have omitted reference to the Basic Sciences of Medicine, which are to be dealt with fully in other lectures.

SURGERY

by

C. F. W. Illingworth
Regius Professor of Surgery

Five hundred years ago the fair town of Glasgow had little need for surgeons. Its people, few in numbers, were of virile stock. Market and cloister brought a modest prosperity and the nearby countryside gave good victualling. In the simple doctoring of this small pastoral community, there can have been few calls for a surgeon's skill, and of these we may suppose that such common tasks as the letting of blood and the lancing of boils played a major part.

Nor, had the need for surgical skill been greater, could it have been satisfied readily. Five hundred years ago the practice of surgery the world over had altered little since the time of the Pharaohs, limited as it was to the treatment of wounds and abscesses and such operations of necessity as could be performed without anæsthesia. It was neither an art nor a science, but a crude menial task, beneath the dignity of physicians, and relegated to men of lowly status who were fain to be ranked with barbers.

That progress has been made since that time, both in the state of surgical practice and the status of its practitioners, is due to the labours of many men in many fields, and our University has shared with other schools the fruits of their endeavours. But, more than this, our University has made its own particular contribution, and indeed some of the most momentous and memorable advances have been made within its very walls. In tracing the history of surgery in this University, therefore, and in following the achievements of its alumni, we shall tread the main highway of surgical advance from 1451 to the present time.

In 1451, even such surgeons as there were would have found little scope for their ambitions in the small town of Glasgow, and so it remained for more than two hundred years. Thus it came about that in 1748, when the young John Hunter left his farm at Long Calderwood to set out on his surgical career, it was to London, rather than Glasgow, that he turned his steps.

Only towards the end of the eighteenth century, when the Colonial trade began to make Glasgow a thriving centre of commerce, did the picture change; but then it changed rapidly, so that by 1815, when the Regius Chair of Surgery was founded, the busy city, with its population now grown to over a hundred thousand, must have provided its first incumbent with ample scope for his teaching and practical skill.

REGIUS CHAIR OF SURGERY

The Regius Chair of Surgery was founded in 1815 under Charter from King George III. The first degree in Surgery (Chirurgiae Magister: C.M.) was granted in 1817. The number of graduates averaged about twenty a year until 1841, but from then until 1861 the number was much smaller, commonly one or two and rarely more than five. This was the period during which the Royal Faculty of Physicians and Surgeons exercised its right to control the practice of surgery in the West of Scotland, to the detriment of University graduates. After the passage of the Medical Act in 1858 the number of surgical graduates again rose, reaching a hundred annually by the eighteen eighties.

The degree of Bachelor of Surgery (Ch.B.) was first granted in 1819, but discontinued three years later until 1897, when it replaced the C.M., as normal requirement for a surgical practitioner. The Mastership now became a higher qualification awarded after special study and on presentation of a thesis. After 1911 its designation was changed to Ch.M.

John Burns, M.D., F.R.S. The first Professor was John

Burns. He was the son of the Reverend John Burns of the Barony Church, the brother of the two founders of the Burns Shipping Line, and uncle to the first Lord Inverclyde.

John Burns was destined to achieve distinction in the world of medicine no less than his brothers in commerce. In 1794, at the age of twenty, he became the first House Surgeon to the Royal Infirmary, which was then newly built on its fine site close to the Cathedral. At the end of his house appointment, he took up general practice. In those days, in Glasgow, Surgery was not a distinct speciality, and throughout his lifetime Burns practised the full range of Medicine with Obstetrics as well as Surgery. Nor was the possession of a hospital appointment deemed essential for one engaged in the practice of Surgery or in its teaching. Burns held the post of Surgeon to the Royal Infirmary only for short periods on two occasions (1797-99 and 1809-10), but from then onwards, and throughout the whole period of his tenure of the Chair, his sole opportunities for the conduct of his surgical work were those presented by his general practice. Even more remarkable to us is the fact that for some years, while he was Professor of Surgery, he was also on the staff of the Infirmary as a physician.

Long before his appointment to the Chair, Burns had gained a notable reputation for his teaching ability. As a Professor at the Andersonian University (which subsequently became Anderson's College of Medicine) he became known as a teacher of Anatomy, Midwifery and Surgery, while in 1797, during one of his brief periods on the Infirmary staff, he was the first to engage in the teaching of Surgery at the bedside. Nor was his reputation a local one. In 1809 he published a book on the *Principles of Midwifery* which carried his fame far beyond his native city. Evidently it was a popular text-book and widely read, for it ran to ten editions and some foreign translations.

His later work on the *Principles of Surgery* makes interesting reading and gives an admirable picture of the scope of surgery at that time. Its five hundred pages are devoted, for the most part, to Inflammation, Suppuration and the Complications of Wounds, while the operations described are mostly those concerned with injuries and the arrest of hæmorrhage. Of the diseases which make up the great bulk of surgical practice at the present day there is no mention. Written in the flowery style of the period, with literary allusions—and allusions not devoid of playful malice towards his surgical contemporaries—it reveals a gentleman of culture and something of a philosopher. Despite these attractive features, alas, the book seems to have been less highly valued than his work on Obstetrics, for it failed to achieve a second edition.

Burns occupied the Chair for thirty-five years. He died at the age of seventy-six from drowning, when the steamship *Orion,* on passage from London to Glasgow, on a clear moonlight night foundered off the rocky coast of Wigtownshire.

James Adair Lawrie, M.A., M.D. Burns was followed by James Lawrie, who occupied the Chair from 1850 to 1859. Little is recorded of Lawrie's works, and he does not appear to have made the contribution to Surgery or to have enjoyed the wide reputation of his predecessor. Perhaps he was content to 'cultivate his garden' rather than woo renown. Certainly he seems to have given useful service to the medical fraternity in Glasgow, for he was one of the promoters of the Medico-Chirurgical Society and for a time he was editor of the *Glasgow Medical Journal.* For many years also he represented the Universities of Glasgow and St. Andrews on the General Medical Council.

Joseph Lister, M.B., F.R.S. (later Baron Lister of Lyme Regis). If the historian can find little of substance to record about the second Regius Professor, it is far otherwise with the third. Joseph Lister's life and works have been the subject of many biographies and innumerable other writings, for they constitute a most important chapter in the history of Surgery and indeed in the age-long story of man's war against disease.

To appreciate Lister's contribution fully, it is necessary to recall to mind the state of surgical hospitals in his day. In 1860 when Lister came to Glasgow, this great city with its crowded population—now swollen to nearly half a million—presented a surgical problem the like of which had not been seen before, nor will again. No longer were its diseases those of a simple farming community, for now busy workshops and streets brought innumerable injuries, city murk and meagre diet fostered malnutrition and deformities, crowded tenements harboured all manner of infective diseases.

These city ills were reflected and magnified in the state of its hospitals, for there the bacteria of wound sepsis flourished, breeding in the fœtid discharges and gaining in virulence as they spread from one patient to the next, so that the wards teemed with suppuration, phagedæna, erysipelas and the dreaded hospital gangrene, and even the simplest operation carried a high risk of death. It was not surprising, therefore, that, although the introduction of anæsthesia had abolished pain, most surgeons feared to operate and their work was still, for the most part, limited to amputations, the removal of superficial cancers, and similar operations of necessity.

Lister's discovery brought this state to an end and indeed marked a new epoch in Surgery, for it paved the way to all manner of elective operations, not only on the limbs but within the body cavities, so that in turn the abdomen, the thorax and the skull yielded access to the healing knife.

The main incidents in Lister's career are well known: his Quaker birth and upbringing, his student days at University College, his move to Edinburgh where he quickly gained the friendship of Syme and the affections of Syme's daughter, his appointment to the Regius Chair in Glasgow in 1860, his return to Edinburgh in 1869 and to London in 1877, his death in 1912. Of his long career only nine years were spent in Glasgow, but it is gratifying to reflect that this short span was the most active and fruitful period of his life, for it covered the time in which his great idea was conceived and brought forth, leaving only its detailed application to be the occupation of his later years.

Now, over eighty years later, one may attempt to assess Lister's work objectively, free from the adulation and equally the antagonism which marked the divisions among his coevals and immediate successors. His debt to Pasteur was, of course, never in question. It was Pasteur who established beyond doubt that fermentation, whether in wines or other organic liquors, is due to the action of living microbes and can be prevented if these organisms be destroyed or denied access. Lister's part was to recognise that Pasteur's discovery could be applied to putrefaction in wounds and that this process also could be prevented by the exclusion of bacteria.

It has been asserted that Lister was not the first to discover the infective nature of wound sepsis nor to treat it by antiseptics, and there is indeed a grain of truth in this assertion. Many years earlier, Gordon in Aberdeen had noted the contagious nature of puerperal sepsis, Semmelweiss in Vienna had shown how to prevent it by hygienic measures, and Oliver Wendell Holmes had brought their findings to the notice of the world. Only a year before Lister's discovery, Spencer Wells had commented on the relation of Pasteur's findings to hospital sepsis, and indeed had clearly recognised bacteria to be its cause. It fell to Lister, however, to see the whole problem clear, to follow the argument to its logical conclusion, and finally, having been accorded the revelation, to devote his whole life to its propagation.

Doubtless if Lister had failed to divine the truth, someone else would have done so very soon, perhaps Spencer Wells himself or some younger man now doomed to obscurity. But such speculations are unprofitable. It is much more to the point to enquire how Lister came to be the instrument; what innate virtue or outward event determined that he should be the one to lay bare the secret. Was it pure chance, or he outcome of long tedious research or, as most people will agree, a fine example of Dr. John Brown's 'happy guessing,' the ευστοχια of Aristotle, blended of profound knowledge, long study and the final flash of genius?

It is clear that the problem of wound sepsis had been in his thoughts for many years, but he was not alone in this, nor was he the only surgeon to seek its remedy. He had, however, the inestimable advantage, rare among surgeons of his day, of a scientific upbringing, which enabled him to appreciate the problem fully and to work logically from one advancing step to the next. His training was indeed that of the research worker. From his father he inherited a scientific bent and acquired proficiency in the use of the microscope. As a student under Sharpey he had preferred Physiology to the usual surgical apprenticeship of the dissecting room. His first researches were on physiological problems. As a young teacher he spoke more on the science of disease than on surgical handicraft. As a young surgeon he had few patients in his consulting-room, but frogs, mice and occasionally even a calf in the wash-house. When Pasteur gave him the clue, he was ready to follow it to a successful conclusion.

In 1869 Lister returned to Edinburgh to succeed his old chief and father-in-law in the Chair of Clinical Surgery. His place was taken by George H. B. Macleod.

Sir George Husband Baird Macleod, M.D.,LL.D., F.R.S.E. Macleod came of a distinguished family of divines. His grandfather had occupied the manse of Fiunary in the parish of Morven; his father was minister to Campsie and later to St. Columba's church in Glasgow. His brother was the famous Norman Macleod of the Barony church and minister to Queen Victoria.

Tall and handsome, of commanding presence and dignified bearing, he became a notable figure in the medical world of his day. He excelled as a teacher, for he had a special gift for imparting instruction, with great powers of illustration and description. As befitted his clerical stock, his teaching was orthodox and dogmatic, his presentation sonorous and elegant. He could fill his class-room and compel his students as his brother held the congregation at the Barony or Crathie church.

In his younger days, Macleod was a teacher of surgery at Anderson's College. On his appointment to the Chair, he was given charge of surgical wards at the Royal Infirmary. Five years later, in 1874, when the newly-built Western Infirmary opened its doors, Macleod was translated thither, and there remained until his death in 1892.

Sir William Macewen, M.D., LL.D., F.R.S. Curators of patronage rarely find their task so easy as did the advisors to the Crown on this occasion, for here was William Macewen at hand, already at the height of his world-wide reputation, a man second only to Lister in his contributions to Surgery, and perhaps his equal or even superior in his contributions to the fame of the Glasgow School.

Macewen had been a pupil of Lister's and was one of the first to adopt and develop the antiseptic system. Appointed as surgeon to the Royal Infirmary at the early age of twenty-eight, he soon outstripped his master in the scope and magnitude of his surgical achievements.

Revelling in the new freedom to which Lister had given the key, and endowed with the energy, enterprise and supreme confidence of the pioneer, he extended the range of surgery to almost every part of the body and established himself as a master of his craft in such diverse fields as the bones and joints, the brain, the ear and the lungs, while in the sphere of science his writings on bone growth, on intracranial infections, on aneurysm and a dozen other subjects have left a permanent memorial to the originality of his mind no less than the wide compass of his interests.

Most of Macewen's original contributions were made during his surgeonship at the Royal Infirmary, and the decade 1880-90 was marked by a succession of notable occasions which gained for him world-wide recognition and raised the Glasgow School to a pinnacle of fame. When the Regius Chair became vacant in 1892 his appointment was a foregone conclusion, and during the next thirty-one years he reigned supreme and unchallenged, solitary, masterful, arrogant, intolerant and indeed selfish, but a magnificent surgeon and in his generation unique in his contributions to surgical science.

Archibald Young, B.Sc., M.B.C.M. Masterful men suffer no rivals, and Macewen founded no school. When he died there were few to follow in his train. His successor, Archibald Young, assumed a task of peculiar difficulty, and it is a tribute to his strength of character and purpose that the traditional lustre of the office was kept undimmed during the succeeding fifteen years.

Young's death is so recent and his memory so fresh in our minds that no more than a brief recital of his work is needed. It is sufficient to put on record that he enjoyed a high reputation for his skill in a wide field of surgery and in particular for his work on the sympathetic nervous system, while his contributions to the surgical literature gained world-wide recognition.

THE UNIVERSITY AND THE HOSPITALS

We have seen that in 1874 the Regius Chair, hitherto related, though informally, to the Royal Infirmary was translated to the newly-opened Western Infirmary. It will be convenient at this point to break the narrative in order to review the development of these and other teaching hospitals and their relationship to the University Chairs of Surgery.

The old Royal Infirmary had been erected in 1792-4 on the site of the ruins of the Archbishop's castle close to the west of the Cathedral. The most active of those responsible for its foundation was the Professor of Logic in the University, George Jardine. Despite this informal connexion the hospital had no direct association with the University and no responsibility to provide for clinical teaching. The earlier Professors of Surgery did not teach in hospital and indeed did not necessarily hold hospital appointments. Even Lister on assuming the Chair was compelled to wait for nearly two years before being elected to a surgeonship on the Infirmary staff. Admittedly the students 'walked the wards' then as they do now, and by so doing gained the practical experience of their craft, but this apprenticeship was a thing apart from their training in the art and science of their profession.

In the eighteen-sixties the growing riverside population to the west of the city imposed the need for a second hospital, and when in 1870 the University moved to Gilmorehill it was clearly desirable to build this new hospital close to it. Thus arose the Western Infirmary. Originally it was designed as a 'University Hospital'; a grant obtained by the University from Government sources provided the nucleus of the building fund, the University Court was to have a controlling interest and the building was planned primarily to provide for the clinical teaching requirements of the two Professors. Later this plan was seen to be inadequate, and eventually it was decided to build a general hospital, to be administered by an independent Board, though with a close affiliation to the University.

Later still (1890) the Victoria Infirmary was built to provide for the needs of the growing south side of the city, and it too became recognised as a teaching hospital, though by reason of its distant situation it never acquired the close University connexion of the older institutions. Still more recently the former municipal hospitals, Stobhill and the Southern General Hospital, have been accorded a similar status, while finally, to carry this part of our history up to the present day, the University, by virtue of its special powers under the National Health Service Act, has been enabled to seek teaching facilities in any hospital throughout the region.

THE CLINICAL AND ST. MUNGO CHAIRS

In the early days of the Regius Chair, as we have seen, there was no formal connexion between the University and the Royal Infirmary, and even in Lister's day the Professor might find himself without a hospital appointment. In the time of Lister's successor, Macleod, it was decided to translate the Regius Chair to the Western Infirmary, and this move was made as soon as that institution was opened in 1874.

In the same year a second Surgical Chair was established with the support of an endowment of £2,500 provided by the family of the late Dr. Moses Steven Buchanan, a worthy surgeon who had taken a notable part in the affairs of the Royal Infirmary. It was named the Chair of Clinical Surgery, and it too was installed at the Western Infirmary, so that now, and for thirty-seven years to come, the Royal Infirmary was deprived of its University connexion.

To repair this loss of teaching facilities, in 1875 the Managers of the Royal Infirmary obtained a Charter which enabled them to set up a new medical school, and with support by public and private subscription it opened its doors in the following year. In 1889 the School became part of St. Mungo's College, a body set up under the Companies Act with a separate Board of Governors, and including a Faculty of Medicine.

It became clear, however, that separation from the University was harmful to both sides, and in 1911 the former connexion was restored. In that year the Chair of Clinical Surgery at the Western Infirmary was suppressed, and replaced by a new Chair tenable at the Royal Infirmary. It was given the title St. Mungo Chair of Surgery, the emoluments were augmented by funds provided by St. Mungo's College and the patronage was vested in a special Court of Curators, nominated jointly by the University, the Managers of the Royal Infirmary and the Governors of St. Mungo's College. Thus arose the situation which has continued until the present day, in which two Surgical Chairs of similar function and equal status are maintained, one at each of the principal hospitals.

George Buchanan, M.A., M.D. LL.D. The first incumbent

of the Chair of Clinical Surgery was George Buchanan. He was the son of Dr. Moses Buchanan, a surgeon and an early historian of the Royal Infirmary. The new Professor had served in the Crimean War and on his return had gained a reputation as a bold and skilful surgeon. Among other notable achievements he was one of the first to excise the upper jaw for malignant disease, and introduced new operations for the cure of hernia and various congenital deformities. He held office for twenty-six years.

Sir Hector Clare Cameron, C.B.E., M.D., LL.D. Hector Cameron, who succeeded to the Clinical Chair in 1900, was a pupil and disciple of Lister and his biographer. Cameron was a man of gracious personality, a speaker with an Augustan love of the polished phrase and a master of English prose. His interests were clinical rather than scientific and his major contribution was to expand and illustrate the new methods of Surgery to which Lister had opened the door. Cameron retired from the Chair in 1911 and thereafter, for a number of years, adorned the office of Dean of Faculties.

Robert Kennedy, M.A., M.D., B.Sc. Robert Kennedy was the first occupant of the St. Mungo Chair which he held from 1911 to 1924. He gained recognition for his researches on the regeneration of nerves and nerve transplantation and became adept in the treatment of injuries and other affections of the nervous system. Kennedy enjoyed a reputation as a bold surgeon and brusque, plain-spoken man, whose uncompromising views on many aspects of surgical treatment brought him into frequent conflict with that other individualist Macewen.

Peter Paterson, M.D., C.M. Kennedy was succeeded in 1924 by Peter Paterson, who held office until 1935 and now enjoys a quiet and honourable retirement.

NON-PROFESSORIAL TEACHERS

These then were the Professors of Surgery, a notable company of men who did much to spread the fame of our University and to enrich the art and science of their profession. But the fortune of a medical school does not rest wholly on the Professors; it draws its strength also from the independent clinical teachers, the physicians and surgeons of the teaching hospitals. Particularly is this so in Scotland where the tradition of clinical teaching holds strong; where every hospital Chief counts it a duty to devote much time and preparation to the instruction of his students and where, to tell the truth, there are some who have outshone the Professor in this particular field.

Among these men, who without University distinction have excelled in this honourable duty, were Beatson, who devoted himself to the study of cancer, founded the Radium Institute of the Cancer Hospital, and gained wide fame as originator of the operation of öophorectomy in the treatment of breast cancer; Maylard and Kennedy Dalziel, two pioneers in the surgery of the abdomen; Pringle, an authority on melanoma and on hip dislocation and a critical student of many other surgical disorders; and Parry, who by his spirited and inspiring teaching attracted large numbers of students to the newly opened Victoria Infirmary. Nor were the special branches of surgery less fortunate, for they included William Mackenzie, a leading ophthalmologist of his day, and J. R. Wolfe who anticipated the modern operation of cornea grafting by seventy-five years, and originated one method of skin grafting; Brown Kelly, who became a recognised authority on diseases of the larynx and is famed as one of the first to describe a well-known syndrome; and his close colleague Gray who gained wide renown for his work on Otosclerosis and other diseases of the ear.

THE CHANGING FIELD OF SURGERY

In following the careers and achievements of the surgical Professors and other teachers, we have caught glimpses as from a moving train of the changes taking place in the surgical landscape from 1451 until the present day. Let us now retrace our steps to study some of these developments more closely.

We have seen that modern surgery did in truth start with Lister, here in Glasgow. He was the Columbus who discovered the New World of Surgery. His pupil Macewen was one of the first and most successful of the prospectors who rushed to traverse and explore the unknown prairie country, and by the time of his death nearly every frontier had been approached. Since then many surgeons in many countries have followed in their wake and consolidated their victories, while such territory as they have failed to occupy has now been sought out and conquered.

The University is five hundred years old, the Gilmorehill building only eighty; but during these eighty years the whole face of Surgery has altered, and Lister, if he could return, would not recognise it. Such septic infections as resisted Lister's carbolic have yielded to sulphonamides and penicillin. Diseases which Lister knew have disappeared from ken, for example, the rickety deformities which Macewen straightened in hundreds and which now are rarely seen. Other diseases that Lister knew not have sprung into being; among them appendicitis and peptic ulcer now head the list of hospital admissions. Finally, achievements which Lister by no flight of the imagination could have foretold have now been brought to fruition—among them the surgery of the gullet, the pancreas, the great vessels and even the heart itself.

These years of progress have brought with them many other changes in the surgical scene. One of the most notable in recent years has been the emergence of the surgical specialities. A hundred years ago, Dr. John Burns could encompass the whole field of surgery and obstetrics while yet in general medical practice: only thirty years ago, Macewen unassisted could still master the whole field of surgery: now their successors are content to win fame in much more limited territories.

Ophthalmology was the first branch of surgery to form

a distinct speciality, following the invention of the Ophthalmoscope in 1850. Later Laryngology and Otology went the same way and by the end of the century Gynæcology also became recognised as a special subject. Our University has set its seal upon these changes by instituting Chairs in two of the subjects (Ophthalmology and Gynæcology) and Lectureships in the others.

In recent years the division of Surgery into separate specialities has gone further, with the formation of special departments of Orthopædics, Neurosurgery, Urology, Thoracic and Plastic Surgery. The Barclay Lectureship in Pædiatric Surgery was instituted in 1919 and the Frederick Young Lectureship in Orthopædics in 1942; while more recently still the special branches of Neurosurgery, Thoracic Surgery and Plastic Surgery have been recognised by Honorary Lectureships.

One important though perhaps not obvious effect of these changes has been to bring more closely together the two great divisions of Surgery and Medicine. It was Pope Innocent III who, in 1215, by his Ordinance *Ecclesia abhorret a sanguine* prohibited clerics from bloodshed and thus confirmed the distinction between priestly physicians and profane surgeons. While the difference of status has long been resolved (though surgeons by an inverted form of pride still disdain the courtesy title Doctor) the difference in function has been maintained so that until recently physicians spurned the knife, surgeons scoffed at drugs. The changes in medical and surgical treatment, and the specialisation called forth by the increasing complexity of both, have done much to break down the barrier. In each particular compartment the surgeon must know more and more about the medical aspects of his speciality. the physician more about operative technique. In places, indeed, the barrier has gone. In some branches, such as Gynæcology and diseases of the eye, ear, nose and throat, every specialist combines the duties of a physical and surgeon, while in others, such as Neurology and chest diseases, the same tendency is apparent. The harmful schism of 1215 may soon be brought to an end.

The lay observer, presented with this confusing picture, may well ask himself what are the scope and limitations of a surgeon's work; in short, what is Surgery? Scientific papers begin with a definition of their subjects, so it is perhaps fitting that this unscientific essay should end on the same key.

The old assumption that a surgeon is concerned only with the manual skill required for performing an operation no longer holds good. The 'operating surgeon' whose work began and ended in the surgical theatre is no more. The modern surgeon is a physician who, as part of his treatment, may have recourse to the knife.

But the record of our University's own sons tells us that Surgery means even more than this. It was said of John Hunter that he found surgery little more than a trade and made it a science. For him, skill in operating was matched by zeal for knowledge. He asked not what was the name of a man's disease but why the disease had started and how it might have been prevented. Lister followed the same path, and his biological investigations into the causes of sepsis changed the whole face of surgery. Macewen, too, though a dexterous operator, attained world fame mainly by the fruits of his scientific enquiries. For us, as for our great predecessors, the practice of surgery brings to light many problems relating to the causes and prevention of disease, and it is part of our duty to endeavour by study and research to provide their solution.

MEDICAL SCIENCES I
(a) ANATOMY

by

G. M. Wyburn
Regius Professor of Anatomy

'Nor can we easier discover the secret recesses, and dark principles of Generation than the method of the fabrick and composure of the whole world. In this reciprocal interchange of Generation and Corruption consists the Æternity and Duration of mortal creatures. And as the Rising and Setting of the Sun, doth by continued revolutions complete and perfect Time; so doth the alternative vicissitude of Individuums, by a constant repetition of the same species, perpetuate the continuance of fading things'—Harvey's 'De Generatione Animalium' (1651).

The Chair of Anatomy at Glasgow University was founded in 1718, in the reign of George I, and until 1818 was coupled with the Chair of Botany. An annual payment of £30 was to be made to the Professor of Anatomy by the Crown. It was the eleventh Chair founded in Glasgow University and was preceded in the Medical Faculty by the Chair of Medicine. When Johnstoun was appointed to the resurrected Chair of Medicine in 1714 it was decided that instruction in Anatomy should be given in the University and John Gordon, a Glasgow surgeon, was allotted this task. Before 1714, it is probable that such anatomical instruction as was available for medical students in Glasgow was given by the Visitor of the Faculty of Physicians and Surgeons. The first Professor of Anatomy was Thomas Brisbane who occupied the Chair from 1720 to 1742. Brisbane had practised as a physician in Glasgow along with his father, Dr. Matthew Brisbane. At this time, the teaching of anatomy consisted of lectures, together with dissections of the human body by the professor and his assistants. The records indicate that the first Professor of Anatomy had little or no interest in the subject, and his duties in this respect were undertaken by a succession of surgical colleagues including his successor, Robert Hamilton, who retained the Chair until 1756 when he succeeded Cullen as Professor of Medicine. Hamilton was essentially a physician, an M.D. of Glasgow and at one time President of the Faculty of Physicians and Surgeons. He did, however, teach anatomy—it is said with considerable skill. In the midst of the recurring Jacobite eruptions and the conflicting loyalties of the time, anatomy provided a safe and neutral subject for discourse and discussion.

In his progress towards becoming one of Chemistry's immortals, Joseph Black made a temporary halt in the Chair of Anatomy from 1756 to 1757. For these first three occupants of the Chair, Anatomy was a digression rather than a main interest.

In the early part of the eighteenth century, there was a general knowledge of the gross structure of the human body. Most of the fallacies and fantasies of mediaeval times had been dispelled by the work and teaching of Vesalius. Microscopy, however, was in its infancy and despite the publications of Malpighi and Leeuwenhoek in the late seventeenth century, there was little known about the microscopic structure of organs and tissues. Perhaps because of this, there lingered on well into the eighteenth century relics of the Galenic tradition. The first students of anatomy at Glasgow University would learn that the brain—the principal organ of the soul—secreted animal spirits which travelled down hollow tubes—the nerves—to control the actions of the body. They would hear that the blood consists of a mass of Cruor, principally of use to generate heat and composed of globules of an inflammable or combustible nature, and a yellow serum consisting of lesser globules swimming in water. Regarding differences between arterial and venous blood, Jinty states in 1757: 'It remains that we make further experiments'.

From 1757 to 1781 Thomas Hamilton—a younger brother of Robert Hamilton—occupied the Chair. He had enjoyed the advantage of studying under William Hunter in London, and brought something of Hunter's enthusiasm to the teaching of anatomy. Like his predecessors, however, he had a divided allegiance—he taught Botany, gave a course in Midwifery and conducted an extensive practice. He was succeeded by his son, William Hamilton, who retained the Chair until his death in 1790. William was the most gifted of the Hamiltons. He took his medical qualification in Edinburgh, and then worked with William Hunter in London and, like Hunter, built up a teaching museum of anatomical specimens in Glasgow. William Hamilton also taught Botany, Surgery, Midwifery, and was the leading obstetrician of his time. He thus displayed the omniscience and versatility which seemed to be required of Professors of Anatomy in those days. Up to this time, Anatomy could hardly be considered a whole-time occupation for its professors, who not only participated in the teaching of other subjects of the curriculum but were active in the practice of medicine. They were preoccupied with disease and its treatment, and had little concern with the great teleological controversies of their day.

In spite of Harvey's vigorous support of Aristotelian epigenesis, the theory of preformation was thoroughly established in the early years of the eighteenth century. It was taught that the germ cell, male or female, was a replica in miniature of the adult form and contained in Lilliputian proportions the postnatal organs and tissues in correct relative positions. The development of the embryo was thus but a growth and expansion of what already existed and there was no need for a mechanism of inheritance. Anatomists were divided into ovists, who regarded all embryos as produced from smaller

embryos in the unfertilised egg, and the more popular ani-
malculists, who made similar claims for the male germ cell.
There was indeed a tendency to endow the ovum or the
sperm with proleptic individuality. Perhaps the culminating
fantasy of the preformationists of this period was the 'world
of the unborn': 'All those other attending Animalcula,
except that single one that is then conceived, evaporate away,
and return back into the Atmosphere again, when it is very
likely they immediately proceeded; into the open Air, I say,
the common Receptacle of all such disengaged minute sub-
lunary bodies; and do there circulate about with other
Semina, where, perhaps, they do not absolutely die, but live
a latent life, in an insensible or dormant state, like Swallows
in Winter.'

Preformationism was, during this time, strengthened by the
lethal effect of the experimental evidence which Spallanzani
had arraigned against the theory of spontaneous generation.
Nevertheless the idea that living units could arise de novo
from organic material retained many adherents, until finally
completely dispelled by the work of Pasteur. Now that the size
spectrum, which includes the particle of bacteriophage and
the colloidal aggregate, can be made visible it may be that the
dogmatic 'omne vivum ex vivo' of the early twentieth century
was somewhat premature. Preformationism lingered on
through the first half of the eighteenth century to receive its
coup de grâce with the dissemination of Wolff's work on
developmental embryology.

For the next fifty-eight years, from 1790 to 1848, James
Jeffray filled the Chair of Anatomy. Jeffray was a graduate in
Arts of Glasgow University and an M.D. of Edinburgh. He
entered on his duties amidst the turbulent unrest of the
French Revolution, and in his early years would feel the
impact of the swaying fortunes of the Napoleonic Wars. The
eventide of his tenure faded into the age of commencing
steam locomotion and the nascent British bourgeoisie of early
Victorianism. His life-time straddled an era of industrial

revolution and the gestation period of modern biological thought.

Jeffray was a man of great ability—a kaleidoscopic personality—with a vast energy consumed in teaching and administration. This protean professor, in addition to Anatomy, for a time taught Botany, Surgery, Midwifery, Pathology and Physiology. He was, in fact, the physical embodiment of the medical curriculum. It is not surprising that, in 1815, Jeffray lodged a strong plea for the establishment of additional Chairs in the Medical Faculty. Jeffray was a builder; he built up and extended the Anatomy Department, which in 1809 had removed to the new Hamilton Buildings. He was responsible for a great increase in the numbers and reputation of the Glasgow Medical School. He also accumulated an impressive museum of anatomical specimens in addition to the Hunterian collection, which from 1809 was made available for teaching. Largely from his efforts, the Royal Botanical Institute of Glasgow was formed in 1816.

Jeffray played a prominent part in the agitation for legislation to procure bodies for dissection, from which resulted the Anatomy Act of 1832. Thus was ended the ghoulish activities of the resurrectionists. Like his predecessors, he was a clinician and, immersed in his multifarious activities, made no significant contribution to anatomical science. It is certain, however, that contemporary biological advances in knowledge would be reflected in his teaching.

During the first half of the nineteenth century, there was a growing discontent with classical theory and the ecclesiastical insistence on the fixity of species. There was a vague groping and fumbling towards 'evolution'—an expression first used by Herbert Spencer. Jeffray must often have paused in his lectures to allude to the new ideas put forward by Erasmus Darwin and Lamarck that species were subject to progressive change and development, due to the inheritance of acquired characteristics. Did he, like his contemporaries Cuvier and Owen, scoff at these heresies and dismiss them as fantasy? We do not know.

There were other significant discoveries at this time which must have excited anatomists. Schleiden enunciated the cell doctrine. Robert Brown described the nucleus and, after Von Baer had discovered the ovum in 1827, Schwann crystallised the concept of the cell as the essential unit of the animal organism. Meanwhile Continental anatomists were finding out more and more about microscopic structure, and to the gross anatomy of dissection was now added histology—a term first used by Mayer in 1819. Jeffray was by this time, however, becoming an old man. He had worked hard for the Glasgow Medical School and was probably content to leave new-fangled notions to the younger men. It is doubtful if his students would hear of Schwann's classification of the tissues or Purkinje's work on the structure of brain substance.

Jeffray was succeeded by Allen Thomson who occupied the Chair from 1848 to 1877. He also was a graduate of Edinburgh University, had been Professor of Anatomy at the Marischal College, Aberdeen and came to Glasgow from the Chair of Anatomy and Physiology in Edinburgh. Unlike his predecessors, he was a biologist and not a clinician, and brought to the Glasgow School of Medicine the refreshing vigour of a scientific mind enriched by much foreign travel and stimulated by contact with the great men of Continental biology—Bischoff, Neumann, Naegeli, Oken, Magendie.

In this short span of a little over a quarter of a century, Darwin's work accomplished a biological reorientation and the discoveries of Simpson, Pasteur and Lister produced a medical renaissance. Meanwhile, John Stuart Mill was preaching equality of the sexes, Disraeli was manipulating the Second Reform Bill and Mid-Victorian intelligentsia were enjoying Matthew Arnold, George Elliot, the Brownings and Meredith. Darwin published his 'Origin of Species by Means of Natural Selection' in 1859. Its impact was immediate and its effect, as a scientific directive, comparable to the influence of Rutherford's work on atomic structure.

The idea of evolution was not new, but the wide-spread appeal and stimulation of Darwin's work was its concrete and simple theory supported by a wealth of biological and ecological evidence. He was the first to give forthright and reasonable expression to a general idea which had been a growing force over many years, in a period when comparative anatomy was impregnated with transcendentalism. Although Thomson accepted evolution and was influenced by the 'Origin of Species', he was temporally too close to it to be caught up in the 'homology hunt' which gained impetus in the immediate post-Darwinian era. A man of infinite patience and equity, he did not gird his loins for the epic battles of his day or ally himself with this or that biological giant to tilt at the windmills of mechanism or vitalism. His views on evolution are expressed in his Presidential address to the British Association—'The Development of the Forms of Natural Life' (1877).

Allen Thomson was the foremost microscopical anatomist of his time, in Britain. He brought histology to the Glasgow dissecting-room, thus introducing the modern synthesis of macro- and micro-anatomy which offers a rational basis for the correlation of structure and function. He gave weekly lectures on the new microscopical anatomy emerging from the publications of Schwann, Remak, Henle and Kolliker—names immortalised in the eponymous nomenclature of histology. Kolliker, renowned as an embryologist and author of the first text-book on histology, was an intimate and life-long friend of Thomson and had a profound influence on his scientific outlook. They spent many summer vacations together at Thomson's house on the Clyde Coast, and elsewhere, and no doubt they would exchange ideas on a wide range of biological topics. Darwin's doctrine of natural selection had focussed scientific interest on the mechanism of inheritance but his theory of pangenesis, like Herbert Spencer's physiological units, implied an inheritance of acquired characteristics which had not been proved. Although Mendel's work was still unknown, Kolliker maintained that variation is not gradual but is sudden and discontinuous, thus anticipating De Vries's mutation theory.

Thomson's publications show a catholicity of scientific work, for example he wrote on the mechanism of accommodation in the eye, sensibility of the skin and glands of the alimentary tract. But his early and abiding interest was embryology—an interest which has been the inspiration of the many contributions to this subject associated with the subsequent history of the Anatomy Department at Glasgow University. He is the author of the article on the ovum in volume five of the *Cyclopaedia of Anatomy and Physiology*. This is perhaps the most comprehensive book of its kind ever produced in this country. Thomson's account of the ovum by itself could furnish material for a text-book. It amounts to a wide survey of the nature of fertilisation and generation throughout the animal kingdom. 'Tis indeed a remarkable contribution. This now seldom read, if not entirely forgotten, monumental work contains items of recondite information only now becoming generally known. For example, his prophetic observation on the external covering of the mammalian ovum anticipates the modern chemical interpretation of this structure. He had, a century ago, devised techniques for the recovery of the mammalian ovum which have been rediscovered, with much publicity, by many of our modern embryologists. Thomson's name may not be linked with any one great discovery in embryology, but he added many new facts and, more important, he made known in this country the work of the brilliant group of contemporary German embryologists, and thus created a school of British embryologists.

He initiated the association between Glasgow and *Quain's Anatomy*, sharing with Sharpey and Cleland the editing of the seventh edition, with Sharpey and Shäfer the eighth, and Shäfer and Thane the ninth. He was elected a Fellow of the Royal Society in 1848 and became one of its Vice-Presidents.

The work he accomplished in Glasgow 'may be said to have been of two kinds; the introduction of modern anatomy and methods of teaching by which he laid the foundation of the eminence and success which the Glasgow School of Medicine has since attained ... the other, also contributory to that end, the planning and erection of the new University buildings in which great undertaking he was from the beginning the moving spirit'. Succeeding Jeffray's long tenure of fifty-eight years, Thomson's methods 'were a new revolution in the old monastic building of that University. As in Edinburgh, when the third Monro at last made way for John Goodsir ... so the Glasgow School of Medicine when Allen Thomson became Professor of Anatomy, began to take a high rank to which the new colleagues who gradually gathered round him have contributed their part'.

The strong winds of post-Darwinism came to Glasgow when John Cleland was appointed to the Chair of Anatomy in 1877 and joined a Senate already rich in men of world fame—Kelvin, John and Edward Caird, and Jebb. Like Huxley, Haeckel and other great morphologists in the second half of the century, his paramount interest was comparative anatomy and the diligent pursuit of phylogenetic and ontogenetic homologies. As is evident from his well-known text-book of anatomy, written in collaboration with Mackay, he was in addition a notable histologist and so maintained the high standard of teaching of microscopic anatomy introduced by Thomson. Although an evolutionist, he vigorously opposed the mechanism implicit in Darwin's theory of natural selection. On the other hand, Weismann's 'continuity of germplasm' epitomised by Butler as 'a hen is only an egg's way of producing another egg' with its crude hint of an underlying teleology was more acceptable to one of his Covenanter heritage. Of commanding physique with the head of a Roman Emperor, he was in temperament a contrast to the placid precision of his former chief and predecessor. He possessed something of the full enthusiasms and pas-

sionate beliefs which added zest to the scientific meetings o
his day.

His interests and writings range over a wide survey of the
problems of structure and function throughout the anima
kingdom, from the anatomy of the sun-fish to the effect of hea
on the heart action of the chick. A number of his publica
tions, along with those of Mackay and Young (members of hi
staff) were published as *Memoirs and Memoranda in Anatomy* ir
1889. Mackay, at that time Cleland's Senior Demonstrator
later became Professor of Anatomy at, and subsequentl
Principal of, University College, Dundee. Included in thi
volume is 'Teratology, Speculative and Causal and th
Classification of Anomalies'. Here discussing the question
of overlapping individualities in double monsters, he gives
glimpse of the vitalist: 'There is some formative influence a
work which tends to mould and control and harmonise th
two, so that they become parts, so to speak, of a wider organi
whole.' This is essentially similar to what Driesch referrred t
in connection with the developmental forces in the embryo a
a 'harmony of composition'—an example of dynami
entelechy.

Cleland's philosophy was a curious blend of eighteent
and nineteenth century—a compromise between his scientif
training and his deep rooted Scottish Presbyterianism. It i
expressed in his lecture—'The Terminal Forms of Life'–
delivered in the St. Andrew's Halls of Glasgow in 1884
'To me the animal kingdom appears not an indefinite growt
like a tree but a temple with many minarets none of then
capable of being prolonged,—while the central dome is com
pleted by the structure of Man' and again 'On these ground
I believe, not that Man is the highest possible intelligence bi
that the human body is the highest form of animal life possib
subject to the conditions of matter on the surface of the glob
and that his structure completes the design of the anima
kingdom'—a philosophy that could only be classified
evolutionary fundamentalism.

In 1887, Cleland published a volume of poems. This, no doubt, upset the popular conception of the anatomist as a gross materialist, the archetype of the Philistines. It is not, however, unique—Leonardo da Vinci and Goethe are other examples of this teratological formation of the aesthete and the anatomist.

Those who deal with the structure of the brain inevitably feel entitled to speculate on its more esoteric functions. Cleland was no exception and a hundred years ago, set forth his ideas in a paper 'The Physical Relations of Consciousness and the Seat of Sensation'. This is compounded of a mixture of right and wrong with classical examples of the 'post hoc, ergo propter hoc', but shows evidence of much thought and a reasoned application of contemporary knowledge. In spite of the work of Broca and Gall, Cleland maintained that there was no evidence of functional localisation in the cerebrum. He insists on 'consentaneous action of the cerebrum'—a half truth. His idea was that consciousness is brought about by a functional continuity from the stimulated part to the brain, constituting as it were (for a brief period) a 'live wire' from source of stimulus to cerebrum. At this critical moment the brain excites the mind: 'As soon as there is continuity of the impressed condition from finger to brain the consciousness is in connection with the nerve and is directly aware of the irritation at the nerve extremity.' Accordingly, the 'mind' is the seat of consciousness but can only act through the brain. As with much of modern theory on the imponderables of brain function, there is the facile shift from brain to mind—that nebulous philosophical concept where 'omnia exeunt in mysterium' and so useful as an answer to the otherwise unanswerable. Current ideas on consciousness and the nature of abstract cerebral activity will doubtless seem equally naïve a hundred years hence. In a later article, Cleland expresses his views on the relationship of brain to mind in terms which might well have come from a twentieth century neuropsychologist: 'It does not seem to have generally

occurred to thinkers to track sufficiently in detail the steps
physical and mental from the stimulation of a sense organ to
the operations of mind and brain consequent on sensation
... There is an element of mental existence independent of
the body, namely, that on which the nerve-change acts in the
case of sensation, and from which that volition comes whose
action is linked with the brain. In that sphere and not in the
shape of potential vibrations laid past in nerve cells, I believe
it is that latent memories are stored; and I know not how
much else there may be within it.' Substitute 'internal cerebral activity' for 'mental existence' and this could be the
utterance of an up to date electronic neurologist.

During Cleland's time the Department was reconstructed
and expanded into its present premises. This included the
present museum, on which Cleland spent much time and
care, and to which he added a large number of specimens of
comparative anatomy, now known as the Cleland collection.
Cleland—a Fellow of the Royal Society—was recognised as
one of the foremost anatomists of the second half of the nineteenth century.

Those of us who were taught by and worked under
Thomas Hastie Bryce may feel somewhat chastened to
realise that when he was appointed Regius Professor of
Anatomy in 1909, the hansom cab was normal transport, the
aeroplane a glorious adventure and the morning coat and top
hat the hallmark of respectability. Evolution was now firmly
established and already biologists were pushing into new
territory in an effort to discover more about the mechanism
of inheritance. The twentieth century has witnessed the
resurrection of Mendel's laws of inheritance, and the rise of
genetics as a separate discipline with all its panoply of chromo-
somes, genes and mutations.

Bryce came of a family, many of whom attained fame and
eminence, but the name will live longest as that of the 15-day
ovum—the 'Teacher-Bryce Ovum'—of international repute.
In his preparation and description of this specimen, Bryce

added greatly to the embryological tradition of the Glasgow Anatomy Department, commenced by Allen Thomson and sustained in Cleland's time by Gemmill, later Professor of Zoology at University College, Dundee. The monograph on this ovum published by Teacher and Bryce in 1908, might well be said to have initiated a 'chain reaction' in the collection and description of young embryos, which up to date has terminated in the beautiful specimens of Hertig of the Carnegie Institute of Washington. These have, in the main, confirmed Bryce's original interpretations. His early work on the blood of Lepidosiren showed that once more a competent histologist occupied the Chair, capable of presenting a balanced account of the gross and microscopical anatomy.

Embryology had thus far been descriptive and comparative. Observers had been content to note the occurrence of the pattern and sequence of events which moulded the final form —the folding of a sheet of cells to make a tube—the splitting to form a space or the migration of cell populations to new positions and functions. Now they wanted to know something of the factors and influences which caused these changes to take place; to translate the vague and mystical Vis Formatrix of the older embryologists into an understanding of the interplay of the physico-chemical forces responsible for morphogenesis. The new approach to embryology was introduced by the experimental methods of Wilhelm Roux and the developmental mechanics of His. Although not directly contributing to experimental embryology, this reorientation influenced Bryce's work and teaching.

Bryce maintained Glasgow's connection with *Quain's Anatomy*, still the most comprehensive work on the subject in the English language. Along with Sir E. Shäfer and Symington, he edited the eleventh edition of *Quain's Anatomy* and was the author of the volumes on embryology, osteology and arthrology, and on myology.

The Bryce era coincided with the great discoveries of fossil man. Although Neanderthal man was unearthed in 1856, he was reinterred as pathological by Virchow. The real interest began with the discovery of Pithecanthropus in 1891, followed by Piltdown man in 1908 and Sinanthropus in 1927. The dramatic discoveries of Dart and Broom of a new species—Australopithecus africanus—have during the last decade or so provided periodic excitement for the paleontologists. It was thus natural that Bryce should teach his students something of the history of their own species—how around 100,000 years ago, our direct ancestors inhabited caves and buried their dead while the great glaciers of the last Ice Age retreated northwards, and how while the Aurignacians made drawings on the walls of their troglodytic homes, their cousin—Neanderthal man—still roamed the surface of the earth. The many thousands of skulls, mainly Scottish, housed in the Anatomy Museum testify to Bryce's life-long interest in Anthropology and Archaeology.

Bryce must have trained a record number of anatomists, among whom were Thomas Walmsley, until recently Professor of Anatomy at Queen's University, Belfast, and Duncan Macallum Blair, his successor from 1936 to 1944. The writer was too closely associated with the next period to view it in historical perspective.

As at the end of the eighteenth century, Anatomy is again on the threshold of new things. The electron microscope has brought new horizons in structure as yet but dimly perceived. Biology and Physics appear to be converging on the ultimate nature of organic and inorganic matter. Our modern mechanists would have it that finally there will be a common focal point. There is, however, always an answer to mechanism, and this time the vitalist's reply is the 'Gestalt' concept. Man is peculiar in that he has attained a position of dominance in the animal world although anatomically an unspecialised animal, compared to previous dominant species. All the weight of biological evidence predicts that what is good in homo sapiens will somehow go on and become better.

Perhaps the twentieth century parallel to the opening quotation of three hundred years ago is the definition of life as a 'Dynamic Equilibrium in a Polyphasic System'—it conveys no meaning but has euphony.

MEDICAL SCIENCES I
(b) PHYSIOLOGY AND BIOCHEMISTRY

by

R. C. Garry
Regius Professor of Physiology

Academic study of function, of what we now call Physiology, was certainly present in the earliest teachings of the Glasgow medical school. From the beginning occupants of the Chair of Medicine had to profess not only the Practice of Medicine but also the Theory of Medicine (Physiology).

This fact is well illustrated by the careers of such men as William Cullen (1710-1790) and Joseph Black (1728-1799).

In 1751, Cullen became the third Professor of Medicine in Glasgow University and also lectured on Chemistry. In 1755 he went to Edinburgh University as Professor of Chemistry and Physic and in 1766 was appointed to the Chair of Institutes of Medicine (Physiology) in the same University. Nine years later he reverted to the Chair of Practice of Medicine, still in Edinburgh, but kept alive his interest in Physiology since he wrote in 1777 a treatise called *Institutions of Medicine*.

Black studied Medicine in Glasgow and in Edinburgh, became Professor of Anatomy and Botany in Glasgow, then Professor of Medicine in Glasgow and finally Professor of Chemistry in Edinburgh.

Until comparatively recent times, too, there was little distinction between Anatomy and Physiology. Allen Thomson (1809-1884) started as extra-mural Lecturer in Physiology in Edinburgh. At the same period in Edinburgh, Sharpey was

235

extra-mural Lecturer on Anatomy. Subsequently, from 1839-1841, Thomson was Professor of Anatomy in Marischal College in Aberdeen, but he returned to Edinburgh and in 1842 became Professor of Physiology in Edinburgh University. Six years later he came to Glasgow as Professor of Anatomy. Sharpey, his erstwhile colleague in Edinburgh, moved in 1836 from his extra-mural Lectureship on Anatomy to the Chair of Physiology at University College in London.

It is thus obvious that the pre-clinical academic disciplines of to-day gradually evolved from a common stock as a result of a growing content of knowledge and due to increasing specialization in technique. In default of some major process of synthesis this tendency will inevitably continue.

PHYSIOLOGY

Physiology, from its derivation, means the science of nature. It was used in this general sense by the ancients and by medieval scholars. Thus, the third Regent of Glasgow College who, in 1577 at the time of the *Nova Erectio,* taught 'Physiology,' professed, not the study of biological function, bu Geology, Mineralogy, Astronomy, Physics and, it is said, eve Astrology. It is not justifiable, then, as some would have it, t see in this Regent the beginning of the Glasgow medical school

We have seen, however, that the early occupants of th Chair of Medicine professed both Practice of Medicine an Theory of Medicine which consisted largely of what w would now call Physiology and Pathology. Thus, in th University of Glasgow, instruction in Physiology was, i effect, given as early as the middle of the eighteenth centur Nevertheless the need to divide the Chair of Medicine di not receive formal recognition until Charles Badham w appointed in 1827. At that time the Crown reserved the rig to appoint a Fellow Professor in either the Theory or Pra tice of Medicine. In 1832 Badham anticipated action on t part of the Crown by handing his lectures on the Theory Medicine to Harry Rainy.

In 1839, when a Liberal Government was in power, the Crown founded the Chair on the Theory of Physic or Institutes of Medicine. Andrew Buchanan, a Whig in politics, was appointed. Rainy, a Tory, was passed over but later became Professor of Forensic Medicine.

Andrew Buchanan (1798-1882) Andrew Buchanan, born and brought up in Glasgow, entered the University at the age of twelve. He also studied in Edinburgh and in Paris. He obtained his M.D. in 1822, became a Fellow of the Royal Faculty of Physicians and Surgeons of Glasgow in 1824 and, in 1828, the Professor of Materia Medica in Anderson's College.

In 1835 he became Surgeon to the Royal Infirmary, a post he held until 1862.

Buchanan taught in the Old College, his facilities were probably extremely meagre, and all that was demanded from him, even in 1861, was a course of one hundred Lectures, and these Lectures embraced Physiology, Pathology, Therapeutics and Hygiene.

Initially Buchanan had no help in the conduct of his classes. In 1859 he was allowed to engage his son as an unpaid assistant. In 1862 he received £50 from the University to buy instruments to illustrate his lectures, and another £50 in 1867 for laboratory apparatus. Still another sidelight on these days is the £5 granted to him to buy a large slate blackboard and the £5 asked to repair and make comfortable the hard seats of his lecture room.

Before the end of his tenure of office, Buchanan had two assistants, one to assist in the teaching of practical Physiology and Microscopy, the other to teach Pathology. Coats, the first Professor of Pathology in this University, was at one time assistant to Buchanan.

For more than half the time of his tenure of the University Chair, Buchanan was a busy surgeon, and he gained renown by the design of a special 'staff' for lithotomy. He wrote on coagulation of the blood, and he anticipated some of Marshall Hall's work on the nervous system.

Andrew Buchanan was a founder and, for some time, editor of the *Glasgow Medical Journal*.

One has the impression that Buchanan was of a somewhat disputatious disposition. He was involved in the famous action at Law between the University and the Royal Faculty of Physicians and Surgeons of Glasgow. He championed the cause of the mere Regius Professors against the Faculty Professors within the University and, towards the end of his academic career, he was at loggerheads with the University Court. He retired from the Chair in 1876.

With his death in 1882 the old order passed away. For well over a generation, Buchanan, in his brougham, with its white horse and coachman, John, had been a kenspeckle feature of Glasgow streets. He was a busy practitioner of Medicine, an active surgeon and a University Professor of a Medical Science now of full academic status. His day was done, yet, in his time, he had been no mean exponent, in teaching and in research, of the subject he professed.

John Gray M'Kendrick (1841-1926). M'Kendrick was a graduate of Aberdeen University. He attracted the attention of Hughes Bennett, Professor of Physiology in the University of Edinburgh, and became Bennett's assistant and also extra-mural Lecturer in Edinburgh on the Institutes of Medicine.

M'Kendrick succeeded Andrew Buchanan in 1876. One gains the impression that he was rather critical of the facilities at Glasgow but, nothing daunted, he set to and soon created a department on the Edinburgh model. He adopted the newer name of Physiology for his subject. The modern era in Physiology in our University began with M'Kendrick who was trained as a physiologist and devoted his entire energies to his academic duties. The average income from the Chair during the two years 1876-77 and 1877-78 was £726 per annum. This sum included the annual Government grant of £150. Out of this income M'Kendrick paid £78 per annum for the services of what we would now call a technician. He also added £10 to the salary of his only graduate assistant, the Muirhead Demonstrator, to make the yearly income of that assistant £100. He had also to supply expendable chemicals and keep his apparatus in repair. He estimated this annual maintenance budget at £40. M'Kendrick, then, could count on an annual income of about £600.

At that time the lecture course extended over only the two terms of the winter session. Practical work was crowded into the summer term and originally was chiefly histological. M'Kendrick rapidly expanded the laboratory work to include physiological chemistry and experimental physiology. The Muirhead Demonstratorship was founded in 1877.

The 'Enrolment Book' of the Department still exists. He never had fewer than 100 students ; in the session 1888-1889 there were 168. In 1893-1894 a 'Ladies Systematic Class' and a 'Ladies Practical Class' first make their appearance; there were fourteen women students in that year.

M'Kendrick appreciated the importance of physical apparatus for physiological research. His interest was in what we would now call Biophysics. In keeping with this outlook he was a friend and admirer of Helmholtz whose life he wrote in 1899.

M'Kendrick made striking advances in physiology of the special senses, being the first to record the retinal potential on exposure of the eye to light. In many ways his outlook foreshadowed that of present-day physiologists with their preoccupation with a physical approach to physiological problems. He also found time to write on the history of Physiology and of science in general.

M'Kendrick was one of the nineteen physiologists who met in London in 1876 to form the Physiological Society. His signature appears in the first Minute of the Society.

The controversy between science and religion did not leave him untouched. He opposed the naive and arrogant mechanistic views so popular in the South.

Shortly before he retired he designed new laboratories for

Physiology in the West Medical Building then under construction. But M'Kendrick was not to occupy the new department. He retired in 1906 at the age of sixty-five, as he said, 'anything but a "done man".' Which was indeed true, for he retired to Stonehaven, took there an active share in civic affairs and became Provost in 1910. He died in 1926.

Diarmid Noël Paton (1859-1928). Noël Paton was the son of Sir Joseph Noël Paton, the artist. He was educated at Edinburgh Academy and at Edinburgh University. Noël Paton as a student was attracted to Physiology by Sir William Rutherford and, after graduation, he returned to work under his direction. He later held an extra-mural Lectureship in Physiology at Surgeons' Hall and in 1888 became Superintendent of the research laboratories of the Royal College of Physicians in Edinburgh.

Noël Paton entered on his new charge in Glasgow in 1907 and insisted on using the title 'Institute of Physiology' for his Department to emphasise continuity with 'Institutes of Medicine.' He inherited a well-staffed department from his predecessor. There was a Lecturer on Experimental Physiology, one on Histology and there was the Muirhead Demonstrator in Experimental Physiology. In 1908 a Lectureship in Psychology was founded in the Physiology Department to commemorate M'Kendrick's work on the Special Senses. This was the beginning of the independent Department of Psychology in the University. Attached to the Physiology Department, too, was the Grieve Lectureship in Physiological Chemistry. The first holder was Cathcart, who was appointed in 1905.

In these days the 'ordinary class' received a daily lecture during the Martinmas and Candlemas terms. As the content of physiological knowledge grew, the lectures gradually spread into the Whitsun term. Laboratory instruction extended over three terms, one term being given to Histology, one to Experimental Physiology, one to Physiological Chemistry. The laboratory classes met twice weekly for two-hour sessions.

Noël Paton was an outstanding teacher. Even with junior classes he kept dogmatism within bounds. He marshalled facts and then demanded that the undergraduates think for themselves, applying the acid test of 'scientific scepticism' to any resultant hypothesis. As might be expected, blackboard illustrations were a feature of his lectures. With a few simple lines he presented the essentials; it was the skill of the caricaturist, more revealing than the painstaking detail of pedestrian illustrators.

Noël Paton's interests in research were catholic and ranged from the metabolism of the salmon to postural reflexes in birds. In the study of metabolic processes he was a pioneer, consequently becoming intensely interested in nutrition and in social problems. He contributed largely to the early study of endocrinology. In these fields, however, it was his fate to be engaged in scientific controversy, in which he was to some extent worsted. As a result, there is a tendency to remember only the work of his opponents and to forget the important contributions the Glasgow School of Physiology made in the first quarter of this century.

Noël Paton at first scouted the significance of vitamins. From the results of a social and dietary survey, he had the audacity to conclude that the physical health and nutrition of the family depend largely on the intelligence and efficiency of the mother! Noël Paton's conception of the function of the parathyroid glands has not stood the test of time. In 1926, he ventured into the field of genetics with his *The Physiology of the Continuity of Life* and was soundly trounced by orthodox geneticists. These same geneticists are not so sure of their ground this day! However this may be, Noël Paton had the knack of attracting young workers to his Department which became a hive of industry. Many of these workers became eminent in Physiology and in the cognate medical sciences. A future Chancellor of Glasgow University, Lord Boyd Orr, was a student demonstrator in 1910 and later a research worker in the department.

Noël Paton was nothing if not forthright in the expression of his views on Physiology and on people. In manner he was often brusque, even impatient. Yet he never bore a grudge, he had the respect of his staff and students, which he reciprocated.

Noël Paton had few interests outside his subject, he was devoted to Physiology, he was proud of his department. Failing health forced him to resign his Chair in 1928. He died on the very day his tenure came to an end.

Edward Provan Cathcart (1877–). Cathcart succeeded Noël Paton, moving from the Chair of Physiological Chemistry to that of Physiology. Never very interested in the more chemical aspects of Biochemistry, he had for some years previously tended to concentrate on the energy metabolism of man. His translation from one Chair to the other was logical and did no violence to his interests.

Cathcart continued his interest in metabolism and nutrition and made valuable studies of the physique of men and women in industry. He could not agree with those who said that under-nutrition and malnutrition were widespread in the community and he revolted against the mechanistic conception of man as a mere machine to be fed with measurable quantities of fuel.

Cathcart showed a growing interest in psychological problems; he introduced a few lectures on normal psychology into his course for junior medical students and, in his later years, he became interested in Histology.

Outside bodies made additional demands on Cathcart. He was Chairman of the Industrial Health Research Board, he served on scientific committees of the Department of Health for Scotland, he was a member of the Medical Research Council, and he succeeded Sir Donald MacAlister as representative of the University on the General Medical Council. He also served for many years as civilian member of the Army Hygiene Council.

During the first year of the Second World War the Physiology Department of King's College, London, was given hospitality in the Glasgow Department. Air attack in 1941 blew in the windows of the Glasgow laboratories but left the walls and roof intact.

Cathcart retired in 1947 after forty years of practically continuous devoted service to his science and his University. He took with him many academic honours and the affection of his old students.

Robert Campbell Garry (1900-). Garry was a Glasgow graduate attracted initially to Physiological Chemistry by the personality and enthusiasm of Cathcart.

Appointed in 1924, first as an assistant, subsequently as a Lecturer and Muirhead Demonstrator in Physiology, he directed his interests towards experimental physiology. For a short period, 1933 to 1935, he was physiologist to the Rowett Research Institute, Aberdeen, where he came under the influence of John Boyd Orr, the Director, and of J. J. R. Macleod, Professor of Physiology in Marischal College, Aberdeen. Thereafter came twelve years as Professor of Physiology in University College, Dundee, the University of St Andrews.

In 1947 Glasgow University 'took over' the medical and dental students of the extra-mural colleges of Anderson and of St. Mungo. For the first time the Department taught students of Dentistry. An ordinance giving the University power to grant the degree of B.D.S. came into force in 1947.

The Glasgow Veterinary College became part of the University in October, 1949. However, students of Veterinary Medicine continued to receive instruction in Physiology in the old Veterinary College buildings in Buccleuch Street.

In October 1949 a six-year curriculum in Medicine was instituted. The first academic year is devoted wholly to the study of the Pre-medical Sciences of Chemistry, Physics, Zoology and Botany. The five subsequent terms are given to Anatomy, Physiology and Biochemistry. At the present time approximately two hundred students of Medicine and fifty of Dentistry enrol each year. In addition, about fifty Science students take a 'Single Course' of one year in the Departments of Physiology and of Biochemistry. Many of these proceed to advanced or Honours courses either in Physiology or in Biochemistry.

For many years a 'Combined Course' in Science and Medicine had been a feature of Glasgow University. This was allowed to lapse during the Second World War, but was revived in 1948 and strengthened by insistence on an Honours degree in Science in the combined course. Such a curriculum lasts for at least seven years, depending on the subject chosen for study to the Honours standard. The choice at the moment rests between Anatomy, Physiology, Biochemistry and Pathology with Bacteriology.

In the teaching of medical and dental students, and of science undergraduates in the early stages, the Departments of Physiology and of Biochemistry collaborate, as in the past, to give an integrated theoretical and practical course on the function of living organisms.

BIOCHEMISTRY

Gently at first, and then with increasing impatience, Biochemistry emerged from Physiology. The designation used initially was 'Physiological Chemistry.' But, with the passage of time, the dependence on Organic and Physical Chemistry increased, and the name now almost universally used is Biochemistry. This new science may now be defined as 'the study at the molecular and atomic level of the organisation and function of biological systems.' The development of Biochemistry was actually foretold by Liebig at a meeting of the British Association in Glasgow as long ago as 1840.

Inevitably, then, Biochemistry developed first on the Continent of Europe; it was not until 1902 that the first British Chair of Biochemistry was founded at Liverpool. Nevertheless, we have seen that, in the latter part of the nineteenth century, Biochemistry began to play an increasingly important role in the Department of Physiology in Glasgow.

In 1905 the Grieve Lectureship in Physiological Chemistry was founded at Glasgow University. Fourteen years later, in 1919, the Gardiner Chair of Physiological Chemistry was established, the third Chair of Biochemistry in Britain. Biochemistry had come into its own, with its own Department, its own staff, although in the teaching of elementary students there remained close integration with Physiology.

Edward Provan Cathcart (1877-   ). Chance drew Cathcart to Biochemistry. He went to Germany to study Bacteriology. One day he turned into the laboratory of Carl Voit, *the* authority on metabolism and nutrition. The die was cast.

Back in Glasgow, after some time in the Lister Institute, he was appointed to the Grieve Lectureship in Physiological Chemistry and soon gathered round him an active group of workers. His study of metabolism in starvation became a classic. Work on the metabolism of protein quickly followed, leading eventually to the publication of an authoritative monograph on the subject.

Cathcart travelled widely. For a while he worked with Pavlov in Russia. But Cathcart never took kindly to animal experimentation. More significant for the Glasgow school was work with Benedict in America on energy metabolism.

In 1913 Cathcart was appointed to the London University Chair of Physiology in the London Hospital. But, in 1919 at the invitation of the University, he returned to Glasgow to fill the newly-founded Gardiner Chair of Physiological Chemistry. He quickly fired the imagination of his students, and became one of the outstanding personalities of the University. For Cathcart was interested in his students not only as metabolic machines, but also as human beings. He could arouse enthusiasm and emotion in individuals and in audiences. Nor did he take kindly to the post-war outlook on many matters. His lukewarmness towards the more modern attitude to nutrition has already been mentioned, and he had the temerity to state that one of the prime needs of mankind is self-respecting work.

When Noël Paton died Cathcart succeeded him in the Regius Chair of Physiology.

Andrew Hunter (1876-   ). Hunter, a distinguished graduate in Arts, in Science and in Medicine of Edinburgh University, carried out research first in Edinburgh, and subsequently on the Continent of Europe.

He later became Assistant Professor of Biological Chemistry in the Medical School of Cornell University in New York. Subsequently he went to the Chair of Biological Chemistry in Toronto University and then succeeded Cathcart in our own University in 1929 as Professor of Physiological Chemistry.

Hunter stayed too short a period in Glasgow greatly to influence his Department. His earlier work had been concerned with the metabolism of protein and its derivatives. Later his attention turned to studies of enzymes and of the conditions affecting their activity, and it was this type of work which he pursued in Glasgow. Hunter was a meticulously careful teacher, his lectures being models of lucidity and of orderly presentation.

In 1935 Hunter returned to the University of Toronto, this time as Professor of Pathological Chemistry.

George Macfeat Wishart (1895-   ). Wishart graduated in Glasgow, both in Science and in Medicine. He joined the Department of Biochemistry and became Grieve Lecturer in 1921. He held this Lectureship, apart from two periods of study abroad, one in Germany, the other in Sweden, and with one short intermission, until he succeeded Andrew Hunter in the Chair in 1935. In 1947 he became Professor of Applied Physiology and Director of Postgraduate Medical Education.

Cathcart's interest in muscle work led Wishart to look more closely into the physical and physiological justification for the methods used in measurement of energy exchange in human beings.

At this time the importance of physical science for research in biology was becoming more widely appreciated. Wishart, with his sound knowledge of physics, found this approach congenial. He worked on the mechanism of oxidation, on the measurement of pH, on the nature of enzyme action.

One of his publications was a most useful book, *Groundwork of Biophysics*.

Wishart's teaching was distinguished for lucidity of expression. He spared no pains to put his wide knowledge of medical and of academic affairs at the service of both graduates and undergraduates.

Towards the end of Wishart's tenure of the Chair of Physiological Chemistry, an important change was made in the curriculum of undergraduates reading for an Honours Science degree in Biochemistry. They now came wholly under the control of the staff of the department, so that Biochemistry became master in its own house, able to decide the fate of its own students.

James Norman Davidson (1911-). Davidson graduated first in Science then in Medicine in Edinburgh University. After graduation he worked with Warburg in Berlin, returning to Scotland just before the outbreak of the Second World War. Thereafter he spent two more years as Lecturer in Biochemistry in University College, Dundee, the University of St. Andrews and then became Lecturer in Biochemistry in Aberdeen University for five years. He subsequently went to the National Institute for Medical Research in London and shortly thereafter to the London University Chair of Biochemistry at St. Thomas's Hospital.

He had always, however, expressed the intention to return to Scotland if opportunity arose and, when Wishart vacated his Chair in 1947, Davidson was appointed. He took up his duties in the beginning of 1948.

With Davidson's advent, Biochemistry in Glasgow University was at last allowed to attain its majority as a distinctive discipline. The name of the Department was changed from 'Physiological Chemistry' to 'Biochemistry.'

MEDICAL SCIENCES II

PATHOLOGY AND BACTERIOLOGY

by

C. H. Browning
Professor of Bacteriology

Pathology appeared relatively late among the disciplines
of the University. However, its first material entry was
both imposing and important, in the form of those portions
of William Hunter's collection of anatomical preparations
which exemplify abnormalities, injuries and diseased conditions. Hunter at one time seems to have meditated a return
to his Alma Mater, and, although this was not realised, it
was no doubt his warm feeling for her and for his native
county, along with Dr. Samuel Johnson's encouragement
apparently, which caused him to bequeath in trust to Glasgow University those specimens among other treasures. He
stipulated that his partner and his nephew, Matthew Baillie
(both former students of Glasgow also), should enjoy the
use of the collection in London for thirty years after his
death to enable them to carry on the great School of Anatomy
which he had founded. But by 1802 the survivor, Baillie,
was ready to surrender the museum as soon as Glasgow
University could house it. The transfer began in 1807 and
was completed in two years. The collection, amassed over
forty years, was very largely the work of Hunter's own hands.
Accompanying it were copies of his catalogue, which was
published in 1841 'for the use of the Medical Students of the
University and of scientific visitors.' According to Teacher
it is a faithful reproduction of the manuscript, but contains

many clerical errors due apparently to the ignorance of
Hunter's original copyist. Nothing further was done with
the collection until the Bellahouston Trustees provided for
its better arrangement and cataloguing. Fortunately Dr. J. H.
Teacher undertook the work with the practical assistance of
Mr. W. Kinghorn in remounting many specimens. Teacher's
catalogue (1900) is not a bare list of the preparations, but
represents an enormous amount of descriptive work and research in the identification of specimens from illustrations
and text of publications of Hunter and of others. For instance,
the Hunterian preparations were extensively reproduced in
Matthew Baillie's *Engravings of Morbid Anatomy* (1799 *et seq.*),
which illustrate his work on *The Morbid Anatomy of Some of
the Most Important Parts of the Human Body* (1793), the earliest
text-book of Pathology in the English language. Teacher's
Introduction to the Catalogue presents convincing arguments
for William Hunter's material claims to fame as a scientific
observer.

In the case of the tumours, Teacher prepared sections and
investigated the histological appearances; as he stated, 'it is
surprising how much light the microscopic examination of
specimens which had been from 150-120 years in spirit was
able to give as to their nature.' The Catalogue is a fine
memorial to its compiler as well as to the original author.

However, the Hunterian Collection for long seemed to
give no obvious stimulus to Pathology here. Of course,
what could be learned from morbid changes by the naked
eye alone was strictly limited. But shrewd observers elsewhere
had made important discoveries by correlating clinical facts
with the gross morbid anatomy and so entities like Bright's
disease of the kidneys were distinguished, and diphtheria identified by Bretonneau. Lister's epoch-making contribution to
Pathology, although of somewhat later date, while he was
Professor of Surgery in Glasgow at the Royal Infirmary,
belongs to this category of syntheses. To quote his own
words (1867), 'I arrived, several years ago, at the conclusion

that the essential cause of suppuration in wounds is decomposition, brought about by the influence of the atmosphere upon blood or serum retained within them. . . . But when it had been shown by the researches of Pasteur that the septic property of the atmosphere depended, not on the oxygen or any gaseous constituent, but on minute organisms suspended in it, which owed their energy to their vitality, it occurred to me that decomposition in the injured part might be avoided without excluding the air, by applying as a dressing some material capable of destroying the life of the floating particles.' The demonstration of the actual pyogenic organisms was not achieved until many years later; also subsequent observations convinced Lister that the chief vehicle of infection to wounds was not the atmosphere, but infected solid objects (1890). However, this does not detract from his unique achievement. None but he had grasped those implications of Pasteur's discovery; thus Lister made the triumphs of modern surgery possible.

Further progress in Pathology had to await the perfecting of objectives for the compound microscope, in which the father of Lord Lister played so distinguished a part, and also the development of reliable microtomes for making thin sections of tissues of the order of 1-2500 to 1-8000 in. thick. Both instruments were already well forward by the middle third of last century and, along with the finding of chemical 'fixatives' which preserved with fidelity the life-like characters of tissue-constituents and stains which coloured them distinctively, opened the way for rapid developments of microscopic anatomy with its applications to Pathology (Morbid Histology). The great generalisation of Virchow (1858), the first modern pathologist, *omnis cellula e cellula,* which revealed the cell as the universal biological unit, came at this time; it has dominated biological thought and directed physiological and pathological investigation ever since, and its truth is nearly as potent now as ever.

In the early phases of the new era, pathologists confined

themselves principally to observational methods in the study of disease by the microscope. The materials for investigation were furnished chiefly by cases of spontaneous disease which ended in death or where during life the morbid product could be removed by surgery. Much knowledge was gained thereby, and the inclusion of animal diseases within the sphere of interest added notable contributions. Later, the value became increasingly evident of producing lesions experimentally and studying their evolution. Thus there developed Experimental Pathology devoted to tracing the structural and chemical changes wrought by disease induced deliberately and their effects on function. The conclusions so reached are in many ways fuller and more convincing than those deduced purely from scrutiny of the end-products. When a very considerable number of important and common diseases were discovered by the work of Pasteur, Koch and others to be caused by infection with living agents, usually of microscopic dimensions or even smaller, which parasitise the tissues, the foundations of Medical Bacteriology were laid. Relatively recently it has been established that what may be called a purely chemical lesion can exist, which so far escapes detection by the most powerful microscopes.

In tracing the further history of our subjects the sequence of Professors at each Infirmary will be followed because, for better or worse, a Department reflects its Head.

Joseph Coats appeared when Pathology was beginning to reap the harvest of those discoveries outlined above and the subject reached the status of a discipline in the true sense in Glasgow, although at first an extra-mural one, when he was appointed Pathologist to the Royal Infirmary in 1870 and began systematic teaching of the subject. He had been pupil and assistant of both Lister and Gairdner and, when twenty-four years old and a medical graduate of three years' standing, had already worked under Ludwig, physiologist, and Recklinghausen, pathologist, and this was followed several years later by a period under the pathologist Rindfleisch. Thus he familiarised himself with the German School of Pathology then pre-eminent. In 1871 he was attached to the Department of Institutes of Medicine (Physiology) of the University as Assistant Lecturer on Pathology. When the Western Infirmary was opened in 1875, Coats came there as Pathologist. In 1877 he started a class of Practical Pathology which was attended at first by about four students. In 1890 he became an independent Lecturer.

PATHOLOGY AT THE WESTERN INFIRMARY

At length, a Chair of Pathology was created and Coats became the first Professor in 1894. An Institute of Pathology was built in the grounds of the Western Infirmary under his guidance in respect of the planning of internal arrangements and with Mr. (afterwards Sir) John Burnet as architect. For the preceding twenty years most of the work had been done by the Pathologist along with one or two assistants in a room twelve feet square and the teaching of classes of over 100 students carried on in rooms where they were so tightly packed as scarcely to have elbow room. At the close of his speech on the opening of the new Institute in 1896, Professor Coats said 'There are still two subjects to which I would like to allude before sitting down. The first is the connection of this place with the University. Our circumstances here are, I think I may say, unique, and I think I may add that they are in a sense ideal. . . . There is thus combined under one roof and under one superintendence both the Infirmary and the University Pathological Departments. The University has the great advantage for its students of all the material afforded by the Infirmary, whilst the Infirmary has the skilled assistance of University men and the stimulus of an educational body in the prosecution of its work. My pathological friends tell me that such a conjunction of interest is a happy ideal which is nowhere else realised. . . . I can say from the inside point of view that we have a laboratory better than anything in this country and,

I believe, better also than in any other.' Nevertheless, so rapid was the growth of the subject that before many years had passed the accommodation had become insufficient for the requirements of the Institute. In 1897 postgraduate courses in Pathology were started in the new Institute. Unfortunately Professor Coats was now in ill health and in 1899 he died at the early age of fifty-three.

The outstanding qualities which Coats brought to the benefit of Pathology in Glasgow were his intense devotion to the subject, together with alertness to test critically every reported important advance. From his own wide clinical experience he held that the science of Pathology must be pursued not only as an end in itself, but also as a means of advancing the work of the clinicians. To further these aims he wrote the *Manual of Pathology,* dedicated to Joseph Lister and W. T. Gairdner, and published in 1883, when for many years there had been no modern text-book in English. It is characteristic of the author that it contains a description of the tubercle bacillus, which had been first demonstrated as the cause of tuberculosis only in the previous year. It was for long a standard work, both for undergraduate and post-graduate study; in twenty years, five editions appeared, the last two of which were revised by L. R. Sutherland, Senior Assistant to Coats and afterwards Professor in the University of St. Andrews. In addition, a contribution 'On the Pathology of Phthisis Pulmonalis' was published in *Lectures to Practitioners,* a joint work with W. T. Gairdner (1888). For many years, from 1877 on, Coats was editor of the *Glasgow Medical Journal,* at first alone and then jointly. He introduced as a special feature abstracts of current medical publications, for the preparation of which he was chiefly responsible; these had an important educative value. He was firmly convinced of the importance of research in the training of young workers; and in the new Institute a number of rooms were provided for this purpose. At the opening ceremony he made this plea, 'I cannot think of a better way of advancing the scientific position of our school and at the same time conferring great benefits on the community than by some man who is able, conferring a moderate endowment on those who may devote themselves to research. . . . It would not take much and I feel sure that it would be well applied.' He did not live to see this hope realised, but the Coats Research Scholarship, founded in 1899, has proved for a number of us the beginning of a career in Pathology or Bacteriology.

This is not the place to deal with the personal traits which made Professor Coats deeply respected by a wide circle and also beloved by those who knew him intimately, or with his intense energy which benefited a multitude of causes, both outside and within the University. All of this has been preserved in the work *Dr. and Mrs. Joseph Coats—a Book of Remembrance compiled by Their Daughters* (Glasgow, 1929). It is essential to add here—Coats made Pathology in Glasgow.

Robert Muir came as Professor in 1899. A distinguished medical graduate of Edinburgh University and member of the Pathology Departments of the University and the Royal Infirmary there, he had been chosen in 1898 as the first Professor of Pathology in the University of St. Andrews. His record of accomplishment as teacher and scientific investigator was already noteworthy and his subsequent brilliant career testified to the wisdom of the Glasgow appointment. In time many young workers were attracted to his Department as assistants or research scholars. Alone or jointly he accomplished a mass of outstanding work in diverse fields of pathological investigation which is discussed later. It should be added, however, that he always welcomed and encouraged individual workers pursuing investigations on topics chosen by themselves; he also willingly suggested subjects for research. The result was a substantial output of papers which stimulated a variety of interests in the Department and proved of inestimable benefit in training resourceful and independent scientists. Among the problems which were tackled fruitfully, to mention only a selection, there were the blood and blood-forming tissues, the nodal tissue of the heart in different vertebrates, the Wassermann 'antigen,' vital staining, tuberculosis in childhood, tissue-culture and the nature of the rheumatic lesion. Many Honours M.D. theses, with the added award of a Bellahouston Gold Medal for outstanding merit, resulted from those independent studies. The Professor might often seem to be little concerned with such work, but the constant and unflinching vigour of his critical vigilance, although manifested in few words, ensured that the truth and nothing but the truth emerged—we do not say the whole truth, because that never is or can be attained in any field of biological experience. Thus the Pathological Institute at the Western Infirmary became the centre of pathological-clinical research in the West of Scotland.

In the course of years the fabric of the Institute was, so far as possible, altered in minor ways to keep pace with growing needs and opportunities, *e.g.,* increased access of precious daylight was secured by enlarging windows. The applications of pathological and bacteriological knowledge in furthering the diagnosis and treatment of the individual patient were rapidly extending, so in 1911 a Laboratory of Clinical Pathology, presented by an anonymous donor, was opened to deal with this branch of the work, including Biochemistry. Unfortunately it had to be placed at some distance from the Pathological Institute, a disturbance of the functional compactness of the School of Pathology, which was such a notable feature. Postgraduate courses in Clinical Pathology were conducted, which were optional for undergraduates at first. In 1913 a storey was added to the Institute. In 1925 a Lectureship in Pathological Biochemistry was instituted under an endowment given anonymously. In 1935 an annexe to the Institute was opened, which was the gift of the Trustees of Mrs. Margaret Macgregor of Stirling; in addition to further laboratory accommodation, this provided a library. In the following year a new Biochemical Laboratory was built adjacent to the Laboratory of Clinical Pathology.

The pathological work of the old Royal Hospital for Sick Children at Garnethill was performed by a member of the Western Infirmary staff of Pathology. On removal of the Hospital to its new site at Yorkhill this practice continued, but provision was made for an independent Department of Pathology and in 1928 a Gardiner Lectureship in the Pathology of Disease of Infancy and Childhood was endowed by Sir Frederick Crombie Gardiner and Mr. William Guthrie Gardiner, the Lecturer being Pathologist to the Hospital; also a Lecturer in Pathological Biochemistry was appointed. Professor Muir did much in many other ways to advance Pathology in the West of Scotland; thus it was under his guidance that the project to found a Western Asylums' Research Institute took practical shape and work started in 1910.

Muir's chief scientific contributions were a series of studies, each carried out over a period of years; these will now be referred to in more detail and their bearing on current knowledge emphasised.

Leucocytosis in infections and leucoblastic reaction of the bone-marrow (period up to 1902). The nature of leucocytosis as a defense response to certain infections had been established, and Ehrlich had shown that the cells of pus were a specific class of leucocytes, the polymorphonuclear neutrophils, so-called from the granules which they contain. Muir studied the source of these cells, which can be produced rapidly and in enormous numbers after infection, for example, with staphylococci. In this work, begun in Edinburgh and completed in Glasgow, he established independently that the leucocytes arise by the proliferation of cells with rounded nuclei containing similar granules, which inhabit the red bone marrow—myelocytes. When a drain on the leucocytes occurs the fatty marrow is replaced by those leucoblastic cells. In the adult, at least, the bone-marrow is normally the sole source of the neutrophil polymorphs (apart from the disease leukæmia); collections of these cells elsewhere in the course of infections, *e.g.*, in the spleen, are not due to their proliferation there, but result from accumulation after transport by the blood. This was proved both in experimentally infected animals and also by observations in natural cases of pyogenic disease in man.

Studies in immunity (1903-1912). The discovery of antitoxins and other antibodies in the fluid constituents of the blood of animals immunised against bacterial poisons or living microorganisms, opened up a rich field for research. Hæmolytic antisera obtained by injecting into an animal red blood cells of a foreign species act on these cells in a manner similar to that of antibodies which kill and dissolve susceptible bacteria, the lysis being due to the co-operated action of immune body (the antibody) and of complement, the latter being a normal constituent of the blood fluid. This hæmolytic phenomenon presents a very beautiful, convenient and precise method of analysing many immunity phenomena. By its use Muir proved that the immune body does not, as was currently supposed, act as a link between the cell and the complement, that is, it does not have the constitution of an 'amboceptor.' The efficacy of complement in bringing about lysis was shown to depend on two properties, the combining and the toxic, which may vary quite independently, and each of which *(inter alia)* is affected by the species of animal yielding the immune body, although the different immune bodies combine with the same components of the red cells. Related zoological species may yield immune body and complement markedly different as regards the above properties. The striking observation was made that the intravenous injection of a fixed amount of hæmolytic antibody brings about destruction, chiefly by lysæmia, of a far greater quantity of red cells than is effected *in vitro,* but the process is much more gradual *in vivo.* By introducing the antibody already combined with the animal's own red corpuscles, it was shown that when the red cells undergo lysis, the antibody is split off *in vivo* and then becomes fixed to further red corpuscles which are lysed in turn. The opsonic action of normal serum was proved to depend on a complement-like component. The phenomenon, independently described by Bordet and later called conglutination by him, was discovered, and this more recently has found in other hands a very successful application in the detection of Rh antibodies. These researches are all of very great biological interest, and some of them have valuable practical uses. The greater part of the work, most of which was done conjointly with Muir's pupils, was published under the title *Studies on Immunity* (London, 1909).

Researches on blood pigments and especially the role of the liver in the metabolism of the iron-containing fraction (1914-1935). These are important chiefly through clarifying problems on which there had previously been diversity of opinion, although the wider significance of certain findings still awaits elucidation. When acute anæmia was produced in the rabbit by intravenous injection of hæmolytic antibody, it was found that iron-containing pigment quickly appeared in large amounts in the parenchyma cells of the liver and kidney. By the time that regeneration of the blood was complete, the iron had disappeared again, especially from the liver, this suggesting that it was used up in the formation of new red cells. On the other hand, much larger amounts of hæmoglobin from the rabbit or horse injected intravenously in the form of a solution, even when given repeatedly, led to only slight accumulation of iron in the liver cells, although much more appeared in the kidney. Thus hæmoglobin as such is apparently not taken into the liver cells and broken down there. Those observations point to the affinity of organ-cells for iron-containing pigment as an important factor affecting its storage. This is strikingly illustrated in the disease hæmochromatosis (bronzed diabetes), where the liver may show one hundred times the normal iron-content, the pancreas and retroperitoneal lymph glands also participating in the storage, although collateral evidence of excessive blood destruction is absent. There is always an associated cirrhosis of the liver which seems to precede the iron-storage. The factors underlying this remarkable state remain obscure, however. Information on the mode of production of bile pigment in tissues outside the liver was got by injecting subcutaneously in mice or rats either homologous red cells or a solution of hæmoglobin. Macrophages which gave the iron reaction soon appeared and after about a week crystals of hæmatoidin (bile pigment) were found within such cells. No formation of pigments was observed outside cells. (In rabbits, however, hæmatoidin was not produced after the same procedures.) Unaltered hæmoglobin in a free state in the blood stream either resulting from lysæmia or after injection of a solution as such, does not pass into the bile. But certain toxic compounds, which need not be hæmolytic, *e.g.,* phosphorus, cause the appearance of traces of hæmoglobin in the bile, both of the gall-bladder and bile ducts, owing to liver damage with escape of red cells into the bile capillaries.

Researches on cancer (1927-1941) culminated in a study of the evolution of malignancy. Out of a very large number of cases of human mammary cancer, a considerable series was collected in which the development of malignant changes could be traced by the microscope. The following conclusions were reached from these. There is a multicentric lesion of the ducts or acini or both, which consists in a gradually accelerating process of growth and dedifferentiation of the epithelial cells. Thus it is not possible to define precisely the stage at which the break through of growth into surrounding tissues occurs, which is the chief criterion of malignancy. Often the malignant change is diffuse, regional rather than focal. The processes are closely similar to those experimentally initiated by a hormonal stimulus, such as œstrone administered to mice. Hence the changes found support the view that carcinoma is the end result of any individual carcinogenic agent and there is no indication of a second agent of different character, *e.g.*, a virus, coming into operation at a later stage and changing reactive into autonomous or malignant proliferation. Also, evidence is lacking that normal cells become converted to malignancy by contact with malignant ones, through a sort of 'autocatalytic' effect. In fact the two classes of cells can be sharply distinguished when growing in close contact, as is seen in Paget's disease of the nipple. This work is a model of interpretation informed by experience and judgment and is likely long to remain the closest approach to truth on the problem attainable by histological methods.

In addition to his scientific researches, Muir was author of two famous text-books, the *Manual of Bacteriology* (jointly) and the *Text Book of Pathology,* the latter originally issued in 1924 and now in its fifth edition. The beautiful photographs in the *Pathology* were the work of John Kirkpatrick who, in addition to his other outstanding qualities as a laboratory worker, for many years made the Department distinguished for the excellence of the illustrations in its publications and the lantern slides shown at meetings of the Pathological Society, etc.

As the years passed the importance of Pathology as a scientific study became increasingly recognised here, and in 1928 it was included among the subjects in which a student of Medicine could obtain the B.Sc. in Pure Science with Honours. Many appointments of trust and scientific distinctions were conferred on Professor Muir, including the F.R.S. in 1911 and a Royal Medal in 1929, the honour of knighthood in 1934, and the Lister Medal of the Royal College of Surgeons in 1936. Twenty-one of his staff and pupils became Professors of Pathology or Bacteriology. As Sir F. G. Hopkins, P.R.S., said, he was a torch-bearer for many years, who illuminated the paths of progress for British Pathologists, he created in Glasgow a centre of pathological thought and teaching second to none in this country, it might be said second to none in the world.

John Shaw Dunn, Professor of Pathology at the Royal Infirmary, succeeded to the Chair at the Western Infirmary in 1936 on the retiral of Muir, whose pupil and assistant he originally was. The temperament and discipline of the naturalist inspired his study of Pathology; he amassed a unique knowledge of gross and microscopic morbid anatomy and the correlation between lesions and their clinical effects. Dunn's experience during the war of 1914-1918, first at a mobile laboratory in France, provided him with the main subject of his life's work, renal pathology, then later, while investigating gas poisoning at Porton Station for the Chemical Warfare Committee, impressed on him the supreme value of the experimental method in the elucidation of disease. Also, war-time investigation by gross and microscopic methods on the nature and mode of spread of the muscular damage in gas gangrene, published along with J. W. McNee, was not only an important scientific contribution, but had an immediate outcome in practical therapy. It was proved that the infective lesion involves individual muscles or portions of muscles and spreads in their length, while adjacent muscles are often intact. Accordingly, instead of performing a mutilating amputation which previously had been the only hope of saving life, it was now necessary for the surgeon only to excise the affected muscles. On the testimony of Sir C. Wallace, these pathological observations saved many limbs. On return to Glasgow, Dunn continued research on various aspects of nephritis, which he had already pursued with much success when Professor of Pathology at Manchester. He set himself to make a comprehensive examination of the validity of the modern filtration-reabsorption theory of kidney function associated with the name of Cushny. To this end all types of human nephritis and also forms experimentally produced by chemical agents were investigated in great detail, both by histological methods and also chemical analysis of blood and urine, and the findings correlated with other bodily changes, especially œdema. He was one of the foremost pioneers in this field and, together with many juniors, a large number of publications of the highest critical quality and acumen were produced. To his great regret he never succeeded in reproducing in animals an acute glomerulonephritis similar to that originally encountered in man as 'trench nephritis' or 'war nephritis.' But he satisfied himself generally as to the filtration-reabsorption theory fitting the pathological data. He offered the only adequate explanation of the nephrosis syndrome, in which water-retention with œdema is associated with little or no disturbance of renal excretion of nitrogenous compounds. According to Dunn's view, based on changes histologically demonstrated, in this condition the glomeruli are all continuously in action instead of, as he believed, normally only a proportion at a time. Thus every kidney tubule receives a diminished amount of the filtrate, the total quantity of which is unchanged. Accordingly, there is then an increased filter-bed in the tubules for reabsorption of the glomerular filtrate, hence the oliguria characteristic of the condition. When, during the late war, injuries occurred from the pressure on muscles of heavy masses of dislodged masonry, the 'crush syndrome,' Dunn took up the problems. In an attempt to discover the mode of production of the renal lesions in such cases he injected into rabbits alloxan (selected because of its chemical relation to uric acid, which causes nephritis). In a proportion of the animals unexpected symptoms occurred, followed by death. The nature of this complication was investigated and lesions of Langerhans' islets in the pancreas were found. In short, Dunn made the altogether novel discovery that alloxan, a substance of defined constitution, exerts a selective toxic action on the insulin-producing cells of the pancreas and so causes diabetes, which is responsive to insulin. But a great amount of experimentation was required before conditions were defined for establishing regularly in rats and rabbits a disease in general respects similar to spontaneous diabetes in man. The importance of this lead was at once recognised in America and elsewhere, and the results were confirmed and amplified with resources which were never at Dunn's disposal. The pity is that he did not live to enjoy the rewards of this spectacular work or to reap the harvest of his long-continued investigation of nephritis. The latter was so complex and made so great demands on knowledge and understanding, especially as he never published any collected account of it, that there was bound to be a considerable time-lag before pathologists and physiologists incorporated the concepts in the currency of their thought. (Fuller details of Dunn's work are given in the Obituary Notice J. Path. Bact., 1944, 56, 577.)

Daniel F. Cappell succeeded to the Chair in 1945. Also a pupil and former assistant of Sir R. Muir, he had been Professor of Pathology in St. Andrews University since 1931. His main earlier researches were on Ehrlich and Goldmann's phenomenon of 'vital staining.' Thus some dyes in colloidal solution and substances in the form of fine particles, when presented to certain living cells become segregated in vacuoles in their interior. Such *intra vitam* staining is a valuable indicator of types of cells which act as phagocytes in the tissues and so arrest and destroy various pathogenic microorganisms, thereby contributing to protection and immunity against infection. Cells had been classified according to their avidity for those stains, but Cappell's work established strong evidence for the view that the degree of vital staining is a measure of the functional capacity of the cell at a given time and not necessarily a specific property. It was shown that vitally staining cells have immense powers of proliferation when stimulated, therefore when they are loaded with stain ('blockade') or large collections of them are suddenly removed, as by splenectomy, new ones are rapidly produced. He demonstrated also that saccharated iron oxide is a vital stain of very low toxicity when injected intravenously; recently advantage has been taken of this in therapy and the method has provided one of the best forms of administering iron. The need for reducing to a minimum the risks of blood transfusion became clamant during the late war, and Cappell took up the problems of blood incompatibility presented by the 'Rh factor'; his observations have had a very significant part in establishing the multiple nature of Rh. His analysis of the data laid the foundation on which Fisher was enabled later to formulate a satisfactory notation of the different Rh blood types. Also, Cappell's work, more than any other in this country, directed attention to the measures required to save the life of infants who, in virtue of Rh incompatibility of their blood with their mothers', are afflicted with hæmolytic disease of the new-born. He has lectured on the subject, by invitation, on the Continent. He was the first to discover in Britain examples of 'inclusion bodies' in the organs of young infants; these were widely distributed, and both nuclei and cytoplasm of cells were affected. The condition is most probably due to a congenital virus infection analogous to that originally described in guinea-pigs, in which similar lesions occur in the salivary glands and other tissues. In 1949 the activities of the Department were extended in an important and interesting direction by the appointment of a Lecturer in the Histopathology of the Skin.

BACTERIOLOGY AT THE WESTERN INFIRMARY

From Pasteur's work, Medical Bacteriology developed at first piecemeal; thus Ogston of Aberdeen in 1881 recognised by the microscope staphylococci and streptococci as the species of microorganisms commonly associated with suppuration in man. But the discovery of the tubercle bacillus in 1882 by Koch established the guiding principles and methods which are valid to-day. He demonstrated the organisms in the lesions, grew them as pure cultures on dead medium and finally, by inoculating animals with those cultures, reproduced the disease. After that, advance proceeded at avalanche-pace and within seventy years a discipline of great precision has evolved with intricate ramifications and applications in the service of man such as could scarcely have been foreseen. Coats was at once receptive of Koch's work. Muir before coming to Glasgow had published with James Ritchie in 1897 the *Manual of Bacteriology*; in 1932 C. H. Browning with T. J. Mackie (Edinburgh) became responsible for this book which is now in its eleventh edition. Teaching of the subject and clinical applications were originally provided for by an assistant appointed 'with special reference to Bacteriology,' who also conducted postgraduate laboratory classes. Then a special Lectureship was created in 1908 with the aid of the Carnegie Trust and in 1919 a Chair was endowed by Sir Frederick and Mr. W. G. Gardiner. Carl H. Browning became the first Gardiner Professor, having previously been assistant to Muir, Lecturer in Bacteriology and, at the Middlesex Hospital, Professor of Bacteriology in the University of London; in 1928 he was elected F.R.S. Bacteriology was conjoined with Pathology when this was included among the principal subjects for the combined degree of B.Sc. with Honours and M.B., Ch.B. In 1950 Bacteriology was included among the principal subjects for an Honours B.Sc. degree in Pure Science.

Research has followed several lines. An investigation of the properties of tissue extracts employed as 'Wassermann antigen' for eliciting the syphilis complement-fixation reaction, led to recognition of the important part played by cholesterol, which is therefore generally added as a constituent of such antigens. The selective antiseptic action of particular dyes and other compounds in suppressing the growth in cultures of certain species only among a mixture of bacteria, found a valuable application in brilliant green for the isolation of 'enterica' organisms, especially the paratyphoid B bacillus, during the war of 1914-1918 (*Applied Bacteriology*, edited by C. H. Browning, London, 1918). The principle of such 'selective media' has now been extensively employed for isolating various pathogenic organisms.

A Special Report of the Medical Research Council on *Chronic Enteric Carriers and their Treatment* was issued in 1933. Work carried out over many years helped to establish the value of the laboratory mouse for investigations on tuberculosis. Under the stimulus of Ehrlich, whose pupil and assistant Browning was, chemotherapeutic research has been pursued here for nearly forty years. In addition to yielding experimental findings of theoretical interest, such as the phenomenon of 'chemotherapeutic interference' in which one trypanocidal agent annuls the action of another *in vivo,* the work helped to sustain interest in chemotherapy in this country. Also, it led to the use in the war of 1914-1918 of aminoacridine derivatives (proflavine, acriflavine, etc.) as 'surface-antiseptics' with valuable properties for local application to infected wounds. In the recent war those compounds were again widely used before the introduction of penicillin, etc., which has the great advantage of acting from the bloodstream on certain grave general infections. Further, certain phenanthridine drugs, prepared by Morgan and Walls at the Chemical Research Laboratory of the D.S.I.R., Teddington, were shown to act powerfully on *T. congolense;* and 'phenidium chloride' and 'dimidium bromide' proved the first highly effective agents for the treatment of the economically serious African trypanosomiasis of cattle. Those chemotherapeutic investigations owe very much to the co-operation of Miss R. Gulbransen, Miss K. M. Calver and Miss M. W. Leckie, also to the support of the Medical Research Council.

Among researches independently carried out are studies on the clinical application of the Wassermann test, largely incorporated in Browning and Mackenzie's *Recent Advances in the Diagnosis and Treatment of Syphilis* (2nd edition, London, 1924); serological investigations on complement, Forssman's antigen, etc., included in *Immunochemical Studies* (editor, C. H. Browning, London, 1925); the carcinogenic action of certain aminostyryl-quinoline dyes; the therapy of experimental staphylococcus infection; the effect of surface-active agents on the swarming of *B. proteus;* and the formation and mechanism of action of staphylocoagulase.

The close association of Medical Bacteriology with Pathology has been maintained throughout and this has proved of the greatest benefit in the training of young workers.

PATHOLOGY AND BACTERIOLOGY AT THE ROYAL INFIRMARY

John H. Teacher was elected the first St. Mungo-Notman Professor in 1911, having been appointed in 1909 Pathologist to the Infirmary with teaching duties. The re-housing and development of the Department were undertaken by him, and his introductory lecture delivered in the new Pathological Institute 'On the History of Pathology in the Glasgow Royal Infirmary' (*Glasgow Medical Journal,* 1912, 77, 10) supplements what has been said earlier. It must be noted here, however, that when women were first admitted to the study of Medicine at Glasgow University, the late Dr. Lindsay Steven taught Pathology to the Queen Margaret College students at the Royal Infirmary. Teacher's interest in Pathology was aroused when in 1894 he became under-keeper of the anatomical and pathological department of the Hunterian Museum and prepared the catalogue already referred to. Before becoming assistant in the University Department of Physiology and, from 1903, in the Department of Pathology with Muir he made observations on a case of the rare and deadly condition then named 'deciduoma malignum'; he supported Marchand's view that it is a malignant tumour wholly derived from the fœtal chorionic epithelium (chorionepithelioma malignum). Work on this subject was continued and a monograph published in 1903. Teacher confirmed the remarkable fact that 'self cure' may occur and that after removal of the primary growth metastases may disappear. In 1907 he discovered in a piece of spontaneously expelled uterine membrane a very early fertilised human ovum. Along with T. H. Bryce a detailed investigation was made and its age fixed at thirteen or fourteen days; it was the earliest specimen then known. The research was published by Bryce and Teacher in a beautifully illustrated book, *Early Development and Embedding of the Human Ovum* (Glasgow, 1908). Later a second ovum, very slightly older, was found at autopsy. This provided material for a further critical monograph *On the Implantation of the Human Ovum*. The chief importance of these works is, of course, embryological; but they directed Teacher's attention to the physiology and pathology of the menstrual process. In recording with Jardine in 1911 the rare lesion of symmetrical cortical necrosis of the kidneys associated with puerperal eclampsia and suppression of urine, he concluded that 'the ultimate cause of it was spasmodic contraction of the renal vessels.' It was not generally recognised till much later that vascular spasm is an important, common factor in the production of renal lesions. He gained a most extensive experience of the pathology of the female genital tract and planned to write a book on the subject; unfortunately at his death in 1930 somewhat less than half was complete. Under the editorship of Miss Alice J. Marshall, M.B., the rest was added by seven contributors and in 1935 *A Manual of Obstetrical and Gynaecological Pathology* was published.

In 1928 a Lectureship on Bacteriology was founded by Mr. William C. Teacher, with which is associated the post of Bacteriologist to the Infirmary.

John Shaw Dunn vacated the Chair of Pathology at Manchester University to become Professor at the Royal Infirmary in 1931. His work here has already been mentioned. An anonymous benefaction enabled a Lecturer on Pathological Biochemistry to be added to the Department in 1934. The post of Director of Research at the Maternity and Women's Hospital was instituted in 1935 with the co-operation of the Medical Research Council.

John W. S. Blacklock, a former pupil and assistant of Muir, then Gardiner Lecturer at the Royal Hospital for Sick

Children, was elected Professor in 1937. His admirable work in setting up a pathological museum at the Royal Hospital for Sick Children and preparing a catalogue calls for mention. He is identified with the problems of tuberculosis in the child population of the West of Scotland. A Special Report of the Medical Research Council (1932) contains his major work on *Tuberculous Disease in Children; its Pathology and Bacteriology*. By painstaking observations and correlation over a long period of the lesions with the types of tubercle bacillus responsible he convinced himself of the reliability of the so-called 'primary lesion' in the lungs of young children as marking the route of entry of the infection. In the great majority of these cases the tubercle bacilli are of 'human type,' *i.e.*, derived from other human beings. Since declared pulmonary tuberculosis in infancy is exceedingly fatal, it was deduced that this disease in adults must be due generally to a fresh infection contracted in later life. Contrary to the findings of some observers on the Continent, here the alimentary tract is not the chief path of entry of tubercle bacilli in childhood and, as alimentary infections are preponderantly of the bovine type, this means that the latter is of subsidiary, although very considerable, importance in human tuberculosis. A joint study of a series of cases of tumour of the surparenal medulla, phæochromocytoma, is a valuable contribution on account of the rarity and of the importance of recognising the condition, so that it may be effectively dealt with by surgery.

George L. Montgomery, Gardiner Lecturer at the Royal Hospital for Sick Children, was appointed Professor in 1948 on the resignation of Blacklock. While on service with the Army as Director of Pathology in the Central Mediterranean and later in the South-east Asia area, he had the exacting task of organising the laboratory service in Burma and has outlined the story in 'A Pathologist on Active Service' (*Proc. Roy. Phil. Soc. Glasg.*, 1946-47, 72, 39). He investigated under experimental conditions the healing of wounds of the lung, a subject of much surgical importance especially under war conditions.

To sum up one aspect of this survey of the last three-quarters of a century, conditions at the present day relative to modern needs, have reverted to those of Coats' early times—too little room to house the staff and apparatus required. But one striking difference between past and present obtrudes—our predecessors devoted much thought and effort to pursuit of their work, while now we must spend too much of our energies on external administrative tasks.

We have given the main facts about Pathology and Bacteriology as regards Glasgow itself, but there is another aspect which should not be overlooked and that is the important part played by Glasgow graduates in other places, both in this country and abroad. The number of those who have come to occupy important posts in those subjects is strikingly large, and equally striking is the quality of their work, whether in investigation, teaching or in other ways, in their respective fields of activity. For there has been no similarity in the subjects in which they have attained distinction, but as a rule each has chosen some subject for intensive study. Initiative and independence have been marked features of their work.

I am indebted to many friends for information used in the preparation of this lecture, and especially to Professors D. F. Cappell and G. L. Montgomery for their participation.

CHEMISTRY

by

J. W. Cook

Regius Professor of Chemistry

This task which I have undertaken, to review in the compass of one short article the history of the Department of Chemistry in this University, is to a large extent an unnecessary task. It is unnecessary because it has already been accomplished, much more fully and more competently than I can attempt to do it, in the recently published volume of essays *An Eighteenth Century Lectureship in Chemistry,* edited by A. Kent. These essays, written by a galaxy of distinguished contributors, were published to commemorate the two hundredth anniversary of the founding of the Department of Chemistry, an anniversary which we celebrated in 1947. Four of the essays consist of lectures which were delivered in the University in May of that year. In assembling the material for the present survey I have drawn freely on the subject-matter of those essays. I am glad to acknowledge, with gratitude, the debt which I owe to the authors of those essays.

Measured by the standards set by the University and some of its more venerable departments the Chemistry Department may seem quite youthful—it was only four years old when the University celebrated its tercentenary. Yet it is a lusty infant, as its severest critics would agree, and incidentally one which swallows a very large share of the sustenance of the University. When Glasgow decided, in 1747, to establish an independent Lectureship in Chemistry there were already in being Chairs of Chemistry at Cambridge (founded in 1702), and at Edinburgh (founded in 1713). Apart from these instances there appears to have been little, if any, prior provision for instruction in Chemistry in the British Universities, so that in spite of its relative youthfulness the Glasgow School of Chemistry is to be numbered among the pioneers.

It was born at a very interesting and appropriate stage in the development of chemistry. Robert Boyle, the Father of Modern Chemistry, had published *The Sceptical Chymist* in 1661, and by his insistence on exact experiment as a basis for chemical theory had sown the seed from which the great nineteenth century tree of chemical knowledge was to grow, and to produce in the present century such rich and abundant fruit. But this seed was slow to germinate. The century which followed Boyle witnessed the rise and fall of the phlogiston theory, an erroneous theory which impeded progress. It was probably a useful and necessary stage in the development of chemistry, nevertheless, and the paradoxes to which it led must have done much to stimulate chemical thought and experimental inquiry.

The proponents of the phlogiston theory, of whom the most influential was the German chemist, Stahl, postulated that the combusion of inflammable materials or the calcination of metals was attended by the escape of phlogiston, a principle of inflammability. The main dilemma to which this view gave rise, as is well known to chemists, was that calcination of metals was found to be attended by *increase* in weight, which was difficult to reconcile with a *loss* of something even so intangible as phlogiston. This theory was finally overthrown in the latter part of the eighteenth century by the French chemist, Lavoisier, when he demonstrated the true nature of combustion, and showed it to consist of combination with the oxygen of the atmosphere. He was led to this conclusion largely by drawing freely on the experimental observations of his contemporaries—on those of Joseph Priestley, the discoverer of oxygen (and of soda-water!); and those of Joseph Black, whose careful quantitative work and recognition that large volumes of carbon dioxide (fixed air) could be held in solid combination with lime or magnesia must have been full of significance to Lavoisier. These men, Black, Priestley and Lavoisier, with Cavendish and Scheele, are commonly regarded as the pioneers who laid the foundations of modern chemistry. Their names will live for ever in the annals of our science. It must always be a matter for pride to our University that they include that of Joseph Black, the second Lecturer in Chemistry, who must be counted among the Immortals of Chemistry.

For the purpose of my general survey it will be convenient to divide the two hundred years or so with which I have to deal into three main periods. These correspond roughly with the three centuries over which my story is spread. The first period, which lies partly, but not wholly, in the eighteenth century is that of the six lecturers, beginning with William Cullen and concluding with Robert Cleghorn. The second period, beginning with the establishment of the Regius Chair, in 1818, covers the remainder of the nineteenth century. The third period, consisting of the present century, witnessed the development of the newer branches of chemistry, including organic chemistry and physical chemistry, and the foundation, in 1919, of the Gardiner Chair. If I may seem to pay inadequate attention to this last period, it is because many of those who have played a part in its development are still living, and in any case it is notoriously difficult to form a just appraisal of contemporary history.

Our Department of Chemistry, then, had its origin in the appointment of William Cullen, in 1747, to the newly-established Lectureship in Chemistry. He was assisted by John Carrick, who had already been assistant to Robert Hamilton, the Professor of Anatomy. Carrick was to have been responsible for much of the teaching of chemistry, but after giving a few lectures he became ill and the entire work was taken over by Cullen. William Cullen was the son of the factor to the Duke of Hamilton. He began his medical training in Glasgow, as an apprentice to Mr. John Paisley, a surgeon and general practitioner and he afterwards went as ship's surgeon on a voyage to the West Indies. He perfected his knowledge of Materia Medica by becoming an assistant to an apothecary in London. Returning to Scotland he set up in practice, and later became the medical adviser to the Duke of Hamilton, afterwards joining forces with his friend William Hunter, whose name is an honoured one in this University.

When, shortly afterwards, Hunter established himself in London, Cullen began to devote himself to his supreme ambition, which was to found in Glasgow a Medical School similar to those of Leyden and of Edinburgh. With this object in view he left Hamilton in 1744, and came to live in Glasgow. Although there was at that time in Glasgow College a Professor of Medicine and a Professor of Anatomy and Botany they did not lecture and were examiners rather than teachers. By arrangement with the Professor of Medicine, Dr. Johnstoun, Cullen was able to give a course of lectures on the theory and practice of medicine during the winter of 1746-47. In the following session he also gave lectures on Materia Medica and Botany. When lecturing on Medicine, Cullen became convinced that the institution of a course of lectures on chemistry was essential to his plan for establishing a regular Medical School. His proposals were approved by the Faculty and they ordered, in January, 1747, that a sum of money should be appropriated for the equipment of a laboratory.

It happened that Alexander Dunlop, the newly appointed Professor of Oriental Languages, had been allowed to defer his duties for a time so that he might act as tutor to a nobleman in Geneva. He proposed that the £30 saved by the University by reason of his delay in assuming office, should be used to equip a chemical laboratory. To this the University added £22, so that the total appropriation was £52; Cullen, as lecturer, was to be paid a salary of £20 per annum. It is recorded that the sum actually expended on the chemical laboratory during the sessions of 1747 and 1748 amounted to £136, and as Dr. Alexander Fleck has remarked, Cullen in this way became the first chemist to go on record as being guilty of an over-expenditure above the amount for which he had obtained sanction.

The number of students who attended Cullen's lectures in medicine and materia medica was small, but a considerable number attended the chemistry lectures. These lectures were designed not only for medical students, but for the general students of the University. In his chemistry lectures, as in his lectures on medicine, but not botany, Cullen made a break with the tradition of lecturing in Latin, and his lectures were delivered in English. This example was soon followed by his professorial colleagues. In 1751, four years after his appointment to the newly created Chemistry Lectureship, Cullen was appointed to the Chair of Medicine in succession to Dr. Johnstoun, who had resigned. After another four-year period, in 1755, the Chair of Chemistry in Edinburgh fell vacant, and Cullen was translated to fill it. In so doing, he set a fashion for migration to the east which was followed by several of his successors in the Glasgow lectureship, namely, Black, Robison and Hope. In fact, from Cullen's appointment in 1755 the Chair of Chemistry in Edinburgh was held for over a hundred years by chemists who had been trained in the industrial west.

Although he is to be regarded as the founder of the Department of Chemistry in Glasgow, as he was of the Medical School, Cullen made little contribution to chemical knowledge. He wrote very little on the subject, and his single published paper in this field was really concerned rather with physics. It was entitled: *On the Cold Produced by Evaporating Fluids*. This was a very significant piece of work as it aroused the interest of Cullen's pupil and successor, Joseph Black. This led Black to the conception of latent heat, which must have played no small part in the deliberations of Black's illustrious pupil, James Watt, and doubtless helped to stimulate his perfection of the steam engine. If Cullen contributed little to chemical knowledge or literature, he nevertheless exercised a profound influence by his teaching, which was clear and full of interest. During his tenure of the Chemistry Chair at Edinburgh, he was called upon to deliver some lectures on materia medica. It happened that Dr. Alston, who held the Chair in that subject, died soon after he had commenced his lectures for the session. Cullen was requested to finish the course which had thus been interrupted. Thomson, in his *History of Chemtry,* cites as evidence of Cullen's popularity as a lecturer that whereas Dr. Alston had lectured to ten students, as soon as Dr. Cullen began a hundred new students enrolled in the class. This may equally well be taken as a mark of Dr. Alston's unpopularity as a lecturer! Cullen urged the claim of chemistry as a subject of philosophical study and as an aid to the industrial arts. He was a strong advocate of the application of chemistry to agriculture, and his early work on the bleaching of linen fabrics is of interest in view of the later discovery of Bleaching Powder in Glasgow by Charles Tennant.

Cullen moved to Edinburgh in 1755, and in the following year he was succeeded in the Glasgow Lectureship by his friend and pupil, Joseph Black. Black was born of Scottish parents, in 1728, near Bordeaux. His father and his maternal grandfather were both concerned with the export to Scotland of the finest claret, or Gascon Wine as it was then called. At the age of twelve the young Joseph was sent to his father's home at Belfast to attend a grammar school, and in 1746 he came to study at Glasgow University. During his medical course he came under the influence of Cullen. He went to Edinburgh to complete his medical studies and he graduated M.D. in 1754. He returned to Glasgow two years later to become Professor of Anatomy and Botany and Lecturer in Chemistry. After a year he decided that his knowledge of Anatomy was insufficient, and, with the concurrence of the

University authorities, he exchanged chairs with the Professor of Medicine. His salary as Professor of Medicine was £50 and his fees were £20 to £30; but he also received the salary of £20 as Lecturer in Chemistry, with fees, so that his total income from his University appointments amounted to about £140 to £160 per annum. In 1763 he persuaded the University to equip a new laboratory and lecture room. This was done at the considerable expense of £500.

Black evidently had no wish to be the leader of a medical school, and does not appear to have been entirely satisfied with his medical lectures. At all events, unlike his chemical lectures, no remains of these were found among his papers. Black's researches on latent heat were carried out during his tenure of the Glasgow lectureship. In 1761 he was able to show that when a quantity of water froze it gave up an amount of heat equal to the amount absorbed or rendered latent during liquefaction of the ice. He gave the first account of these investigations in 1762 to a literary society which met in the Faculty-room of the College. Curiously enough, this important work was never published although it was discussed by Black in his chemical lectures. The measurements which Black made of the latent heat of steam were afterwards repeated with better apparatus and greater accuracy by his pupil, James Watt.

Black's other main series of researches, on magnesia, fixed air, lime, and mild and caustic alkalis had been carried out earlier in Edinburgh; they formed the subject of his M.D. thesis. This work is an interesting early example of the impact of politics on science. The researches seem to have originated in the fact that both Sir Robert Walpole and his brother were troubled with urinary calculi. They supposed that they had benefited from a medicine invented by a Mrs. Joanna Stephens. Through their influence she received five thousand pounds for revealing the secret, which was published in the *London Gazette* in 1739. The medicine, consisting of a fearsome mixture of calcined egg-shells, snails and various plants, is described in full by Ramsay. Cullen and Black, and their colleagues were not much impressed with the efficacy of such caustic remedies, and Black began his experiments with the object of discovering a milder alkali. This is not the place to detail this classical work, which was the first systematic chemical investigation involving the use of the balance and helped to elevate chemistry to the rank of an exact science. It undoubtedly served as a model for the later researches of Lavoisier in which he elucidated the nature of combustion and calcination. Black published, in all, only three papers, and he discontinued experimental research after his work on latent heat had been completed. The high quality of his work was recognised by his election to many foreign academies, including the Imperial Academy of St. Petersburg. Curiously enough, he was never elected to the Fellowship of the Royal Society of London.

A discovery in a somewhat different category was disclosed by Black to a party of his friends whom he had invited to supper. This was soon after the publication of Cavendish's work which had shown that hydrogen was at least ten times lighter than common air. Black filled the bladder of a calf with hydrogen, and when he set this free for the entertainment of his friends, it ascended to the ceiling and remained fixed there. This phenomenon was easily explained by the company. It was obvious to them that a small black thread had been attached to the bladder, that this thread passed through the ceiling, and that someone in the room above had pulled the thread and thus caused the bladder to ascend. This experiment of Black, was never published nor even described to his class. It may have come to the knowledge of the French physicist, Charles, under whose supervision ten years later, in 1783, the brothers Robert constructed a hydrogen balloon, and in it made the first successful ascent.

In 1766, at the age of thirty-eight, Black left Glasgow for Edinburgh for the second time, once more to succeed his teacher, William Cullen, this time as Professor of Chemistry in Edinburgh, a post from which Cullen had resigned on his appointment as Professor of the Institutes of Medicine (Physiology). Although Black lived for another thirty-three years, his researches virtually came to an end with this move, and he devoted himself almost exclusively to his teaching duties. It was probably his indifferent health and delicate constitution which induced Black to abandon his chemical researches, and even to eschew the effort of preparing for publication an account of his own discoveries. He was a gracious man of many accomplishments, and possessed of a calm and unruffled disposition. In Glasgow he formed a close friendship with the celebrated Adam Smith—a friendship which lasted throughout their lives. Dr. Smith, according to Thomson, used to say that 'no one had less nonsense in his head than Dr. Black'; and he often acknowledged himself obliged to him for setting him right in his judgment of character. Black enjoyed great renown as a lecturer. It is recorded that his audience continued to increase from year to year for more than thirty years. Thomas Thomson, who attended his last course of lectures, described him as the most perfect chemical lecturer in his whole experience. Lord Brougham, the Lord Chancellor of England, wrote: 'the gratification of attending one of Black's last lecture courses exceeded all I have ever enjoyed. I have heard the greatest understandings of the age giving forth their efforts in their most eloquent tongues— have heard the commanding periods of Pitt's majestic oratory —the vehemence of Fox's burning declaration—but I would prefer, for mere intellectual gratification—to be once more allowed the privilege—of being present, while the first philosopher of his age was the historian of his own discoveries, and be an eye-witness of those experiments by which he had formerly made them, once more performed by his own hands.'

Even the death of Joseph Black was calm and methodical. It took place in the closing weeks of the year at the end of the eighteenth century, and it is recorded that 'he expired without any convulsion, shock or stupor, to announce or retard the approach of death.'

Black's influence was exercised at a very formative period in Scottish culture, and in a century of very considerable expansion by Glasgow University. He consolidated and developed the work which Cullen had begun, and when he relinquished his posts in Glasgow, the new Medical School was well established and the Department of Chemistry firmly founded. Black's own influence was immense. All five of those who succeeded him in the Chemistry Lectureship were his pupils; namely, Robison, Irvine, Hope, Cleghorn and Thomson. Other of his pupils founded chemical schools throughout the world. Smithson Tennant developed the backward Cambridge school; John Morgan and Benjamin Rush founded the Chemical School at Philadelphia; Ogilvie went to Aberdeen, and Garnett to the new Anderson's Institution in Glasgow, now the Royal Technical College. Black's most illustrious pupil was undoubtedly James Watt, who remoulded the steam engine. He was one of a number of Scots who, in Birmingham, took part in the activities of the Lunar Society, which did much to bring into greater prominence the application of chemistry to arts and manufactures.

I have dwelt at some length on the achievements and personality of Joseph Black, for he is certainly the most distinguished man who has taught chemistry in this University. I can make no more than passing reference to those who held the lectureship during the remainder of the eighteenth century. There was John Robison, the son of a Glasgow merchant, who, after serving in the Navy returned to Glasgow to study chemistry under Black, whom he succeeded in 1766. Three years later, Robison resigned and went to Russia, where he became Inspector-General of the Imperial Corps of Marine Cadets at Cronstadt. The winter climate there did not greatly attract him, and he returned to Scotland in 1774 to become Professor of Natural Philosophy in Edinburgh. William Irvine, who succeeded Robison in the Glasgow lectureship, was also the son of a Glasgow merchant. A physician of some standing, he never really settled down to medical practice and preferred scientific work. Irvine was appointed in 1766 to a new lectureship in Materia Medica, the institution of which had been earlier advocated by Cullen, and he succeeded Robison in the chemistry lectureship in 1769, thereafter holding both lectureships until his death in 1787. What reputation he has seems to be founded on his association with Black, whom he assisted in researches on Heat. Irvine himself extended this work and applied his own interpretations, after Black's departure to Edinburgh. He was also interested in applied chemisty and gave assistance in the developing of local industries which were concerned with chemistry. Irvine's death, at the age of forty-four, terminated negotiations in regard to an official appointment in Spain, where he was to have devoted attention to glass-making and metallurgy.

Irvine was succeeded by Thomas Charles Hope. An Edinburgh man, he was son of the Regius Professor of Botany in the University, which he entered as a student at the age of thirteen. He was just twenty-one when he was appointed to the Glasgow lectureship in chemistry. Like his teachers and colleagues he had subscribed to the phlogiston theory. Learning of the experiments of Lavoisier, however, he became so impressed by the French chemist's views on combustion, that in his first year in Glasgow he taught them to his class. This was the first occasion on which the doctrines of Lavoisier were publicly expounded in Britain. Hope succeeded his uncle as Professor of Medicine in 1791, whereupon he resigned the chemistry lectureship. It was then that he carried out his research on a mineral from Strontian, in Argyllshire, and he isolated and named the first known compound of the element strontium. Hope was the first to determine the exact temperature of the maximum

density of water, but perhaps the greatest service which he
rendered to science was in recommending Humphry Davy
to Count Rumford to fill the post of lecturer at the newly
founded Royal Institution in London. On Black's death
in 1799, Hope was appointed to succeed him as Professor
of Chemistry at Edinburgh, a post which he filled with
distinction for forty-five years.

When George IV visited Edinburgh in 1822 there was
an embarrassing lack of portraits of this monarch. The gap
was filled by engravings of Raeburn's portrait of Hope,
with the addition of the sash of the Order of the Garter
across the chest as the sole alteration. These 'false Hopes'
are stated to be now very scarce and to command a high
price.

The last of the chemistry lecturers of the eighteenth century was Robert Cleghorn, who was appointed in 1791 and
held the position until he resigned in 1817. Singularly little
is known about him. The demands on his time made by
an extensive medical practice and by the positions which
he occupied in public and professional bodies left him little
time for original work. He was evidently an acceptable lecturer, if we may judge from the comment of his successor,
Thomas Thomson, who was himself an enthusiast for practical chemistry. Thomson wrote 'My own class is much
more expensive than any other in the College. Chemistry
may, indeed, be taught at a very small expense and in this
way the teacher may be popular and the audience delighted.
This was the system followed by my predecessor who at a
very trifling expense delivered a course of lectures that
charmed his hearers. My object being to teach the science
and to raise up a race of practical chemists my expenses are
necessarily much enhanced.'

I have not perhaps sufficiently emphasised the fact that
these six lecturers who taught chemistry in this University
in the eighteenth century were, with the exception of Robison,
all medical men. The lectureship was a lectureship in the

Faculty of Medicine, and many of the incumbents held also medical teaching posts. Some of the students, but by no means all of them, were primarily students of medicine. This close association between chemistry and medicine was one of the outstanding characteristics of that period in the history of the University and was of mutual benefit to both partners. With the coming of the nineteenth century this intimate relationship began to dissolve. There are signs that it may now be reviving. It is certain that there was never a time in which the science of chemistry was more able to make substantial contributions to medicine. There was never a time when they were more needed. It is not without significance that the Nobel Prize for Medicine for 1950 was shared between a physician and two chemists. This is symbolic of the new partnership between medicine and chemistry and, I think, also of the extent of the contribution which chemistry can make to this partnership.

I come now to the nineteenth century and the foundation of the Regius Chair. The first incumbent of this chair was Thomas Thomson, of whom I have already spoken. He was born at Crieff, in Perthshire, a distinction which my colleague, the present Gardiner Professor, almost shares with him, for Professor Robertson was born within a few miles of Crieff. Thomson was appointed to the Chemistry Lectureship in 1817, on the recommendation of Sir Joseph Banks. At the instance of the Duke of Montrose a chair of chemistry was instituted by George III, and Thomson was elected to the Chair in 1818, with an annual salary of £50. He continued in office until he died, in 1852, in his eightieth year, although in his later years his duties were largely taken over by his nephew, who assisted him. He studied at St. Andrews and Edinburgh, and was the last of Black's pupils to hold the Glasgow lectureship.

Thomson was an ardent experimenter, but although he carried out a large amount of careful work, and published more than two hundred papers, he did not make any great discoveries. He was probably the first of my predecessors to teach his students practical chemistry. This he had already done in Edinburgh, where he conducted a laboratory for practical instruction in chemistry at least as early as 1807. This was probably the earliest British laboratory of its kind. His first laboratory in Glasgow was in a damp ground-floor room. In 1831 he moved into a new laboratory in Shuttle Street, near the College. The authorities of that day evidently mistrusted the chemists, and were reluctant to have a chemistry laboratory within the College itself. But after twenty years fears were allayed. I have in my possession a document which has just celebrated its centenary, for it is dated 7th February, 1851. It is a copy of an advertisement, offering for sale a Tenement at the corner of West College Street and Shuttle Street, the upper part of which was used for the chemistry class room and laboratory, and the lower part for shops. The advertisement intimates that the Faculty of the College contemplated the erection of a Chemistry Class Room *within* the precincts of the College. That project was never realised for the Shuttle Street laboratory continued in use until the removal to Gilmorehill.

Sir Robert Christison described Thomson as 'a very little, well-made man, with small, sharp, handsome features, a calm, contemplative eye, and smooth untroubled brow.' This description is entirely borne out by his portraits. He was not only an active worker at the laboratory bench, he was also a prolific writer on chemical and other topics. At the age of twenty-three, he became editor of the *Supplement* to the *Encyclopaedia Britannica,* to which he contributed several articles. His *System of Chemistry,* first published in 1802, was the first comprehensive text-book of chemistry in the English language, and his *History of Chemistry* is almost as well known. As Thomson remarks himself in his *History,* he introduced an account of Dalton's atomic theory in the third edition of his *System of Chemistry* (published in 1807), and it was in this way that the atomic theory was first made known to the chemical world. Thomson had learned about the theory from conversation with Dalton. To some extent, then, there is justification for claiming that the atom of the chemist was promulgated from Thomson's laboratory in Glasgow. This Daltonian conception of the atom lasted for a century, until the discovery of radioactive disintegration caused it to be superseded by the more complex atoms of the physicist. The recognition that there are atoms of different masses, but almost identical properties played an important part in this new conception of the atom, and it is interesting to recall that the existence of these so-called isotopes was first demonstrated by Soddy during the present century, when he was Lecturer in Physical Chemistry in Glasgow. It is a popular misconception that all of the modern work on the unravelling of the secrets of the atom has been due to physicists. While it is true that the artificial breakdown of the atom was first accomplished by physicists, it is also true that the process known as nuclear fission, by which atomic energy is released, was first brought about by a German chemist, Otto Hahn, who received the Nobel Prize in Chemistry for this work. The production of energy on a large scale by this fission, as in the atom bomb, was made possible only by the skill of the American chemical engineers, who solved the problem of the separation on an adequate scale of the particular isotope of uranium which is needed.

Thomson, like all save one of his predecessors in the chemistry lectureship, was a doctor of medicine. He was succeeded in the Regius chair by Thomas Anderson, who was the last of the incumbents to be medically qualified. After graduating M.D. in 1841, Anderson went abroad and studied first under Berzelius in Stockholm, and then under Liebig in Giessen. Anderson was evidently regarded by his contemporaries as a chemist of some distinction, although little is heard of him now. He was an original member of the Chemical Society on the Council of which he served from 1852 till 1855. He was an honorary member of the Royal Academy of Sciences of Upsala, and was awarded the Keith medal of the Royal Society of Edinburgh and a Royal medal by the Royal Society of London. In view of this latter award it is remarkable that Anderson was not a Fellow of the Royal Society, although his predecessor had been.

Like Cullen and some of the other incumbents of the Glasgow lectureship, Anderson was interested in agricultural chemistry, and in fact during the whole of his tenure of the Regius Chair he found time to act as chemist to the Highland and Agricultural Society. In 1860 he published a book, *Elements of Agricultural Chemistry,* which was stated to have been welcomed both by farmers and professional students as a clearly written practical summary of the state of the science at that time. I may perhaps interpolate here that agricultural chemistry, which has received attention in Glasgow for two centuries and is now being actively pursued at the West of Scotland Agricultural College, will shortly become more closely associated with the University again. Provision is being made for both teaching and research in agricultural chemistry in the new block of the Chemistry Department now being constructed.

Anderson's chemical researches were mainly in organic chemistry, a branch of chemistry which was then in its infancy. He studied the products formed by destructive distillation of natural materials, and his best known work was concerned with the pyridine bases present in bone oil. It is said that at this period, 'those who knew the subject of his work detected his presence in a mixed company as much by scent as by vision.' When the move to Gilmorehill took place the large supplies of residues which had been accumulated in the course of this work were transported from the Old College, and provided William Ramsay with material for his early work on pyridine bases which he carried out when he was assistant to Anderson's successor, John Ferguson. Anderson died in 1874, having been Regius Professor for twenty-two years. Although the new buildings at Gilmorehill were occupied during his professorship, he appears to have played very little part in the transfer, as he was afflicted with an illness in 1869, which largely incapacitated him for his remaining years. It was Ferguson, then Anderson's assistant, who was largely responsible for planning the new laboratory and supervising its equipment.

John Ferguson took some part in the life of the University for sixty years, from his matriculation as a student in 1855 until his retirement from the Regius Chair in 1915. His last official position was that of Curator of the Hunterian Library. I was a boy of fifteen when Ferguson died, and there are still many in Glasgow who knew him. He was familiarly known as 'Soda,' a designation which was well recognised far beyond the confines of Glasgow. I have never discovered the precise significance of this nickname. It may have originated in the fact that he was, in the words of one of his biographers, 'sometimes a little caustic.' He was, I think, the last official link with the Old College in the High Street. Ferguson was a man of scholarly attainments. He had a distinguished career as a student of Arts, and in addition to other prizes, he gained the Cleland Gold Medal for the best 'Essay on the Winds,' and the Ewing Gold Medal for the best 'Historical Account of the Papacy as a Temporal Power in Europe.' He was a good linguist and a man of culture, being especially fond of music. It is recorded that 'from his presence, his courtly manners, and exact knowledge of ceremonial etiquette, he became an almost regular representative of the Senate at academic functions in this country and abroad.' It is interesting to note that even as late as 1863, chemistry was taught only in the Medical Faculty, and Ferguson had to enter that faculty to study the subject.

Ferguson was, above all, a bibliophile, and could scarcely bear to destroy any printed matter, so that he became surrounded by, and perhaps almost buried in, his books and papers, both in the University and at home. He became a leading authority on the literature of alchemy and early chemistry, and his *Bibliotheca Chemica,* a detailed descriptive catalogue of the James Young collection at the Royal Technical College, is regarded as his *magnum opus,* and will ensure his name a place with posterity. This monumental task occupied him for nearly thirty years. A large part of his own extensive collection of alchemical literature is now one of the treasures of the University Library, and is stated to be an even finer collection than that which formed the subject of the *Bibliotheca Chemica.*

It is to be hoped that chemistry will always attract men of Ferguson's scholastic attainments to keep alive its great past, and to give meaning to the philosophy and ideas of those who have shaped its course down the ages. But if Glasgow was uncommonly rich on this score in having Ferguson, it was the sufferer in other respects. For Ferguson cared little for experimental work, and during his tenure of the Chemistry Chair the University contributed relatively little to the vast flood of chemical knowledge which was rising during one of the most formative periods of chemical development. To a considerable extent, however, this deficiency was compensated in Glasgow by the activities of a succession of distinguished chemists who contributed much to chemical knowledge by their labours at the Royal Technical College during that period. In spite of the comparative quiescence of experimental chemistry under Ferguson, he had the capacity to inspire men who subsequently achieved fame in this realm. One need mention only William Ramsay, John Millar Thomson, Arthur Smithells, J. J. Dobbie, and G. G. Henderson. The influence of a professor on his students is determined not so much by the nature of the pursuits in which he engages as by the kind of man he is. Ferguson is stated to have been an excellent teacher in his early days, and to have given his students a clear and methodical and philosophical introduction to the study of their subject.

Ferguson was not only the last link with the Old College,

he was also the last of the Victorians, and I come now to the twentieth century. My time is almost spent and I can do no more than cast a few very brief glances back over these fifty years. They have brought many sweeping changes. In the early years of the century, lectureships were established in Organic Chemistry, Physical Chemistry and Metallurgical Chemistry. This last, first held by C. H. Desch, has now been transferred to the Royal Technical College. To the organic lectureship, T. S. Patterson was appointed in 1904, being elevated in 1919 to the newly instituted Gardiner Chair. Patterson was a cultured man of scholarly attainments, and he was inspired by Ferguson with an intense interest in the history of chemistry, to which he made several notable contributions. He was also a most exact experimental worker and his published scientific papers number more than a hundred. If he had been less absorbed in rather unimportant details and had taken a more comprehensive view of the problems in which he was engaged he might have been included among the foremost chemists of his day. I have already referred to Frederick Soddy, who was appointed in 1904 to a newly established lectureship in Physical Chemistry. He was succeeded in 1914 by A. W. Stewart, later a professor in Belfast, and he in his turn was succeeded by Dr. Robert Wright who is now living in retirement in the same city.

The most outstanding figure in twentieth-century Glasgow chemistry was G. G. Henderson, who was appointed to the Regius Chair in 1919, after having already occupied the Chair of Chemistry at the Royal Technical College for twenty-seven years. He was an organic chemist of distinction, but it is perhaps not unfair to say that his most outstanding research work was done before he came to the University. He was a man of great influence in chemical circles, both locally and nationally. He was revered by most of those who knew him, and he is one of the few men I have known to whom I have never heard a disparaging reference. He, with Patterson, was responsible for planning the new building which now houses the Chemistry Department, and Henderson's name is fittingly attached to a fine large laboratory for organic chemical research. In 1912 the Royal Technical College became affiliated with the University for purposes of certain degrees in Applied Science, and this was followed in 1915 by the institution of a degree in Applied Chemistry. This degree, for which Henderson was doubtless in large measure responsible, has served a very valuable purpose in providing a satisfactory training for men embarking on careers in industrial chemistry.

On Henderson's retirement in 1937, he was succeeded by George Barger, a dominating personality with an international reputation in organic chemistry; he was so nearly medical in his research interests as to represent a modern counterpart to the eighteenth-century lecturers whom I have discussed earlier. Barger died after holding office for only a year, and so was unable to exercise any lasting influence on Glasgow chemistry.

I have come to the end of my survey. I have written mainly of the personalities who have held, first the Lectureship and then the Chairs in the Department of Chemistry. If I could have described the students who studied under them, perhaps a much more interesting story would have been unfolded. The number of distinguished chemists of our own time who have been Glasgow students gives some inkling of the vast army of illustrious men who must have studied under my predecessors during these two hundred years. I have not had time to pay tribute to the valuable work which has been done during the present century by the student society known as the Alchemists' Club. The future historian who may recount the chemical works carried on here during this century will have to take note of the activities not so much of the professors as of the much more numerous lecturers and their research students. This Chemistry Department, which began with a lecturer and a small group of students, in a class-room probably shared with others, has grown to an impressive Institute with a staff of more than thirty lecturers and assistants, and a muster of students of close on a thousand. Whereas we began in one faculty we have now invaded four, and we play some small part in the education not only of the ortho- dox products of these four faculties, but also of dentists, agri- culturists and veterinary practitioners. Our new buildings, when completed, will have cost considerably more than half a million pounds. Our annual expenditure exceeds fifty-five thousand pounds. Is all this outlay justified, and are we getting value for our money? It is not for me to say. It would be interest- ing to hear the verdict of my successor who may be privileged to give the sixth centenary lecture one hundred years hence. But by that time our whole civilisation may have passed into oblivion!

NATURAL HISTORY

by

John Walton
Regius Professor of Botany

At the time of the *Nova Erectio* in 1577, one of the three regents in the College was entrusted with the teaching of physiology, a subject which then covered practically all branches of natural knowledge, including Botany, Mineralogy and Zoology. There was no regular medical instruction before 1637, and it was not until 1712 that a Chair of Medicine was finally and permanently established. When the Chair of Medicine was first established in 1637, it was still the age of herbals when herbals were the principal medical text-books. We have only to glance through the fine collection in the library of the Royal Faculty of Physicians and Surgeons in Glasgow to see that herbals were the most important part of the library of a physician as late as 1700. Botany was the first separate science to be taught by a special instructor for a lectureship was established in 1704. It is known that private herb gardens existed in Glasgow in the eighteenth century, for it is recorded that Dr. John Woodrow cultivated one by the Molendinar Burn near the site of the present St. Andrew's Square. There was also a Mrs. Balmano, a druggist, who had a herb garden near the site of the present Balmano Street close to the City Chambers. Her shop was at the sign of the Golden Galen's Head.

In the eighteenth century the development of botanical teaching was, as one would expect, closely linked with the development of the medical school, and indeed all physicians still required a knowledge of the properties of herbs in the preparation of drugs and simples. Many would probably

collect their own plants and would have to be able to iden-
tify those which were required. It is therefore not surprising
that the University had to turn to physicians for teachers of
botany and that Botany was the first of the Natural Sciences
to acquire an independent status.

In the records of the University there occur under the date
1704, the words 'The Faculty enact that part of the great
yard behind the gardener's house, be improved for amenity
of the College and for improvement of students in the knowledge of Botany,' and under the same date, 'The Faculty,
having resolved to prosecute their own act of July 4th anent
the improvement of some parts of their great yard for botany
and a physic garden, do now think it necessary to name one
who shall have the charge and oversight thereof, and who
may instruct the scholars who shall apply to him for the
study of botany, and being informed that John Marshall,
chirurgeon in Glasgow, is capable of discharging that trust,
and being specially recommended by the Dean of Faculties'
letter, therefore the Faculty does nominate the said John
Marshall to the said employment.' It is clearly implied that
there had been teaching of botany in the College prior to
1704, and it has been taught without interruption to the
present day.

In September of the same year, Marshall was appointed
keeper of the physic garden. He had studied in Paris in
1677 and had no doubt seen physic gardens there and was
able to introduce to Glasgow new ideas for the lay-out of
such gardens. He was granted a salary of £20 and an allowance for a gardener. The University conferred on him the
degree of M.A. in 1706, and in 1708 Queen Anne allo-
cated £30 yearly to the 'Professor of Bottany' (sic), and
Marshall may have used the title of Professor. His classes
were of an informal character and consisted of practical
demonstrations conducted by him or by his gardener in the
physics garden. He died in 1719.

In 1718, in order to develop the teaching of Anatomy, a

combined Chair of Anatomy and Botany was established, and in 1720 Thomas Brisbane, M.D., of Leyden, was appointed to it. However, Marshall seems to have carried out the duties of lecturer until the year of his death. It is surprising that Brisbane was appointed to teach Anatomy, for he is reported to have had an intense dislike of dissection and seemingly completely neglected his duties as far as anatomy was concerned. So much so that the Commission of Visitation to the University in 1727 insisted that he teach Anatomy yearly, if at least ten students presented themselves, once a week from November to May when the Botany course began. Here we have the first indication of a summer term for botany. He had at least one student of note, the Marquis of Graham, 'who,' according to a contemporary, 'studied medicine, especially botany, a long time in this University.' The Marquis may be regarded as the lordly prototype of those interesting and often picturesque 'hardy perennials' who graced our classes until 1939, when the advent of unsympathetic action by the Ministry of Labour effectively discouraged them. In those early days, noble birth appears to have had some advantages, for students so favoured were entrusted with a key to the physic garden but were not allowed to lend it to others.

Robert Hamilton was appointed to the Chair in 1742. The standard of instruction is said to have fallen to a low level under Brisbane. Cullen, who came to Glasgow in 1744, worked independently of the University and began teaching botany in addition to other sciences. When in 1750 he accepted the Chair of Medicine he collaborated with Hamilton, who was an active botanist and interested in the garden and greenhouses, where there was a 'banana tree' and other interesting plants under cultivation. A great improvement in botanical instruction was effected during Hamilton's time, and one of his students, John Hope, who graduated in 1750 in Glasgow, later became King's Botanist for Scotland and University Professor in Edinburgh.

u

A second physic garden was laid out in University lands between Blackfriars Church and Blackfriars Wynd with conservatory and hot beds, but, on Hamilton's departure for Edinburgh, it appears to have fallen into disuse. It produced at least one botanical triumph. According to the *Edinburgh Evening Courant* of the 20th April, 1776, a plant of *Rheum palmatum* (a rhubarb) was grown which when dug up and washed weighed 45 pounds. He was succeeded by Thomas, brother of Robert Hamilton who died in 1781, and later by William Hamilton, son of Thomas, who occupied the Chair from 1780-1789.

The Hamiltons, although they made little contribution to botanical learning, seem to have kept in touch with advances being made elsewhere and carried out some simple experimental work. There are in the University Library and the Department of Botany, manuscripts one of which is a syllabus of lectures in botany by William Hamilton, the others appear to be notes taken by students. One of the class tickets issued by William is preserved in the University Library and is illustrated in the late Dr. J. M. Cowan's book *Some Yesterdays* (Glasgow, 1949). It is clear that the lecturer was not only familiar with the anatomical and microscopical discoveries of Hooke and Grew but with the work on plant physiology, including plant nutrition, by Hales, Knight, Cæsalpino and Duhamel. There are also references to the effect of plants in purifying the atmosphere, the action of perspiration (transpiration) and the movement of sap.

There is, as one would expect, a good deal of attention paid to the Linnæn artificial system of classification, but the other systems are also discussed. There are observations on the nature of soils and practical aspects of botany in gardening and in obtaining natural substitutes for foreign medicinal plants.

During the period of 1754-1789 the records give evidence of much activity and considerable expenditure on material and labour for the garden. In 1789 Robert Lang was appointed gardener 'at the wages of £17 a year, with the grass of the College garden, valued at £8, an allowance for tools and a house rent free.' On William Hamilton's death his trustees offered all the collections, preparations and hot house to the University for £298, the College refused to pay more than £243, but the trustees refused to accept this sum. The hot house was subsequently acquired by Hamilton's successor, Jeffray.

Jeffray found the twofold duties of the Chair too much for one man, and the botanical teaching in 1799 was entrusted to an assistant, Dr. Thos. Brown, a surgeon in the Royal Infirmary. On Brown's death his collections of minerals and fossils were shared between Glasgow and Edinburgh. An allowance of £20 a year was granted for the supply of plants for the botany class, for the College garden had fallen into disuse and teaching material had to be sought elsewhere.

In 1816 Robert Graham was appointed lecturer in Botany under Jeffray and became the first Regius Professor of Botany in 1818 when separate Chairs of Anatomy and Botany were established. About 1814 the Royal Botanical Institute of Glasgow acquired eight acres of ground in Sandyford Place and in 1817 the University contributed £2,000 for its development. Graham was responsible for the layout of the garden which by 1822 contained about 9,000 species of plants and is reputed to have ranked as highly as any other garden of its kind in Britain. Unfortunately Graham's period of office in Glasgow was short (two years), but he held the Edinburgh Chair with great distinction. Robert Brown, the greatest of all Scottish botanists and perhaps the greatest, and certainly the most versatile, botanist of his time, was offered the Chair but refused it.

However Glasgow did not suffer greatly, for in 1820 (Sir) William Jackson Hooker succeeded Graham. His application for the Chair was strongly supported by Sir Joseph

Banks. Born in 1785 at Norwich he was educated in the Grammar School there. While learning estate management in Suffolk, he spent much time in studying natural history and developed a special interest in birds and insects. These interests led to his election to the Linnæn Society at the early age of twenty-one, a record at that time. He made botanical tours in Scotland in 1807 and 1808 and in Iceland in 1809. In 1814 Switzerland, Italy and France were visited and he made the acquaintance of de Jussieu, Lammarck and Humboldt. He settled down in the small Suffolk town of Halesworth and published in 1816 his *British Jungermanniae,* a work which may be considered one of the more important early contributions to the scientific study of the Liverworts. This was followed by the first volume of *Musci Exotici.*

Hooker had had no experience as a teacher, but he seems to have made a great impression on the students of his first class on medical botany, for in the Botany Department Library there is a letter written by Hooker from his house at Halesworth to a student thanking him for a silver vaculum for which the class had subscribed. The University shortly afterwards conferred on him the degree of LL.D. He had a strenuous time preparing his lectures as he had little knowledge of plant anatomy and physiology. He found too that in Scotland the Linnean or artificial system of classification was still in use. His contacts with de Jussieu and de Candolle had converted him to recognise and use the natural system, a less empirical scheme of classification than that of Linnæus, so with his characteristic energy he wrote and published a year after his appointment *Flora Scotica.* In it he compares the two systems so as to encourage his students to accept the new. He organised botanical excursions for the students and in a few years became a very accomplished lecturer.

He helped to develop the Sandyford Garden, and the number of species in cultivation (9,000 in 1821) was increased to nearly 20,000 by 1840.

With teaching duties limited to the medical class in the summer term, he spent the rest of the year working at his herbarium and writing. His output of published work was considerable. Between 1827 and 1842 he published several volumes of *Icones Plantarum* which when completed consisted of ten volumes containing a total of about 1,000 plates of illustrations, *Icones Filicum* in two volumes (1829-31) and the *British Flora* in two volumes (1830-31). He also made voluminous contributions to botanical journals. His herbarium received constant attention and ultimately became one of the finest private collections in the world.

Associating with him in Glasgow and collaborating with him in many of his tasks were Greville, George Bentham, Walker Arnott (his assistant for a few years and one of his successors in the Glasgow Chair), Richardson the Arctic explorer, and W. H. Harvey of Dublin who became famous as an Algologist. Bentham's microscope is preserved in the Department of Botany.

Hooker had a struggle to get what he considered adequate recognition of Botany as part of the medical curriculum, and, during the time he spent in Glasgow, he pressed for the recognition of extramural courses as qualifying candidates for the M.D. examination.

He is perhaps best known among botanists for his work on the Bryophyta and the Ferns. His work on the Phanerogams is partially overshadowed by the achievements of his son, Joseph, who was born in 1817 at Halesworth. Joseph was educated at the Glasgow High School and University. He graduated M.D. in 1839 at the age of twenty-two years.

During Hooker's tenure of the Chair, Glasgow became one of the principal centres of Botanical Science. His influence on botanical development of the time was profound, in the words of his son Sir Joseph Hooker, at the opening of the present Botany Department building in 1901, 'he had resources which enabled him to overcome all obstacles: familiarity with his subject, devotion to its study, energy, eloquence, a commanding presence, with urbanity of manners, and above all, the art of making the student love the science he taught.' He was extraordinarily prolific as an author of botanical works, and the unfailing accuracy with which these were illustrated is astonishing for most of them were drawn by his own hand.

Hooker left Glasgow in 1841 to assume the Directorship of Kew Gardens.

In 1807, the year in which the Hunterian Museum was completed, a Chair of Natural History was established and Lockhart Muirhead, M.A., LL.D., was appointed to it. Under the title Natural History were included Geology and Zoology. Lockhart Muirhead was also University Librarian and registrar for Medical students until 1827. He was succeeded in 1829 by William Couper, who was also appointed Keeper of the Hunterian Museum. Couper was not regarded very highly by some of his contemporaries. It has been written that 'his professorship was bestowed on him in consequence of the skill with which he directed volleys of minerals against the soldiers of the 71st Regiment at the Battle of the College Gardens in 1810 and the Keepership of the Hunterian he obtained as the reward of his extraordinary valour in defending the Museum from the violence of the red coats.' According to Professor John Ferguson he was an absolute nonentity who neglected his lectures and gave but occasional demonstrations of minerals in the Museum. Others, however, have recorded that he was a skilful descriptive mineralogist.

In 1841 John Hutton Balfour was appointed to the Chair of Botany which he occupied for four years. The Botanic Garden at Sandyford had been by now completely shut in by streets and houses, and the atmospheric pollution had so increased that the more delicate plants refused to grow. Its value as a site, however, had greatly increased. Balfour therefore helped to carry out Hooker's plan for a new Garden on the present site in Kelvinside. This garden, like the old one, was not the property of the University but belonged to the

Royal Botanical Institution of Glasgow. In 1845 he resigned on being appointed to succeed Graham in Edinburgh, where he was largely responsible for the foundation of the Botanical Society of Edinburgh. During the last few years of his life he had the young Joseph D. Hooker as assistant.

George Arnott Walker Arnott, laird of Arlary in Fife, succeeded to the Chair in Glasgow in 1845. In 1821 he had been admitted to the Faculty of Advocates but never practised in law. He subsequently became Deputy Lieutenant of Kinross-shire and a magistrate for Fife. He was a friend of Hooker, and at the latter's suggestion worked in Paris on Mosses and went on botanical tours in Spain and Russia. He accompanied Bentham to the Pyrenees in 1825. His collaboration with Hooker extended from 1830-1840. During this period he and Hooker examined the plants collected by Captain Beechey in the Pacific. In the Botanical Department Herbarium there are large numbers of specimens representing the first collections of Chilean plants that had been made by Beechey, Gillies, Cumming and others. This Chilean herbarium and some fine examples of *Welwitschia mirabilis* are practically the only reliques of the Hooker period in Glasgow.

Walker Arnott worked diligently on the description of the new plants from India, Senegambia and South America and built up an excellent herbarium. He was in close touch with Wight, and a large representation of Wight's collections are to be found in the herbarium. He became an authority on diatoms. His herbarium and botanical collections were acquired by the University.

The occupant of the Chair of Natural History from 1857 to 1866, Henry Darwin Rogers, was not only distinguished as a geologist but was the first, and so far only, American citizen appointed to a Chair in this University. He may be rightly claimed as the initiator of the fine tradition of Geological teaching and research in Glasgow. Rogers was descended from a Tyrone family. His father fled to America after the rebellion of 1798 and for a time was Professor of Natural Philosophy and Mathematics in the College of William and Mary at Williamsburg, Virginia. Rogers and his three brothers all rose to eminence in American science. He held various school and university teaching posts. In 1831 his interest in Socialism led him to visit Europe with the son of Robert Owen of New Lanark Mills. He studied chemistry under Edward Turner, then secretary to the Geological Society of London, who was responsible for exciting in him an interest in Geology. He returned to America in 1833 and in 1835 was appointed to the Chair of Geology and Mineralogy in the University of Pennsylvania.

In 1836 he was appointed State Geologist and issued six annual reports. In 1855 he visited Edinburgh to arrange for the publication of his final report. While he was there he was, by the influence of 'powerful friends,' appointed by the Crown to the Chair of Natural History in Glasgow. In 1858 Zoology became a compulsory subject for Medical students, and so compelling was his enthusiasm that, in addition to the Zoology course, he held a class in Geology specially for them on Saturday afternoons. He conducted geological excursions. On one visit to Arran he was accompanied by six students and his assistant, John Young. He was an excellent lecturer and was regarded as the leading structural geologist of his time, and to him has been assigned the discovery of the significance of overthrust faults in mountain formation. He published about seventy important scientific papers between 1835-1868. The work which stands out above all is *The Geological Survey of Pennsylvania*. Professor Gregory regarded him as 'the direct forerunner of Suess' and the founder of modern theory of 'the origin and distribution of mountain chains and the major relief of the Globe.' He died in 1866.

Rogers was followed in the Chair of Natural History by John Young, M.D. Young was born in Edinburgh in 1835, educated at the High School, where he won many prizes.

He proceeded to the University and studied medicine, graduating M.D. in 1857. He was appointed assistant physician to the Royal Edinburgh Asylum. He appears to have enjoyed and taken a great interest in his work for about three years, and then he took the somewhat surprising action of accepting a position in the Geological Survey. Sir Roderick Murchison was at that time director, and Professor A. C. Ramsay, Scottish director. Young had been a close friend of Archibald Geikie during his school days and had evidently had his interest in Geology stimulated by frequent geological excursions with him in the Edinburgh district.

Ramsay entrusted to Geikie, Young and Peach the investigation and mapping of the drift deposits first in Fife and the Lothians and then in Peebles. Young became a well-known figure in the Southern Uplands for, in addition to his official work, he appears to have given freely of his spare time in providing medical assistance to isolated shepherd families. With encouragement from T. H. Huxley he also undertook research on fossil fish.

He was appointed to the Chair of Natural History in Glasgow in 1866. He was scarcely settled in his duties when the removal of the University and Hunterian Museum from High Street to Gilmorehill was put into effect. Young held in addition to the Professorship the Keepership of the Museum. His assistant was John Young, who had been appointed by Rogers, and their time was fully occupied at first in the removal of the Hunterian Collections. In 1876 the Honeyman-Gillespie Lectureship in Geology was established, and Young was appointed lecturer. He gave courses of instruction in Zoology and Geology. He was the first to introduce practical classes in Zoology.

Young was a man of many interests, probably too many for him to acquire a position of eminence in any one of them. He was often brusque and outspoken, and tended to frighten the more timid students and antagonise his colleagues until they found that under the formidable exterior there was sympathy and understanding. Young adopted a cynical manner which seems to have inspired his students with enthusiasm. He considered that lectures were a waste of time and that a student's time was better spent in reading. He took an active part in extramural matters, and was a keen advocate of higher education of women, and with others worked for the establishment of Queen Margaret College and its final amalgamation with the University. He had a clear and retentive memory and his knowledge of the Hunterian Collections was unequalled. The University was specially fortunate in having one with Young's catholic interests in charge of the Hunterian Museum during the removal from the old premises.

In 1868 Alexander Dickson succeeded Walker Arnott in the Chair of Botany. Dickson was a student of medicine in Edinburgh but turned to natural science. He lectured in Botany at Aberdeen, and later held the Chair of Botany in Dublin. After two years in the Chair in Glasgow, he went to Edinburgh as Professor of Botany and Regius Keeper of the Botanic Gardens. He was laird of Hartree and Kilbucho and was a popular figure in Edinburgh society. In spite of his interest in outdoor sports and social engagements, he published a considerable number of short scientific papers.

Dickson was followed by (Sir) Isaac Bailey Balfour, son of John Hutton Balfour, who had occupied the Chair for six years before succeeding Dickson in Edinburgh. Balfour was born in Edinburgh and later graduated in science in Edinburgh University. He studied under Sachs at Wurtzburg and de Bary in Strassburg. He assisted Huxley in Edinburgh. He graduated in Medicine in 1877. In 1874 he visited the island of Rodriguez and, after his appointment to the Chair in Glasgow, went and studied the flora of the island of Socotra. The results of this expedition were published by the R.S.E. in a volume with 300 quarto plates of illustrations.

In 1885 he was appointed to the Chair in Oxford, but

in 1888 returned to Scotland to Edinburgh, where he occupied the Chair of Botany until his death in 1922. He is best known for his transactions of Bary's Comparative Anatomy and Sach's Lectures on the Physiology of Plants, and was very largely responsible for the foundation of the Annals of Botany in 1887.

Bailey Balfour's short tenure of the Chair left but little impression on the University. He had, however, made a beginning in establishing laboratory practical classes. The laboratory consisted of two fairly large rooms in the East Quadrangle. The lectures were given in one of the lecture rooms of the Faculty of Arts.

Bailey Balfour was succeeded in 1885 by Frederick Orpen Bower, who, during his forty years' occupancy of the Chair, was responsible for the transformation of the Department of Botany into a modern laboratory. When Bower arrived in Glasgow, botany was taught only to medical students and his teaching was carried out in the summer term. He followed Bailey Balfour in taking advantage of this by spending the greater part of a year in Ceylon. In 1893 the Faculty of Science came into being, and in 1901 the present Botany building was declared open for classes by Sir Joseph Hooker. It was the first of the science departments to be installed in a separate building.

Associated with Bower as lecturers or assistants during his period of office were Dr. J. C. Willis, Dr. Gwynne-Vaughan, Professor W. H. Lang, Professor McLean Thompson, R. C. Davie, Dr. D. Patton, Dr. J. Thompson and later Dr. S. Williams. Dr. Robert Kidston of Stirling also co-operated in a voluntary capacity with Bower, Gwynne-Vaughan and Lang.

Kidston's association with the Department was most fruitful. With Gwynne-Vaughan he produced a monograph of the Fossil Osmundaceæ and with Lang the first descriptions of the Middle Devonian plants from Rhynie in Aberdeenshire. This latter work has been so far the most important contribution to Palæobotany in this century. The Kidston collection of fossil plant sections, which includes all the type specimens of the Rhynie plants and his library of palæo-botanical books and pamphlets, was bequeathed by him to the Botany Department.

Under Professor Bower the Department had developed into a large institution. Bower came of a Yorkshire family and in his early years studied at Cambridge. Later he worked under Sachs at Wurtzburg and de Bary at Strassburg. In 1880 he became assistant to Daniel Oliver at University College, London, and in 1882 lecturer in Botany under Thomas Huxley at South Kensington.

He was one of a group of British botanists who, after experience of the German and French universities, returned to this country and introduced a new outlook and new life into British Botany, which then had become almost completely submerged in the purely systematic side of the subject. Experimental work and laboratories developed rapidly. He will be chiefly remembered for his work on the morphology of the Pteridophyta. The theme on which much of his writing was based was that the sporophyte generation of the Pteridophyte has developed as an intercalation in the more primitive sexual life history in response to the environmental conditions of life on land. His argument may be followed in his books the *Origin of a Land Flora* and *Primitive Plants*. His great three-volume work on the Ferns is a description of the main divisions of that group of plants in an evolutionary sequence. He used developmental and anatomical data in addition to the superficial criteria previously used by systematists in their schemes of classification with outstanding success. Professor W. H. Lang has written an excellent biography and bibliography to which the reader may refer for a full account of Bower's activities, publications, honours and distinctions. In 1938 Bower wrote an autobiography in which he gives an interesting account of the activities of some of the distinguished botanists with whom he was contemporary.

Bower took a very active part in University affairs and in

the Department of Botany has left permanent records of his long period of tenure of the Chair in the collections and library and in the planning of the main buildings.

Professor Drummond who succeeded him occupied the position until 1930, when he was appointed to the Chair of Botany at Manchester. During this short period the teaching of genetics as part of the Honours Course in Botany was one of his chief interests. He also did much to promote interest in the Officers' Training Corps, of which he was commanding officer.

The teaching of the subject of genetics, which had been carried out as part of the Honours Courses in both the Botanical and Zoological Departments, was entrusted in 1945 to Dr. Guido Pontecorvo, who was appointed Lecturer in Genetics in the University. In 1947 Genetics became an independent degree subject, and in 1949 the Department of Genetics, under the direction of Dr. Pontecorvo, was established in part of Anderson's College which was reconstructed for the purpose.

Since Professor Drummond's resignation from the Chair of Botany, an annexe has been built on the east side of the Botany Department for Plant Physiology and Mycology. This was made possible by the generosity of Sir Daniel Stevenson who gave £5,000 for this purpose. The Stevenson Laboratory, as it is now called, was opened by Sir Albert Seward in 1937. Owing to the increasing number of students and need for additional accommodation for the staff, the large botanical museum has been divided up by the construction of two floors. This provided in 1950 seven additional rooms and a smaller but adequate museum.

The Chair of Geology was founded in 1903, and John Walter Gregory was appointed to the Chair at the age of thirty-one years. He had graduated in London and at first held the post of assistant in the Geological Department of the British Museum. He was a great traveller. He had visited the Rocky Mountains in America, the West Indies and

Kenya. The last was an unfortunate experience but illustrates his determination and resourcefulness, for, owing to dissensions in the party and other difficulties, Gregory had to reorganise the expedition and finally set off by himself with a party of native carriers and explored 1,650 miles of country in less than five months. He all but accomplished the first ascent of Mt. Kenya, and studied the tectonic features of what he named the *Great Rift Valley*. In 1896 he took part in Sir Martin Conway's expedition to Spitsbergen and was the first to make a crossing of the interior. In 1900 he was appointed to the Chair of Geology in Melbourne. This gave him the opportunity of exploring and carrying out surveys in Victoria.

From the time of his appointment to the Chair in Glasgow in 1904 he carried on his work on Corals, Bryozoa and on economic and general geology. His thirst for travel was, however, insatiable and between 1904 and the year of his death in 1932 he visited Cyrenaica, Southern Angola, India and the Alps of Chinese Tibet. He returned from the British Association meeting in Australia in 1914 by way of the Trans-Siberian Railway. After his retirement in 1929 he lived in Essex, but in 1932, at the age of sixty-eight, he set out with a party he had organised to explore the geology of the Peruvian coastal belt and the desert area between it and the Andes. In negotiating the rapids of the Urubamba his canoe was upset, the three other occupants of the canoe managed to get ashore but he was drowned. He was buried by the river, and a cairn marks the grave.

Gregory was a stimulating writer and teacher. He was the author of twenty books and over three hundred scientific papers. He achieved much as a teacher in popularising geology. His principal contributions to science were his works on tectonic geology. No other British Geologist it is said achieved such a world-wide reputation or had such a large circle of friends in every continent.

On the fly-leaf of one of his notebooks used in Peru he had written the following lines:

'I wandered till I died
Roam on! The light we sought is shining still
Dost thou ask proof? Our tree yet crowns the hill
Our Scholar travels yet the loved hill-side.'

Gregory was succeeded in 1929 by Sir Edward Battersby Bailey, who came to the University Chair from the Geological Survey. Bailey's interests were principally centred in Highland geology and tectonics. In 1937 he left the Chair to assume the directorship of the Geological Survey of Great Britain. The Chair of Geology was then occupied by Sir Arthur Trueman from 1937-1947 who subsequently became chairman of the University Grants Committee. Dr. Tyrrell was associated with Gregory, Bailey and Trueman and was responsible for the instruction of Petrology. His text-book of Petrology is very well known and widely used.

In 1903 the Chair of Zoology was founded, and John Graham Kerr was appointed first Professor of Zoology. Although there had been a Chair of Natural History from 1807 to 1902, Zoology had been subordinate to Geology in the interests of all those who occupied, it and Graham Kerr was really the first person whose chief interest was to teach Zoology in the University. He was responsible for the planning of the present Zoology building. He did much during his long tenure of office (1902-1935) to develop Zoology as an important subject in the University. He also did much to encourage the development and activities of the Millport Marine Biological Station. He was in addition an active politician and retired from the Chair when he was elected a Member for the Scottish Universities in Parliament. On his retiral in 1935, Dr. Edward Hindle succeeded him in the Chair. The war years interfered with further developments and Hindle undertook the very onerous post of Officer Commanding the Students' Training Corps in the University. In 1944 he resigned from the Chair and was appointed Scientific Director of the Zoological Garden, London.

NATURAL PHILOSOPHY

by

P. I. Dee

Professor of Natural Philosophy

Period of the Regents, 1577-1727. The teaching and study of
Natural Philosophy has continued in Glasgow University
from the earliest years, when the Regenting system was set
up. Under the *Nova Erectio* of 1577, the four subjects of study
which were laid down as qualifying for the degree of Master
of Arts were Greek, Logic, Ethics and Physics—each Regent
carrying his class from Greek to Physics through the four
years of study. Physics included not only the subject-matter
which would now be understood by that name, but also
the teaching of pure mathematics, astronomy and geography.
It is hard to find any evidence as to what constituted the form
of instruction in physics in those early years, but undoubtedly
it must have conformed largely with the Aristotelean Scholasticism. The new outlook in science, originated by Galileo and
perfected by Newton, did not become widespread till the
second half of the seventeenth century. We see, perhaps, its
first influence in *George Sinclair,* the first Professor of Mathematics in Glasgow University, but one whose chief interest
appears to have been in physical science. His contributions
to science appeared in a number of treatises on mathematics,
hydrostatics, coal, astronomy, navigation and other subjects.
Although Sinclair's work contains many obscurities, it is to
his credit that he wished to establish hydrostatics as a subject
for experimental enquiry, whilst James Gregory, of St.
Andrews, regarded it as closed by the pronouncements of
Aristotle. During Sinclair's time, there appeared in the
records of the University the first evidence of expenditure of

funds for the acquisition of apparatus. Thus in the statement of the needs of the University, which Principal Dunlop was commissioned to lay before the King in 1691, apparatus for 'experimental philosophy' was included; in particular, optical instruments, such as a prism, and a telescope eight feet long were acquired.

Robert Dick (1727-1751). When the Regenting system was discontinued, the Commissioners of Visitation allowed the Masters of the three Philosophy classes to elect which classes severally they were to take. Carmichael chose Moral Philosophy, Loudon chose Logic and the first Chair of Natural Philosophy fell, therefore, in 1727, to Robert Dick—the third Regent. Prior to this date, there is little real evidence of serious achievement in Natural Philosophy at Glasgow University. 1727 was also the year of Newton's death, and many of his active contemporaries were working in London; Hooke, Boyle and others. How quickly their discoveries in optics and in dynamics spread to the teaching in Glasgow it is difficult to assess. From this time onward, however, it is clear that experimental demonstrations bulked more largely in the teaching of the subject, and during the period of about thirty years, in which Dick and his son held the Chair of Natural Philosophy, accounts amounting to over £300 for instruments can be traced in the minutes. A complete apparatus for electrical experiments is mentioned among 'additional articles' procured in 1749. In 1730, payments began to be made to Henry Drew for assistance in working the instruments and showing experiments in the course which Dick conducted twice a week in experimental philosophy. Drew is the earliest laboratory assistant of whom we have record. The subjects of study in the Natural Philosophy class of this period were mechanics, hydrostatics, pneumatics, optics, astronomy and natural history. The course consisted of lectures 'in which, facts being taken for granted without any experiments, the consequence of them are demonstrated by Geometry, Plane and Solid, and by the art of numbering.'

These lectures were held on four days of the week. Also, on two evenings, a course was given in experimental philosophy, at which the 'facts which are taken for granted on the other four days of the week are ascertained by a direct proof to the senses.' These subjects of study were continued after Professor Dick's death by his son *Robert Dick,* who held the Chair from 1751 to 1757. Of him, his colleagues said that 'he had the clearest conception and soundest judgment accompanied by a modesty which was very unusual.' The second Professor Dick is perhaps most noted for his encouragement of James Watt, in whom he took much interest when he came to Glasgow in 1754. It was on Dick's advice that Watt went to London to learn the art of mathematical instrument-making, and it was through his introduction that he found employment there. It was also on Dick's suggestion that on Watt's return to Glasgow in 1756 he was appointed mathematical instrument-maker to the University and was given a room in the College. It was in a room of the Natural Philosophy Department that Watt perfected his steam engine.

John Anderson (1757-1796). Robert Dick was succeeded by the robust personality of John Anderson, who formerly had held the Chair of Oriental Languages, and was appointed to the Chair of Natural Philosophy at the age of thirty-one. In Murray's *Memories of the Old College of Glasgow,* we are told that 'Anderson . . . was an active and intelligent man and, although he was not a student or a scholar, or an investigator, he might have been a useful member of the Faculty if he had not allowed vanity, arrogance and a pugnacious disposition to master him.' Again, according to Murray, 'Anderson, known to his students as "Jolly Jack Phosphorus," was a man of good parts, of various accomplishments and a popular lecturer. . . . He was, however, impossible as a colleague; he was meddling and disputatious, obstinate and inconsiderate, and involved the University in protracted, useless and costly litigation.' Samuel Johnson, after the celebrated 'Journey to the Hebrides,' had supper in Anderson's house in the College, but he also met many other Professors on this visit, and it would be ungenerous to attribute too heavily to Anderson the stigma of Johnson's later remark in a letter to Mrs. Thrale, 'I was not much pleased with any of them.'

Anderson delighted in visiting the workshops of artisans and mechanics, and, to his more formal University classes in which the treatment of Physics was often necessarily mathematical, he added evening lectures to what he described as his 'anti-toga' class. These lectures were attended by large numbers of mechanics, artisans, and other inhabitants of Glasgow. There is a widespread impression that Anderson was the first to encourage the attendance of mechanics at evening demonstrations of experimental Philosophy. It is certainly true that he made these lectures immensely popular, the normal attendance being about two hundred at a time when the population of Glasgow was perhaps not much more than 40,000, but there is evidence that the practice was also frequent during the time of the Dicks.

In his general University class Anderson gave an account of the history of Physics and its main theories, and demonstrated mathematically the practical consequences of these. Students were required to give—in Latin—written and even oral answers to physical problems. His 'anti-toga' class was, of course, treated in much more popular fashion. The students watched but did not themselves perform physical experiments.

Anderson published two works on Natural Philosophy for the use of his students. Firstly, in 1760, there was a *Compend of Experimental Philosophy,* followed, in 1786, by his *Institutes of Physics.* These books contained only the general headings of the subject-matter covered in his annual lectures, together with conclusions drawn from experiments performed at the same time. He justified the publication of such outlines by the remark, 'In this manner, it seems proper to guard against the inaccuracies into which young students are apt to fall, while the publication of more than such Outlines might lead them to lay aside the custom of making notes;

a custom by which their attention and ingenuity are constantly exercised, and the Lectures and Experiments become, as it were, their own.' The 'Institutes' was divided into fifteen parts, with titles such as Electricity, Magnetism, Gravitation, Mechanics, etc. It is interesting to note that parts entitled Mineralogy, Botany and Zoology were also included. The preface to this work finishes, 'By the experimental course the students are instructed to see and to value experiments, which is of much importance, because theories without experiments have been the great bane of Philosophy in every age and in every country. The reason of this is well known. It is easy for anyone who has a good imagination to make a theory, and a theory is pleasing to the indolence and to the vanity of its author. But if we would be philosophers, we must despise every theory which does not rest upon decisive experiments or well-established facts, we must remember that the Law by which a Cause acts may be investigated, though the cause itself be unknown; that the investigation of that law is often of great importance in the useful arts, without regard to any theory whatever, and that it is at the same time the only way of making progress in philosophy; for, according to the famous maxim of Lord Bacon, "*Non fingendum, aut excogitandum, sed inveniendum, quid Natura faciat, aut ferat.*" ("We must not suppose nor feign; but we must find out what nature does and brings forth.")'

In Anderson's treatment of the subject-matter of this book, the scientific propositions often illustrate practical problems drawn not only from industry, but also from nature. A few examples may serve to illustrate the nature of instruction in Physics at that time, and also the character of the author. In Part VIII, Mechanics; Section XI, Proposition VI states, 'The lateral strength of a hollow cylinder is to that of a solid cylinder as the section of the first excluding the bore, to the section of the second, and the diameter of the first to the diameter of the second nearly,' with a Corollary, 'Hence the greater strength acquired by forming the same mass of matter into a tube instead of a solid cylinder of the same length, when the increase of the size is not inconvenient; and hence the strength of the stalks of vegetables, and of the bones of animals.' Again, Section II, Proposition XI states, 'The sum of the motions of several bodies in any given direction, is the same as the motion of all the bodies in the same direction, when moved with the velocity of their common centre of gravity,' and concludes, 'Of the centre of gravity in quadrupeds, birds and men, when sitting, standing, at rest, in motion, with or without burdens, and in a variety of attitudes that requires agility and strength.' Parts V and VI, dealing with Electricity and Magnetism, are almost entirely confined to statical effects, the properties of electric currents being at that time barely recognised. But in Section XV of Part V, several propositions deal with lightning conductors, and in 1772, the year following Benjamin Franklin's visit to Glasgow, the first lightning conductor in the city was erected upon the College steeple. Part I of this book is entitled 'Somatiology,' a word of Anderson's own invention, and deals with Space, Time, Matter, Motion, and the Particles of Matter. The section on Space and Time is very short. Present-day students, wrestling with the Theory of Relativity, may well agree with at least part of Anderson's conclusion: 'Though we know not enough of space and time to gratify our curiosity; yet what we do know, is sufficient for the happiness of life.' The sections on matter constitute a kind of chemical dictionary with classification of matter into different orders and divisions. Dalton's Atomic Theory had not yet of course been advanced and, in fact, in one Proposition, Anderson states, 'The difficulty of conceiving the endless divisibility of matter, is no just objection to its truth.'

Anderson himself did very little scientific work, but he was intensely interested in military matters. He invented a six-pounder gun and gun-carriage, and even prepared a new alloy and devised new methods of casting this weapon. Among the many desirable properties which he claimed for it was one that 'when it bursts, it splits and does not fly into fragments.' He also designed fire balloons for use by the French to carry propaganda across the German frontier and again, at the time of a scare of a French invasion, he was responsible for the design of the fortifications of Greenock.

Much of the surviving information about Anderson concerns his unfortunate feuds with the other Professors in the University, characterised by him in his famous will as 'Drones, Triflers and Drunkards.' He fought several actions in the civil courts. One of these concerned a student who had insulted the Professor and later came to the class with a group of companions armed with bludgeons. Anderson was much too impatient an individual to await the decision of the College authorities upon this matter. He held strong views on the methods of keeping the College accounts, and when on one occasion the 'Visitors' were slow to act, he himself raised an action in the Court of Sessions. Perhaps the chief of these battles was his Petition to the King for a Royal Visitation to investigate alleged injustices by the College to students and inhabitants of Glasgow. He obtained no support for this Petition from his fellow Professors, although he did have substantial support from past graduates and townspeople. The Petition did not succeed.

In his famous Will, Anderson bequeathed the whole of his property, except ' . . . Everything that is now within a painted Chest with three locks standing upon Iron Brackets in the Red Room of my House in Glasgow College' . . . 'to the Public for the good of Mankind and the Improvement of Science in an institution to be Denominated "Anderson's University".' He actually named the eighty-one Trustees and thirty-six Professors who were to hold office in this new University, where . . . 'the almost constant intrigues which prevail in the Faculty of Glasgow College about their Revenue and the Nomination of Professors, and their Acts of Vanity, or Power, Inflamed by a Collegiate Life' would be excluded,

and where . . . 'the neglect of duty in the Professors of
Glasgow College, will naturally, in some degree, be cor-
rected by a rival School of Education.' Superficially, the
whole conception seems rather ridiculous, since Anderson
in fact left no funds to further his purpose. He did, however, leave an excellent library of over 2,000 books, and a
collection of physical apparatus which was the most valuable in Great Britain if not in Europe. With these and with
funds gathered by public subscription opened by the Trustees,
a nucleus was, however, formed and the year 1796 saw the
start of the first session of 'Anderson's Institution' with nine
hundred and seventy-two students, about one-half of whom
were ladies. In this latter connection, we might note the
Ninth Article of his Will which contains the paragraph,
' . . . another Course shall likewise be given by the same
Professor; at least once every year, to be called "The Ladies'
Course of Physical Lectures," in which no Mathematical
Reasoning shall be used' . . . 'The intention of this Course of
Lectures is that the Ladies in Glasgow may have an opportunity, for a small sum, and in the early part of life, of
being at several of these Courses of Lectures, by which their
education for domestic affairs will not be interrupted . . . and
such a stock of general knowledge will be laid in as will make
them the most accomplished Ladies in Europe.'

Although Anderson doubtless had many faults, he was
certainly a strong character, and his Memorial exists to-day
in the Royal Technical College of Glasgow which is an
off-shoot of the Anderson College envisaged in his Will.

James Brown (1796-1803). The subject of Natural Philosophy seems temporarily to have languished in Glasgow
after the time of Anderson. His successor, James Brown,
having taught for one session, conceived himself to be in
ill-health and, from then until his retiral in 1803, did not
appear in Glasgow. Such tuition as there was in Natural
Philosophy during this period was given by a series of young
assistants, not particularly qualified in the subject. In 1803,

the Faculty decided to ask for reports by eminent medical men upon the state of Brown's health, whereupon Brown tendered his resignation, it being, however, agreed that he should continue to draw an annual allowance of £165 for life. Brown, therefore, taught in the College for one session, held the Chair for seven years, and his annuity for thirty-three.

William Meikleham (1803-1846). Brown's successor, William Meikleham, had, by 1813, according to Coutts, 'grown tired of the arrangement by which £100 was withdrawn annually from his emoluments to augment the annuity to the inert Dr. Brown.' Thereafter, the Faculty decided to take over responsibility for the whole of this annuity.

Meikleham had been Professor of Astronomy before he took over the Chair of Natural Philosophy. Kelvin says that he 'taught his students reverence for the great French Mathematicians, Legendre, Lagrange and Laplace.' A contemporary writer, however, states that most of the students could not profit by his lectures on account of their ignorance of mathematics.

Meikleham's own health broke down in 1838 and, for the last eight years of his tenure of the Natural Philosophy Chair, the teaching of the subject was carried out largely by Professor Nichol of Astronomy. It is interesting to note that it is during this period that the young Kelvin was a student at Glasgow University.

William Thomson (Lord Kelvin) (1846-1899). Physical Science in Glasgow University during the nineteenth century is dominated by the figure of William Thomson, late Lord Kelvin. From the time that his father, James Thomson, came to Glasgow as Professor of Mathematics in 1831, when Kelvin was a boy of eight, until his death in 1907, Kelvin was associated with Glasgow University, first as a student, matriculating at the age of ten, then, on his return in 1846 from four years at Cambridge, as Professor of Natural Philosophy; finally, after his retiral, as Chancellor.

That he was not merely the brilliant and precocious

student shown by his early academic records but was, rather, destined to become one of the world's leading scientists was foreshadowed by the publication, at the age of seventeen, of his first scientific paper, entitled *On Fourier's Expansions of Functions in Trigonometrical Series.* This paper dealt with certain aspects of Kelland's criticism of Fourier's famous book upon the *Analytical Theory of Heat.*

With Thomson's election to the Chair of Natural Philosophy at the age of twenty-two, the history of the Department is transformed. For the first time, the Glasgow School of Natural Philosophy takes its place in the forefront of scientific advances rather than, as in previous years, at the best, recounting the discoveries made elsewhere.

Upon Thomson's appointment to the Chair, he was exhorted to include experimental physics in the work of the Department, and one of the immediate consequences of his appointment was the development of the experimental laboratory on a much larger scale than previously. Thomson once said in later life, 'When I entered upon the Professorship of Natural Philosophy at Glasgow, there was absolutely no provision of any kind for experimental investigation, still less idea even for anything like students' practical work.' Remarks of this kind should perhaps not be taken too literally. I suspect that the Principals of Universities regard them as the normal consequences of every election to a Chair. There is a record, in the first five years of Thomson's appointment, of the sanction, by the Faculty, of expenditure totalling £550 on apparatus, and it appears that most of this was required for research in electro-magnetism. Towards the end of 1855, the first teaching Physical Laboratory was established below the Natural Philosophy class-room, in which some of the students could assist in the experiments being then conducted by Thomson. This laboratory is to be distinguished from the earlier demonstrations given during the time of the Dicks and Anderson, for which there was already an apparatus room adjoining the lecture-theatre.

The physical laboratory bore little resemblance to a modern teaching laboratory. There was no systematic instruction in experiment; instead, the interested students, most of whom were destined for the Church, were given an opportunity, under the guidance of Thomson's assistant, MacFarlane, of carrying out observations of experiments relating to Thomson's current researches. It is traditional that this laboratory was in the deserted wine cellar of an old professorial house, and this may well be so. It soon spread, under Thomson's guidance, to include the James Watt room and later the Blackstone room, which was no longer required for examinations.

During the ten years following his appointment, Thomson did his most important work in Pure Science, culminating in 1852 in his statement of the second law of Thermodynamics. Thomson's fundamental researches were always closely related to contemporary affairs. His interest in Heat and Thermodynamics was doubtless inspired by the Industrial Revolution, then in full swing, and the increased use of coal and steam as the source of energy for manufacture and locomotion. Although steam engines had been made for over a hundred years, the basic principles underlying their operation were not at all understood. The experiments of Joule had established the quantitative equivalence between mechanical energy and heat, but Carnot's paper upon the efficiency of heat engines assumed that energy was produced by heat falling from one level of temperature to a lower one without a change in its total amount. It is clear that this conception was contrary to the requirements of Joule's experiment, where the amount of mechanical work done by the engine must be related to the disappearance of an equivalent amount of heat. In 1851, Thomson discovered how the points of view of Carnot and Joule could be reconciled, and shortly afterwards enunciated the famous Second Law of Thermodynamics. It is true that Clausius had arrived independently at the same conclusion, but Thomson went much further and showed how the second law could be applied to a large range of phenomena in Physics. Wherever one effect of temperature is known, another can be predicted with the aid of this law; hence it has been said that the second law doubles every discovery of the effect of temperature on bodies. With its aid, Thomson made many discoveries in thermo-electricity, magnetism and electricity.

But as the age of steam power reached its climax, the electrical age was just beginning. It is interesting to note that the beginning and end of what may fairly be termed the electrical age coincide very well with the dates of the birth and death of Lord Kelvin. The most elementary laws of electricity were discovered only in Kelvin's lifetime. Yet here again, before the age of thirty, he made many basic investigations. A paper in 1853, entitled 'Transient Electric Currents', explained how oscillatory discharges may take place in an electric circuit and gave a mathematical calculation of the frequency of such oscillations. This is the basis of the tuning used to-day in every wireless receiver. The oscillators which Hertz used more than thirty years later in the first successful demonstration of radio waves were designed according to the principles described in this paper. In an extraordinary letter to Faraday in 1847, Thomson drew analogies between electric and magnetic forces and elastic strains and made speculations about their propagation. But unfortunately he disowned any intention of regarding his suggestions as constituting more than a useful analogy. He said, 'I did not venture even to hint at the possibility of making it the foundation for a physical theory of propagation of electric and magnetic forces.' He went on to say that if such a theory could be derived then, in conjunction with the undulatory theory of light, it might be possible to explain the known effects of magnetism on polarised light. How close he was in these researches and conceptions to the discoveries of Maxwell and Hertz which, more than thirty years later, were to unfold the Electromagnetic Theory of Light! Had he proceeded with these studies, he might well have combined in his own life the work of Kelvin, Maxwell and Hertz, and ranked in fame with Newton. But this was not to be.

Thomson's work upon the propagation of electric currents through cables, mathematically analogous to the conduction of heat in solids, acquired great topical significance in view of the proposed Atlantic cable. Thomson's intense interest in practical science was now revealed, and the story needs no re-telling of how, from then until the final success in 1868, he threw himself into the many problems of the telegraph, sailing repeatedly with the cable-laying ships, personally making the continuous electrical measurements and super-vising the very means of cable-laying until, after innumerable disappointments, the work was brought to a successful con-clusion. During this period, with the help of his students at Glasgow University, Thomson designed the first sensitive electrical measuring instruments.

Another most important 'off-shoot' of this work derived from Thomson's struggle for precise electrical specification of the cable. Careful investigations on the first unsuccessful cables showed that impurities in the copper of only one per cent. could increase the electrical resistance by as much as forty per cent. He investigated this subject quantitatively and deliberately obstructed other business at board meetings until the cable manufacturers accepted a specification of the electrical resistance of the cable. Out of this and out of his great interest and later work upon the accurate standardisation of electrical units, has grown the National Physical Laboratory where standards are now maintained and instruments checked in order that the measurements of scientists and industrialists everywhere may be identical and mutually acceptable. For the cable enterprise, Thomson was honoured everywhere and knighted by the Queen, and a story is often told of how, while Thomson was in London for this purpose and his classes were being taken by a man named Day, a student wrote upon the blackboard, 'Work while you yet have day for when the Knight cometh no man can work.' Fortunately the claims of Engineering did not completely divert Thomson from his interests in Pure Science, and many great papers on hydrodynamics and water waves were still to come. Throughout the rest of his life he also gave the weight of his great reputation and learning to further widespread developments of the electrical age. During this period he also became an enthusiastic yachtsman, designed the famous magnetic compasses and even succeeded in persuading the British Navy to adopt them.

In his later years, Kelvin gave much effort to attempts to find a realistic model for the ether. His strong mechanical sense led him to feel that Maxwell's electro-magnetic field theory was too abstract, and with great subtlety he developed his gyroscopic models of the ether, ending inevitably in the 'failure' to which he referred in his famous Jubilee speech: 'One word characterises the most strenuous efforts for the advancements of science that I have made perseveringly during fifty-five years. That word is failure.' This was no expression of false modesty. Kelvin had been born and bred into a tradition of regarding basic Newtonian ideas as sufficient to explain the whole of terrestrial mechanics and planetary motions. Throughout his life his objective had been to explain comprehensively, heat, light, electricity and even the nature of matter itself, in terms of mechanics. He once said, 'I never satisfy myself until I can make a mechanical model of a thing.' Herein lay his great strength, but also his weakness. He believed in the finality of engineering concepts. The whole trend of modern physics suggests that a limit to the usefulness of mechanical models of nature may have been reached. Perhaps the best description of his work was that made by the President of the American Society of Civil Engineers at the Kelvin centenary: 'We recognise in Kelvin the great leader who brought together Pure Science and Applied Science, who brought the profoundest conceptions of science into the service of the constructive arts.'

Kelvin's teaching abilities have been variously assessed. It is strange that his long period as a teacher in Glasgow University should not have been graced by any very distinguished pupils. His Ordinary Class in the sixties contained some hundred students, the bulk of whom consisted of law, medical and divinity students preparing for the ministry of the various Scottish Churches, Natural Philosophy being then one of the subjects for the Arts degree. Every morning, except Mondays and Saturdays, the Professor lectured twice, first upon Ordinary Physics, accompanied by experimental illustrations, and later upon Mathematical Physics. Thomson's method of teaching and of conducting the class was in every way characteristic of himself. It was founded on the assumption that the effective education of a student depended upon what he did for himself in making use of opportunities provided. The subject matter of his early lectures are, of course, to be found in permanent form in the famous book entitled *Natural Philosophy*, which he wrote in collaboration with Professor Tait of Edinburgh. This book first appeared in 1867, but the collaboration between the two Professors extended over eighteen years. Advanced proofs of fragments of the book were printed off from time to time for the benefit of the class who, being kept informed of its progress, were made to feel almost participators in the work itself. Oral examination was a characteristic feature of the class work. Each student in turn was called upon to stand up and answer some question bearing on a preceding lecture. For a record, Thomson used a 'call box' with three compartments, each student's name being written on a separate card and kept within the box. One compartment contained the names of students who had not yet been called up. The second contained the names of students who had satisfactorily passed the test. The third contained the names of those whose answers had not yet satisfied the Professor. These compartments came to be popularly known by the names, Purgatory, Heaven and Hell. Frequent demonstrations of physical experiments were given—some of which I hope to repeat at the close of this lecture. In an account of the work of this class prepared for me by Dr. Green, who worked with Kelvin and who, until his recent death, was a lecturer in the Department, we are told that, 'In the actual carrying out of the demonstrations, all trace of the orthodox Professor disappeared and only the keen, ardent, natural man remained, eagerly expectant, rejoicing in the success or downcast by the failure of the matter in hand.' When success was achieved, the uproarious delight of the class was perhaps due more to the enthusiastic pleasure manifest in the Professor's demeanour than to satisfaction in the demonstration of a scientific truth. 'What more powerful persuasion,' asks Dr. Green, 'could students receive, to become workers in physical science, than to see the pleasure it afforded to its devotee? What stimulus to self-effort could be better than the realisation of the value to every man of unbounded pleasure in his daily work? The class was a place of work, of busy life and of laughter.' It was impossible for Kelvin, with his multifarious lines of scientific interest and enterprise, both academic and industrial, to use old-fashioned lecturing methods. He, therefore, often spoke of current activities in the world of scientific enterprise and told what Joule and Faraday were doing, or what progress was being made in his own work of recording and predicting the tides. What he actually spoke of on these occasions was doubtless often above the heads of his listeners, but the enthusiasm and interest aroused in his listeners has many times since been recorded.

Andrew Gray (1899-1924); James Gray (Cargill Chair, 1920-1935). In 1899, Andrew Gray was appointed, on Kelvin's retirement after fifty-three years' occupancy of the Chair. Gray was then Professor of Physics at Bangor University, and had earlier been Kelvin's assistant. The Department then occupied part of the south front of the present Arts quadrangle and in Gray's opinion was very crowded and badly equipped. His first task, therefore, was to persuade the University to build a new Department. Kelvin objected strongly to the suggestion that the teaching accommodation that he had used for nearly thirty years was not good enough for his successor; but the business of collecting funds went on, and, in 1906, the present building was opened at a reputed cost of over £40,000. Gray, who had been a stonemason in his youth, superintended the building to the last detail, and indeed it was well designed for physical experimentation.

Present members of the Departmental Staff who attended Andrew Gray's classes remember him as a dignified and imposing figure, bearded of course, whose morning entry evoked a natural and instantaneous response by the class to rise for morning prayers, which were always conducted with a great depth of spiritual feeling. His formal lectures were very precise, and gave a marked impression of intolerance of ignorance which made him difficult to approach. He knew Greek and Latin well, and there were frequent references to the Classics . . . 'You will remember how Agamemnon lay awake at night in his tent, thinking things over in his mind.'

It was no enviable task to succeed Lord Kelvin, and Andrew Gray was never very popular with his students, some of whom asserted that he simulated the characteristics of his predecessor. Even his slight limp was alleged by hard-hearted students to be modelled upon that of Lord Kelvin. Perhaps the seat of the rumour lay in his rather frequent reference to 'my distinguished predecessor,' and his fondness for reproducing lecture-room demonstrations with Kelvin's apparatus exactly as Kelvin had done them.

Although to Andrew Gray teaching came first and research second, he encouraged research to the limit of the Departmental resources, but he never allowed it to interfere with teaching. His own work was mainly upon the mathematical analysis of gyrostatic motion. He published two treatises which, for many years, remained standard text-books. These were *Gyrostats and Gyrostatic Motion* and *Absolute Measurements in Electricity and Magnetism*. He also published several papers on generalised dynamical theory. Andrew Gray's son, James Gray, later the first occupant of the Cargill Chair of Applied Physics, was a Lecturer in the Department at this same time. Father and son were joint authors of a text-book entitled *Treatise on Dynamics*. Whilst Andrew Gray was primarily interested in the mathematical analysis of gyroscopic motion, his son excelled in the invention of mathematical applications of gyroscopes, such as mechanisms to counteract precessional motion, stabilising devices, etc. James Gray's success in this work during the 1914-1918 War resulted in an award to him of £4,000 by the Commission on Awards to Inventors. His apparatus for finding and maintaining the true vertical on aeroplanes and airships was adopted for bombing purposes by the R.N.A.S. in 1917.

Andrew Gray recognised at an early date that the teaching of Engineering students required courses quite distinct from those given to Arts and Science students, and these separate courses were already in existence when in 1920 the Cargill Chair of Applied Physics was founded and endowed by the gift of Sir John Cargill, merchant of Glasgow, the duties of the new Professor being 'to take over the teaching of Applied Physics within the Department of Natural Philosophy.' James Gray was, as I have already said, appointed to this Chair and assumed responsibility for the courses in Physics for students of Engineering and Medicine.

H. A. Wilson (1924-1925). Following Andrew Gray's retiral in 1924, his successor, H. A. Wilson was appointed. Wilson held the appointment, however, for one year only, returning in 1925 to the Chair of Physics he had previously vacated at the Rice Research Institute in Houston, Texas. During his short time as Professor, the separation between the two Departments of Pure and of Applied Physics was made unnecessarily distinct. Wilson, however, made an appeal for separate funds for research activities which resulted in the creation of the Kelvin Research Fund in commemoration of the Centenary of the birth of Lord Kelvin.

Edward Taylor Jones (1926-1943). After a short interval, Wilson was succeeded by Edward Taylor Jones in 1926. It is, perhaps, too soon to assess his influence in the years to 1943, when he retired, but several of his graduate students and research students have attained positions of distinction in academic life, in Government service and in industry.

Thomas Alty (1935-1948). Thomas Alty succeeded James Gray in the Cargill Chair in 1935 and, in the period from 1945 until 1948, the work of the Department was shared between the two Professors of Natural Philosophy and of Applied Physics; the rigid boundaries of administration which had previously existed between the teaching of Pure Physics and Applied Physics being swept away. When Alty retired, in 1948, to become Principal of the University of Grahamstown in South Africa, the University Court assigned the Cargill Chair to Theoretical Physics, and the first appointment under these new conditions was that of John C. Gunn, who still occupies that Chair. It would perhaps be inappropriate on this occasion to refer to the present work and activities of the Department, but it may fairly be asserted that at the present time there is considerable activity both in the teaching of all branches of Physics, and in research in the field of nuclear physics and the physics of elementary particles. For this work, the wholehearted support of the University has been supplemented by generous financial assistance from the Nuffield Foundation, and later, by the Department of Scientific and Industrial Research, in the provision of the large-scale and expensive apparatus which is necessary in this modern field.

At the close of the lecture, historic apparatus was exhibited and the following lecture demonstrations were performed. The numbers in brackets refer to the indexing of the articles in the Departmental museum.

1. Demonstration of the production of an electric spark from a very early frictional electricity machine (M.4).

2. Demonstration of a model of the 'water dropper' induction machine of Lord Kelvin.

3. Demonstrations of angular momentum as originally performed by Professor Andrew Gray.

    (a) The revolving stool demonstration.

    (b) Three gyroscopes, mounted in a column on a rotating pivot showing self erection into a common vertical axis.

    (c) A gyroscope in a pivoted box.

4. Demonstration of Robins' ballistic pendulum (KMI.2), as performed by Lord Kelvin, using firstly Lord Kelvin's gun (KMI.3), (uncharged, to illustrate Newton's I Law) and secondly a loaded modern rifle. An optical lever attached to the pendulum illustrated Lord Kelvin's method of optical magnification which he first applied to the design of sensitive galvanometers.

5. Two of Lord Kelvin's acoustic demonstrations.

    (a) The monochord, to illustrate the dependence of the frequency of a bowed wire upon its length.

    (b) The French horn (KMI.8), to illustrate the vibrations of an open pipe.

Apparatus exhibited.

1. A demonstration wheel and axle of the eighteenth century, used in Anderson's lectures to artisans and mechanics (M.6).

2. Kelvin apparatus.

    (a) The 'Cable' galvanometer (KMG.1).

    (b) The Quadrant electrometer (KE.7).

    (c) The absolute electrometer (KE.2).

    (d) The current balance (KB.7).

    (e) The pitch glacier (KMI.4).

(*f*) The class call box, named also the 'Purgatory' box (MI.7).

3. The glass plates used by the Rev. John Kerr in his discovery of the electro-optic effect. (KE.2 and KE.4).

I am indebted to Professor J. C. Gunn for much information which is embodied in this lecture and for his advice and assistance in its preparation. In the sections dealing with the Natural Philosophy Class under Lord Kelvin I have drawn freely from the manuscript of a book which was in course of preparation by the late Dr. G. Green, one time lecturer under Lord Kelvin and a member of the staff of the Natural Philosophy Department until his retiral in 1945.

I wish also to express my gratitude to Mr. J. T. Lloyd, Senior Technician in the Department of Natural Philosophy, for the care and enthusiasm with which he prepared and performed the lecture demonstrations.

ENGINEERING

by

James Small
Professor of Mechanical Engineering

Engineering appeared in the history of the University long before it became an established department of study. There was that George Sinclair (of whom more than one of my colleagues in this series of addresses have spoken), the mathematician of the seventeenth century who, in the interval between two periods as Regent, set up as an engineer and surveyor, and whose achievements extended to the draining of mines, the superintendence of the works for Edinburgh's first water supply and the authorship of treatises on Mathematics, Hydrostatics, Coal, Astronomy and Navigation— and of a book on witchcraft and ghosts! And he was not the only professor in the early annals of the College of Glasgow to engage in some pursuits that to-day would fall within the scope of engineering.

It was in 1757, however, that the College first harboured an engineer in the real sense of the term, when it set up James Watt within the precincts, but it was more than eighty years later that Engineering as a study found its place in the curricula. Founded in 1840 the School of Engineering is not old as compared with some other schools of study within the University, but it is the oldest University School of Engineering to be found anywhere. It is true that there are institutions which lay claim to some slight priority in their Engineering chairs; but at the time their chairs were founded these institutions were still to attain to an accepted University status.

My professorial colleagues who have been telling the story

of the ancient disciplines in which they are interested, have sometimes been able to enliven their tale with accounts of the foibles of some of their predecessors—their temperamental whims, their irregularities of conduct, their blatant dereliction of duty or their failure to contribute anything either to the development of their field of study or to the good standing of the University! These colleagues have the advantage of me as the recorder of a department, for the succession of Professors of Engineering have all been respectable and conscientious; if they departed at all from a normal tenour it was when they proved themselves men of outstanding genius.

There is no record of the influences that were brought to bear upon the Government to found a Chair of Engineering. One thing is clear; the University itself took no part in it. But Glasgow was closely identified in the public mind with the name of Watt in the history of mechanical development. That great man had died in 1819. The centenary of his birth fell in 1836, and received widespread notice. The British Association met in Birmingham in 1839, and the opportunity was seized for more celebrations in honour of Watt because of his connections with that city. The place of meeting chosen for 1840 was Glasgow. If a Chair of Engineering was to be set up in one of the old universities, then it may be supposed that Glasgow was a natural choice.

In whatever way it was brought about, however, it was in that year that Queen Victoria 'considering it would be of importance in the education of youth and for the public advantage,' to use the words of the royal warrant, erected a Chair of Civil Engineering and Mechanics in the University and appointed to be the first professor Lewis D. B. Gordon, of whom few had heard.

The times were not propitious for the introduction of Engineering by royal decree into an academic environment for the long dispute was raging over the royal patronage and the rights of the regius professors. The Senate requested Gordon to meet it on 27th October 'in reference' as the minute says, 'to his not encroaching on or interfering with any of the present classes in the University,' and they appointed him 'to write and deliver in presence of the Senate as a trial of his abilities' a Latin essay with the title 'De relatione scientiae ad artes industriae' on 10th November.

In a letter written many years later, Gordon identifies the classes on which he was not to encroach when he says, ' . . . I was met with much jealousy by the Professors of Natural Philosophy and Mathematics.' For a young man of twenty-five, he showed much firmness in the letter he sent to the Senate. After giving the assurances that there would be no such encroachment as they feared, he said, 'In thus satisfying the desire of the Senate, as I trust I have done, I beg respectfully to state at the same time that my willing compliance with their desire on this point must not be construed into an admission on my part that my reception into the office in the University to which I have been appointed is in any degree contingent on my giving such an explanation . . .' Gordon, it would appear, had even now enlisted in the defence of the rights of regius professors.

He delivered his Latin essay, however, and, having presented certificates as to the oath of allegiance and the confession of faith and having subscribed the usual undertaking as to his duty to the University, he was admitted.

The teaching session was well under way but he was not yet officially provided with a class-room. On 13th November he wrote to the Principal, asking that suitable accommodation should be appropriated to his purpose and asking that, in addition to a lecture room, he might have a place in which to display certain models and apparatus. Here is perhaps the first hint of an Engineering laboratory. In due course the committee of the Faculty of the College, which was appointed to consider Gordon's letter, reported as follows: ' . . . There is no accommodation within the walls of the College for the purpose, nor any means of providing such accommodation.' They submitted 'that the only accommodation which the Faculty can afford to Mr. Gordon is the use of the Chemistry class-room at such times and to such extent as may not interfere with the convenience of the Professor of Chemistry, and they recommend that Mr. Gordon be authorized to lecture in that room accordingly.'

They had unfortunately failed, however, to consult the Professor of Chemistry, Thomas Thomson, before making this report. That gentleman had a considerable amount of apparatus set out in his lecture room—most of it no doubt obtained at his own expense—and he quite reasonably refused to open the room for the use of students other than his own. His objections were accepted by Gordon, who made further representations to the Faculty, only to receive the same answer as before.

The Lord Advocate was obliged to bring the weight of his office to Gordon's support, stating that he had been 'called upon as one of the legal advisers of the Crown to consider the propriety of instituting in name of Her Majesty the proceedings that may be necessary for ascertaining the rights and privileges of the Regius Professor,' and in response to this the Faculty put all the blame on the Professor of Chemistry.

As by now the session was well advanced into 1841, the question arises as to whether Gordon did actually teach any students during his first year as professor. There is clear evidence that he did. It is likely that he met them in premises arranged for privately outside the precincts; for the class of Civil Engineering and Mechanics is included among the printed prize-lists for the session 1840-41 and four different names appear among the prize-winners.

In the course of the dispute about class-room accommodation, the Lord Advocate made certain observations about the use of the rooms in the College: 'The Law Class Room,' he says, 'is appropriated to the Professor of Law for one hour only, vizt., from 8 to 9 a.m. but . . . even for that hour it is unoccupied as no Law class has been taught during the present session . . .'

The upshot of it was that Gordon was given the use of the Law class room. It is more than possible, however, that the matter was thus decided only because there was no one then effectively occupying the Chair of Law who might protest. Gordon was not long left in peaceful tenancy, for in 1843 Allan Maconochie took over the duties of the Law Chair, and in October of that year the Faculty had to deal with a letter from him raising strong objections to Gordon's use of the room. It is a letter which, as recorded in the minutes, displays a legal innocence of punctuation. It runs: 'Being confined to my residence in consequence of a severe attack of illness I am prevented from stating to you in person the following communication which however as it is not expedient that it should be longer delayed I beg to present to you in writing vizt. That with the greatest respect and deference I beg humbly but most firmly and advisedly to object and protest against any Professor and more especially when his Profession constitutes him a member of a Faculty altogether distinct from that to which I belong in this University being intruded during the following session into the class room appropriated to the teaching of Law contrary to the established custom in this and all other Universities . . .' and so on in his first sentence of close on two hundred words. His object emerges in the second or third sentence where he asks the Faculty 'by timeously ordering the removal to a more appropriate site of the boxes of Stones and Machinery pertaining to the teaching of a branch of Science altogether disconnected with that of Law' to obviate the unseemly necessity of his taking other measures. As a parting shot he asserts that 'the Honorable the Faculty of the College have no power whatever to infringe his privileges or more right to intrude another teacher into his chair than it has to authorise the Professor of Anatomy to hang his supernumerary Horrors or carry on particular dissections in the Divinity Hall . . .'

Alternative accommodation was found and the issue dropped out of the records.

Perhaps I should mention a fact of some interest here. Gordon's class really comprised two courses, one concerned with what we to-day call Civil Engineering and another with what we think of as Mechanical Engineering. From the beginning, Gordon referred to this course as Applied Mechanics.

There are some gaps in our information about Gordon the man. The University has hitherto had no portrait of him, but some of our curiosity about him is satisfied by a copy of a memoir by his friend, Thomas A. Constable, printed for private circulation in 1877, a copy of which was found among the late Dr. David Murray's books now in the University Library.

Gordon was born in Edinburgh on 6th March, 1815, his father being a Writer to the Signet. He received his early education at Edinburgh High School and at a private school at Finchley. He decided to train himself for a career in Engineering, and when seventeen years of age worked for nine months at bench and forge in the engineering works of a Mr. Stirling in Dundee. Thereafter returning to Edinburgh he attended the Natural Philosophy class of Professor Forbes and the Natural History class of Professor Jameson.

In 1834, when the British Association met in Edinburgh, Gordon made the acquaintance of the great Marc Isambard Brunel, who was so favourably impressed with the young man that he invited him to join him in the work of the Thames tunnel on which Brunel was then engaged. He remained with Brunel for some years, but at the age of twenty-three he decided to devote himself to a short course of study at the Freiberg School of Mines. Here he made contacts with leading figures in applied science and acquired a mastery of the German language and a love for its literature.

He was thus enabled to translate some of the work of one of his German professors. It appears that he also spent a short time at the Ecole Polytechnique in Paris before he returned to Scotland, where he at once set up in practice in Glasgow as a civil engineer in partnership with Laurence Hill, Junior.

A year after his return, and when he was twenty-five years of age, Gordon was appointed to the Glasgow professorship. But the business of the partners continued. Among many commissions they undertook was a survey of the lochs which might serve Glasgow with pure water, and it was Gordon and Hill who first recommended the use of Loch Katrine. Another was the design and construction of the great chimney of Messrs. Tennant at St. Rollox, 447 feet high, which was, up to a generation ago, a landmark in Glasgow and a work of great boldness for its time.

Since the income of the professor as such at this time came from the fees of the students, and these were few in number, it could not be otherwise than that the incumbent of the Engineering Chair should have other resources. The teaching session extended only from November to May and as the professor had in those days no academic duties during the rest of the year, he was then perfectly free to pursue the practice of his profession. But even during the session the demands on the professor's time made by his lecture work were not heavy, and no doubt he did much professional work during the winter months. There were periods when the Engineering classes, like some of the Medical classes, met only in the evenings.

It is clear that even in the early years of his professorship, Gordon's business activities became extensive and he acquired quarters in London.

With Charles Liddell he acted as engineer for several railways in England and Wales, and designed many iron bridges. With R. S. Newall he developed and improved upon the idea of the wire rope, which Gordon was responsible for introducing to this country from Germany, and he was a partner with Newall in the firm of R. S. Newall and Company of Gateshead, which in time applied the wire rope technique in the manufacture of submarine cables. The firm also laid thousands of miles of marine cables, and it was to devote himself to its interests that Gordon resigned in 1855. He continued thereafter to flourish greatly in his business, but, four or five years after his retirement, he became afflicted with a disease which deprived him in time of the use of his legs, and for many years he was an invalid confined to his chair; but he maintained a lively contact with many engineers and exhibited a keen interest in every aspect of science and the teaching of science. As evidence of this it may be recalled that the late Dr. Henry Dyer, the first Principal of the Engineering School in Tokyo, who, on his return to this country, was well known in the public life of Glasgow until his death not many years ago, was appointed to his Japanese post on the recommendation of Macquorn Rankine whose student he had been; but on the constitution of the School, its staff and administration he was advised by Lewis Gordon. It is perhaps with surprise that those who remember Dyer realise how closely Gordon is linked with our time.

Gordon's contribution to the literature of engineering is not inconsiderable. He read several papers to the Philosophical Society of Glasgow and other bodies. His sense of his responsibilities as a teacher is made clear in the publishing of his *Engineering Aphorisms and Memoranda* and *A Synopsis of Lectures on Civil Engineering and Mechanics,* in addition to his translations of the German texts. He survived his successor by some years, and in 1876 was engaged in the project of collecting Rankine's papers for publication when he died.

It is on record that Macquorn Rankine deputised for Gordon during his absence from January to April in 1855, and it is clear from the extracts which are extant from Rankine's journal that Gordon desired Rankine to succeed him. Constable says that indeed Gordon delayed his resignation until he was sure that Rankine would succeed him. At this point John M. Pagan, Professor of Midwifery, as Coutts records, recommended that the Chair of Civil Engineering and Mechanics should be suppressed. To get the full significance of this, however, it is necessary to go to the records of the University, where we find that Pagan—himself a regius professor like Gordon—proposed that the Senate should represent to the Government 'that notwithstanding the high talents and acknowledged ability of the late Professor, the number of students attending the class of Civil Engineering had been very small and that the endowment might with propriety be devoted to purposes of greater and more immediate importance in connection with the higher branches of University Education.' The Government by this time were endowing the Engineering Chair to the extent of £275 per year which, modest as it was, was the largest endowment made, while Midwifery got but £50. These sums were no doubt fixed after consideration of the amount accruing to the professors from ordinary academic sources.

Attention has been called to words used by Macquorn Rankine as Chairman of the Mechanical Science Section of the British Association in Glasgow in 1855. Referring to the Engineering classes at the University of Glasgow, he says: '... the attendance (notwithstanding the great ability and energy of the Professor, Mr. Lewis Gordon) was at the outset so small that he was induced for some sessions to discontinue his lectures. But ... Mr. Gordon resumed his lectures last winter, and obtained at once a numerous attendance of students...'. The question arises, when and for how long the classes were suspended. Rankine is presumably speaking loosely in using the phrase 'at the outset,' as he is in the same speech in referring to his Chair as 'a Chair of Mechanics.'

Neither the minutes of the Senate nor those of the Faculty mention suspension of the Engineering classes, nor can we obtain positive evidence of it from extant Calendars and Prize Lists. In a letter to his brother on 11th June, 1847, Kelvin says, 'I think it is very likely that he (Gordon) will remain in London and give up his professorship' (Thompson's *Life of Kelvin*). But this prediction was not then fulfilled, for Gordon's 'Engineering Aphorisms and Memoranda' are described by him as a synopsis of lectures to be delivered in 1847-48. Gordon married in November, 1850, and set up house in London. In a letter to his father, written on 15th November, 1851, from Abingdon Street (which may have been the location of his professional quarters), Gordon said: 'I am in considerable doubt about going to Glasgow at all this year. I have not advertised nor taken any trouble in the matter, nor do I at present intend doing so. But I am not quite certain about this being the correct thing' (Constable's *Memoir*). It is remarkable that Pagan, in his motion in 1855 for the suppression of the Chair of Engineering, did not refer to the absence of the classes but to the fewness of the students. Nevertheless Rankine's words can hardly be set aside, and it is probable that the classes in Engineering were suspended during the period 1851-1854.

No more was heard of Pagan's motion and, at a meeting of Senate on 3rd December, 1855, the Commission from Her Majesty was read appointing William John Macquorn Rankine to the Engineering Chair. The Senate placed on him the obligation 'to write and deliver as a trial of his abilities a Latin dissertation on the subject "De concordia inter scientiarum machinalium contemplationem et usum".' Rankine did this a week later, signed the necessary undertakings and was admitted.

His reception by the Senate was apparently cordial, not only for his own sake but because Engineering was no longer without its devotees in the Senate. William Thomson, later Lord Kelvin, had been appointed to the Chair of Natural Philosophy in 1846. His elder brother James had attended Gordon's classes and was now established as an engineer.

There can be little doubt that the interest of the Thomsons in engineering and applied science brought valuable support to the Engineering Chair and, in spite of Dr. Pagan, by 1855, when Gordon resigned. it was well established and accepted.

Macquorn Rankine (according to P. G. Tait's *Memoir*)

was born in Edinburgh in 1820, and, although he attended Ayr Academy in 1828 and Glasgow High School in 1830, he seems for health reasons to have had little school education and to have had mainly private instruction. Yet when at fourteen years of age he was presented with a copy of Newton's *Principia* in the original Latin he studied it so carefully that he could later remark, 'This was the foundation of my knowledge of the higher mathematics, dynamics and physics.'

Like Gordon before him, he attended Professor Forbes' Natural Philosophy class at Edinburgh. Here, though only sixteen years of age, he gained a gold medal for an essay on the Undulatory Theory of Light. At the same time he studied music, read much of metaphysics and assisted his father in superintending the works of the Leith Branch of the Edinburgh and Dalkeith Railway. Later he became a pupil in the office of a noted civil engineer.

While still only twenty-two years of age, he sent several papers to the Institution of Civil Engineers for some of which he received prizes. Until 1848 he was engaged in a number of civil engineering projects, but now he gave his special attention to the subject of molecular physics and commenced his work on the Mechanical Action of Heat which he continued to supplement for some years. In this he developed for the first time a theory of heat on the hypothesis that in an elastic fluid the quantity of heat is accounted for by the energy of motion of the molecules. This work brought him election to a Fellowship of the Royal Society in 1853. About this time, and to the end of his life, Rankine was much in touch with William Thomson; but so original and independent were his scientific writings that they may have owed less to Thomson than did Thomson to them. It is interesting to recall that the frequently quoted saying of William Thomson, 'I never satisfy myself until I can make a mechanical model of a thing' came into one of the Baltimore Lectures in which he turned aside to express some criticism of Rankine for not having adopted the same attitude to a problem. The great mathematical physicist found the great engineer too abstruse!

After his appointment to the Chair in 1855, Rankine applied himself to the writing of text-books on every aspect of Engineering, including Naval Architecture. He contributed numerous papers to the proceedings of learned societies. In 1857 he took an active part in founding the Institution of Engineers and Shipbuilders in Scotland and became its first President, and a frequent contributor to its transactions. In the words of Sir James B. Henderson, 'He was undoubtedly the most prolific writer of his time ... on engineering subjects, and in many sections he was in fact creating the Science as he wrote.'

It is fitting that there should be given here a brief description of the work Rankine did upon the structure of the Engineering course within the University and its effect upon the status of the subject.

It is to be remembered that the subject of Engineering was attached to the Faculty of Arts, but it was not recognised as a subject qualifying for graduation in Arts; and the majority of the early students studying Engineering seem to have been men who added this study to the usual course for a degree in Arts. Rankine in 1859 persuaded the Senate to consider the award of a Diploma in Engineering Science, but they submitted the question to the Universities Commissioners as to whether they might grant such a diploma. Late in 1861 the Commissioners said that in their opinion the University could confer no other distinction than a degree, and that in any case Engineering was not 'a proper department in which a degree should be conferred.' Rankine did not let the matter rest. He had presumably strong support in the Senate, for he at once reopened the question and gained the Senate's approval for the award of a Certificate of Proficiency in Engineering Science to those who satisfactorily completed a specified course of work. On this occasion the matter was not referred to the Commissioners; the new system was brought into effect in 1862. The form of the certificate was soon afterwards decided, and in May, 1863, the first was signed by the Principal, sealed by the Clerk of Senate and awarded.

At that time the graduation ceremony was a more private affair than it is to-day. In the presence of the Senate the ordinary graduands in Arts and Medicine were capped by the Principal in his capacity as Vice-Chancellor and thereafter those who had satisfied the examiners in Engineering came forward to receive their certificates from the Principal's hands. It might well be imagined that in these circumstances the distinction between a degree and a Certificate of Proficiency was going to be difficult to maintain; and so it proved.

Various steps were projected to promote the study of science in the University. One proposal was to institute examinations in science only within the Arts curriculum. This did not satisfy Rankine, who wished a degree to be awarded to those who completed the course for his Certificate of Proficiency and, because of the practice in Arts, it was a master's degree which he had in mind. The Senate blew hot and cold over it—mostly cold, and nothing was done. In 1870 the Engineering students prayed the Senate to institute a degree in Engineering Science; but legal opinion, which was sought, was against it on the ground that it would be outside the powers conferred on the University by the Bull of Pope Nicholas V (1451) or by the *Nova Erectio* (1577)!

Rankine possibly had been made aware that the Representation of the People (Scotland) Act of 1868 provided authority for establishing his purpose, and he now pressed for a B.Sc. degree in Engineering. The Senate paused to consider rather the whole question of degrees in Science, and in 1872 the B.Sc. degree was established, though in a form which soon called for modification.

In that year Rankine died at the age of fifty-two.

In the words of Principal Caird he was a man 'of marvellous versatility of gifts and of untiring power of application who, still in the prime of life, had already achieved results for which the longest life might seem scarcely sufficient.'

Before I pass to Rankine's successor, I should like to suggest that if to this series of Fifth-Centenary Lectures there had been added one on the history of the Training Corps, Rankine would have had an honoured place in it. He was, I think, the originator of the idea. It was in July, 1859, that he proceeded to form the Glasgow University Rifle Volunteers, which in 1860 became part of the 1st Lanarkshire Volunteers with Rankine in charge of the 1st Company and William Thomson in charge of the 2nd. One would like to linger over the picture of those dignified and hirsute Victorian gentlemen as amateur soldiers. Kelvin still took part in this activity even after the accident which brought on his lameness. But he resigned at length, for as he said in the typical rather heavy Kelvin style of humour, the more he was ordered to march the more he halted.

Rankine was also the first Convener of the Senate Committee on the Education of Candidates for Commissions in the Army. His interest in military training no doubt arose from the fact that his father had been a lieutenant in the 21st Regiment.

On the death of Rankine, James Thomson, much encourraged by his brother who was now *Sir* William, became a candidate for the Glasgow chair. He was now nearly fifty-one years of age, had occupied the Chair of Civil Engineering in Queen's College, Belfast, since 1857, and his scientific work both before and during this period had been outstanding. It was not surprising that the University of Glasgow had conferred the LL.D. on him in 1870, his election to it having been promoted by Professors Blackburn and Rankine. He was therefore a very strong candidate for the Chair.

With his brother he had entered the University of Glasgow when thirteen years of age and had taken the M.A. degree with Honours in Mathematics and Natural Philosophy when he was eighteen. He had decided to adopt civil engineering as his profession and, like Rankine before him, went into the office of Sir John McNeil in Dublin. But, owing to a breakdown in health, he had to return to Glasgow after only a few weeks.

About the same time, Lewis Gordon was appointed to the new Chair of Engineering, and, during the second session of Gordon's professorship, James Thomson attended the Engineering classes. His name appears on the prize-list as the 'Most distinguished Student and Essayist in the Class of *Applied Mechanics,*' and the subject of his essay is given as 'Overshot Water Wheels.' It is acknowledged that it was Gordon who gave him his introduction to the subject of hydraulics in which in a few years he did some of his greatest work as scientist and inventor.

For a time in 1843 he was employed in the works of Fairbairn and Company at Millwall, but ill-health again interfered with his course of practice, and he returned to Glasgow, where he devoted himself to his inventions of water turbines and to the study of a variety of subjects which yielded a number of important contributions to the transactions of learned societies. Among them was the classic paper on 'Lowering of the Freezing Point of Water by Pressure' which showed that thermodynamics had a fundamental applicability to the physical sciences which even transcended its use in the analysis of heat engines.

After some years Thomson's health greatly improved and he was able to take up actively his profession of engineering. In 1849 he went to London, and it is on record that he worked with Professor Gordon who, though still carrying on his professorship in Glasgow, had quarters there. In 1851 he settled in Belfast as a civil engineer, where he found scope for his inventions in hydraulics and where he became Engineer to the Belfast Water Commissioners. In 1857, he was appointed to the Chair of Civil Engineering in Queen's College, which he occupied for sixteen years, that is, until 1873, when he succeeded Rankine at Glasgow.

Here he found himself in congenial company. Besides his brother William, there were among the professors several who had been his class-mates or associates during his early years in the Old College.

The induction to the Chair still involved the reading of an essay in Latin—a practice which continued till 1894—and Thomson chose as its title, in its English rendering, 'On the Principles of Estimating Safety and Danger in Structures in respect to their Sufficiency in Strength.'

His professorship in Glasgow saw a continuation of his work on the flow of fluids leading to the publication of a considerable number of papers. He maintained his interest in thermodynamics though he published no more papers specifically on that subject. The principle of similarity and the application of the theory of dimensions to different aspects of Engineering were given much attention.

The range of his interests beyond Engineering is shown by the following selection of titles from the list of his papers published after his return to Glasgow as a professor: 'The Grand Currents of Atmospheric Circulation,' 'The Jointed Prismatic Structure in Basaltic Rocks,' 'The Plasticity of Glacier Ice,' 'An Integrating Machine,' and 'The Origin of Winding of Rivers in Alluvial Plains.'

Thomson continued the development of the Engineering school and modified the course to suit contemporary needs. The B.Sc. degree which had been introduced was still administered by the Arts Faculty and was awarded in Engineering to those who satisfied the examiners in two Arts subjects as well as in the Engineering group of subjects. Thomson took the first step to alter this by having a practical course which he introduced, coupled with Geodesy, recognised as equivalent to one of the Arts classes.

He saw the first Engineering degrees awarded in 1876 or 1877 and the founding of the George Harvey Prize and the Young Demonstratorship. During his tenure also took place the first stirrings towards the introduction of a separate class in Naval Architecture, and at last the founding of a chair in that subject. The whole curriculum had hitherto been the same for all students; but a separate branch was now required in which special attention could be given to Naval Architecture and Marine Engineering.

Because of failing eyesight, Professor Thomson was obliged to resign from the Chair in 1889.

The careers of Rankine and Thomson coincided with a period of rapid development in the scope of physical science and at such a time the language of physical science had to be formed. They both introduced many new terms and some of these are now in everyday use. Rankine coined the term 'potential energy,' and it was he who first used the terms 'stress' and 'strain' as applied to elastic bodies. James Thomson was responsible for 'radian' and 'poundal,' and the term 'torque' first appeared in print in one of his examination papers here. When these are added to the many new terms introduced by Kelvin, one might almost say that the speech of physical science has a Glasgow accent!

James Thomson's successor was Archibald Barr, who had at one time been his assistant in Glasgow and who had for five years been Professor of Engineering at Leeds. Barr commenced his engineering career at fifteen years of age as a student apprentice in Mechanical Engineering on the 'sandwich system'—perhaps the first person to do so—and this marked a change in the nature of the succession to the chair, for his predecessors had all received the greater part of their training in what we now call Civil Engineering.

In the academic field Barr's work lay largely in interpreting to a generation of students the teachings of his predecessor. On several occasions he quoted Goethe, 'There are many echoes in the world, but few voices,' and he modestly regarded himself as an echo but hoped that he was a faithful echo. This was perhaps not an untrue judgment of the place he occupies in the history of engineering science, but it is (even so) far from an unworthy one, for few of us can hope even as echoes to be as faithful and clear as Barr was with his great gifts of lucidity in exposition and aptness in the choice of words.

And as a speaker on the less serious occasions of University life Barr was regarded by some as second only to Macneile Dixon.

In the development of the school, Barr made a great mark. It fell to him to take part in shaping the Faculty of Science which was instituted by the Universities Commission in 1893. He took part in the setting up of a Lectureship in Electrical Engineering in 1898 and in modifying the curriculum so that, while keeping to the Rankine tradition of a broad training in the fundamentals for all students, he provided for the special interests of Civil, Mechanical, and Electrical Engineers and Naval Architects. The setting up of the Dixon Chair of Mining Engineering in 1902 added one more branch of special interest.

It was Barr who, by dint of much effort, succeeded in having funds earmarked and money collected for building the present laboratories which in their day were worthy of the subject and creditable to the University. These were opened by Lord Kelvin on 3rd September, 1901.

When Barr was at Leeds he had joined with his colleague, Professor Stroud, in evolving the Barr and Stroud Rangefinder—a venture which was attended in due course with great success.

This collaboration of the Physicist and Engineer may have determined the title of Barr's induction essay—he still had the Latin essay to read to the Senate—'Quomodo Physica ad Artes Mechanicas adhibenda sint.'

It was in 1912 that an ordinance of affiliation made attendance at certain classes in the Royal Technical College acceptable for the purpose of graduating at the University. It is doubtful if Barr gave this move his full support, but it was no doubt his success in designing rangefinders and his pre-occupation in the manufacture of them which caused him to resign in 1913.

John Dewar Cormack, a distinguished student of Barr's, was Professor of Engineering in University College, London, after having served for four years as Lecturer in Electrical Engineering at Leeds and for five years as assistant to Barr in Glasgow. On Barr's retirement Cormack returned from London to take his place. The outbreak of war in 1914 led to a dispersal of the staff and a complete suspension of the teaching of engineering till 1919. Thereafter there was a period of great activity and development in which Cormack found scope for his ability as an administrator. Extensions to the Engineering buildings were commenced in 1920.

In 1921 proposals from the Science Faculty Committee of the Students' Representative Council were submitted to the Senate that there should be established a separate Faculty of Engineering, that there should be a four years' course and that there should be separate Chairs in Civil Engineering, Mechanical Engineering, Electrical Engineering, Mining and Naval Architecture. It must be gratifying to students to know that such far-reaching proposals coming from such a source were not only considered but were in practically every respect brought into effect.

These aims were in some ways served by the Institution of Engineers and Shipbuilders in Scotland, which in 1921 handed over to the University, for the purpose of founding two professorial chairs, a large sum of money which had been collected to mark the centenary of the death of James Watt. The chairs set up were those of Electrical Engineering and the Theory and Practice of Heat Engines.

The new Faculty of Engineering was formed in 1923, and the new curriculum which made the degree an Honours Degree was inaugurated in that year.

The Heat Engines Chair is now to be merged in a professorship of Mechanical Engineering, and this will complete the fulfilment of the students' proposals of 1921.

Of the incumbents of the James Watt Chairs, Professor Goudie has died. It would be inappropriate to attempt an appraisal of the place occupied in Engineering by one so close to our time. But his interest in music, exhibited in his founding of a prize in that subject (among other benefactions to the University) and in the share he took in the founding of the University Orchestral Society, is in keeping with a musical tradition within the Engineering Department. Macquorn Rankine had a cultivated musical taste, but he frequently entertained his friends by singing humorous songs to his own accompaniment at the pianoforte—both words and music being of his own composition. The personnel of the present Engineering Faculty are much in evidence in the councils of the Orchestral Society.

The Chair of Naval Architecture has played no small part in the success of the School. Its inception was no doubt due to Rankine, for, though it was not established until ten years after his death, his close friendship with John Elder must have been in the mind of that great shipbuilder's widow when she decided to found, as a memorial to her husband, the Chair of Naval Architecture, just as in 1872 she had of her generosity secured to the Engineering Chair a much-needed supplement to its endowment.

In 1880 the Senate considered a memorial from a large number of shipbuilders, marine engineers, shipowners and others interested in the construction of ships, proposing to establish in the University a lectureship in Shipbuilding and Marine Engineering. With the co-operation of the Institution of Engineers and Shipbuilders in Scotland, a course of lectures was introduced in 1881 as an experiment for a limited period, with a past president of the Institution, J. G. Lawrie, as lecturer. The Institution was preparing a scheme for the endowment of the lectureship when in 1883 Mrs. Elder provided the funds for the establishment of the professorship. The first incumbent of the new Chair, and indeed the first Professor of Naval Architecture in the world, was Francis Elgar, a former student of the Royal School of Naval Architecture and Marine Engineering in South Kensington. He was admitted to his office in January, 1884, but his tenure was brief for in 1886 he had to resign on being appointed Director of H.M. Dockyards. He later returned to the Clyde as naval architect to the Fairfield Company.

He was followed at the University by a fellow-student of the Royal School, Philip Jenkins, who died in 1891. Jenkins' successor was Sir John Harvard Biles who occupied the chair for thirty years. Percy Hillhouse, who was then appointed, was the first product of the Glasgow School of Naval Architecture to hold the professorship, for he was one of Elgar's first students. He succeeded him also as naval architect at the Fairfield yard.

The Departments of Engineering and Naval Architecture have always had a considerable number of foreign students, but that has been especially true of Naval Architecture. Thus, while the ties of the school are close with the great shipbuilding industry at home, it has many valuable and strong links with other lands.

The Glasgow University Engineering Society—itself sixty years old—keeps in touch with thousands of graduates—distributed all over the world—through its Year Book and Register.

Glasgow Engineering alumni fill a number of important Chairs in this country, and a great many elsewhere in the English-speaking world.

The Department from which they sprang tries not to be unworthy of them. It is alive—and though its physical growth is at present arrested by circumstances peculiar to the times in which we live, its vitality is unfailing.

It is proud of its past as it has reason to be, but its business is with the future and with humble confidence it looks forward to the years—nay, the centuries—that lie before it.